BOOZEHOUND

BOOZEHOUND

ON THE TRAIL OF THE RARE, THE OBSCURE, AND THE OVERRATED IN SPIRITS

JASON WILSON

TEN SPEED PRESS
Berkeley

Copyright © 2010 by Jason Wilson

Published in the United States by Ten Speed Press, an imprint of the Crown Publishing Group, a division of Random House, Inc., New York.
www.crownpublishing.com
www.tenspeed.com

Ten Speed Press and the Ten Speed Press colophon are registered trademarks of Random House, Inc.

Portions of this book have been adapted from previously published material in the *Washington Post*, *The Smart Set* from Drexel University, *Imbibe Magazine*, and *Condé Nast Traveler*.

Library of Congress Cataloging-in-Publication Data

Wilson, Jason, 1970–
Boozehound : on the trail of the rare, the obscure, and the overrated in spirits / Jason Wilson.—1st ed.
     p. cm.
Summary: "A journalistic excursion into lesser-known, forgotten, and misunderstood spirits from around the world, with recipes"—Provided by publisher.
Includes index.
1. Liquors. 2. Cookery (Liquors) I. Title.
TP590.W55 2010
   641.2'5—dc22

                                        2010013363

ISBN 978-1-58008-288-4

Printed in the United States of America

Front cover photograph copyright © Dave G. Houser/Corbis
Cover design by Ed Anderson
Text design by Toni Tajima

10 9 8 7 6 5 4 3 2 1

First Edition

FOR JEN

CONTENTS ⌒

INTRODUCTION ⌀

The Booze Beat

AS LONG AS YOU REPRESENT ME AS
PRAISING ALCOHOL I SHALL NOT COMPLAIN.

—*H. L. Mencken*

A FEW YEARS AGO, I was at a fancy party with several people who have successful careers in what's commonly called lifestyle journalism. We were drinking special cocktails made with a very special gin that had been infused with cucumbers and rose petals, and mixed with rose water that had been specially imported from Lebanon.

I was chatting with a beautiful, sexy friend who wrote for a magazine that covers luxury spa vacations. She got that job, in part, because she wrote a travel book about bathing culture that one critic claimed "bred a new publishing hybrid, the beauty-travel memoir, Bruce Chatwin by way of *Allure* magazine."

As we chatted, I shared some good news with her: I had just been hired to write a column for a major newspaper about spirits and cocktails.

"You should really meet my friend," she told me. "He's the perfume critic at the *Times*."

"Really?" I said. "Let me just see if I'm hearing this correctly. The luxury spa columnist would like the spirits columnist to meet the perfume columnist."

"Yes," she said, with a beautiful, sexy smile.

"Wait," I said. "Did you just hear that?"

"What?"

"Oh, nothing," I said. "I just thought for a second that I heard the sound of the Apocalypse happening."

I often said things like this in the beginning of my new job. I'd grown up, after all, in a family of men who made their money packing fruit and vegetables—real work. I knew what it was like to wake up for work at 4 a.m., to haggle over crates of cantaloupe at the produce terminal before sunrise. By thirteen, I knew what it felt like to unload a truckload of onions in the July sun; how your arms were ripped up by the fifty-pound red mesh bags. My father mangled his thumb in a machine that stitches together bags of potatoes. I could imagine my grandfather saying, "Spirits and cocktail columnist? Really? I'm spinning in my goddamn grave." At least that's how my misguided thinking went in those early days.

When I was in school, I'd dreamed of becoming Ernest Hemingway. Now, I travel and drink and write about my traveling and drinking. Close enough, I guess—though likely closer to the paunchy, boozy, crazy late Hemingway than the younger, dashing one who ran with bulls, drove ambulances in the Great War, and wrote classic novels. It's sort of like dreaming of becoming Elvis when you're young, and then actually becoming Elvis years later—but maybe you've become the wrong one, the Elvis who performed, sweaty and overweight, in rhinestone jumpsuits. Regardless, it's difficult (not to mention unseemly) to complain when work entails polishing off tasting flights of special reserve bourbons or single malts or añejo tequilas at 11 o'clock in the morning. I've come to love spirits, and to admire the people who make them and the places they come from. I hope to convey some of that love to you.

When I'm working, I often think of that poor woman, Jig, in Hemingway's classic story "Hills Like White Elephants." Sitting at a bar in a Spanish railway station on a hot afternoon, trying to avoid another pointed quarrel with her boyfriend, she orders a glass of anís at the railway station bar. "I wanted to try this new drink," she says to her companion, in one of the most cynical lines in American literature. "That's all we do, isn't it—look at things and try new drinks?" Looking at things and trying new drinks. That's a pretty fair description of my job. Any given day I might be tasting a *rhum agricole* made with pure Martinique sugarcane, or sipping an eau-de-vie distilled from some rare alpine berry, or quaffing an herbal *digestivo* concocted from an obscure Milanese recipe, or contemplating the renaissance of American rye whiskey, or comparing sherry-casked Norwegian aquavit to unoaked Danish aquavit. Some friends suggest I should have lived in another century, wandering about town with a cape, a monocle, and a stick. Which may be true, but not for the reasons they would likely suggest.

Along the journey, I've learned that booze—like it or not—plays a central role in the history of humanity. There's a reason the word *spirits* came to be used for alcoholic beverages: the ancient idea that liquor was magical and transcendent, and that when one uncorked and imbibed such liquids, a supernatural force would be unleashed. Spirits are cultural touchstones. They mark geography. They mark time. I am struck by how often I open a bottle and am transported to the particular moment when I first tasted this or that flavor or style. I'm also inevitably reminded of the people with whom I'd shared that time, place, and bottle. Thus the booze becomes a part of life, its tastes and aromas becoming intertwined with memory. Drinking, I believe, can be an aesthetic experience similar to enjoying books or art or music. Learning how to taste spirits, then, becomes no different from study in any of the other humanities: learning how to read works of Russian literature or how to look at German Expressionist paintings or how to listen to *Rigoletto*. At least, that's one way of looking at it.

Here's another way to look at it: Critics and scholars poke around inquiring into every aspect of popular culture, from creepy Japanese comic books to successful professional poker strategies to the filmography of the 1980s rap trio the Fat Boys. Entire forests have been pulped so that we can read social histories on the toothpick, the color mauve, and the candy bar. So why not endeavor to study spirits? Let's be honest: As cultural activities go, there are few more popular than drinking. No matter what the moralists, the scolds, or the self-appointed health advocates tell you, drinking can be one of the most fun things in the world to do. Billions of human beings share this opinion. I am covering a fifty-four billion dollar industry that has seen nothing but astronomical growth in the past decade—a 66 percent rise in U.S. sales since 2000.

The reality, however, is that I am a spirits writer from a country and an age in which many citizens remain extremely skeptical of what they call (clinically) *alcohol*. Or (pejoratively) *hard* liquor. Or worse, *hooch* or *firewater*—even *poison*. We're a people still living with the failed legacy of Prohibition. Even today, nearly eight decades after its repeal, fifteen states continue to ban liquor sales on Sunday. I, perhaps ironically, live in a town where alcohol sales are still banned every day of the week. I have to actually leave town limits to buy booze. The Prohibition experiment sealed off access to many of the wonderful spirits that people once enjoyed, never to be seen again. To add insult to injury, I am of a generation whose baby boomer parents—who'd rebelled against their own parents' midcentury cocktail culture—were largely incapable of teaching us how to drink properly.

I got my first inkling of how little I'd known about drinking on a cold autumn afternoon, back when I was a young and clueless college student. A successful, older mentor took me out for a drink. The reason why is lost to me now, but surely it involved some pointed career advice that I never followed. Anyway, this septuagenarian gentleman—who in my hazy memory wore a brimmed hat and a flower tucked into his lapel and carried a pocket watch—took me to a hotel bar. I was dressed, as usual, in a well-worn flannel shirt, wrinkled khakis, running sneakers, and a beat-up baseball cap. As we sat, he announced to the bartender with a wink, "Jimmy, as of today, I'm putting you on official notice. I've switched to my winter drink."

Without a word, the bartender, dressed in white coat and tie, promptly mixed and served him a Stinger. The gentleman laid a crisp hundred-dollar bill on the bar and told me to order, so I asked for a vodka and tonic, hoping it seemed more sophisticated than the cheap beers and shots that I normally drank with my fake ID. The gentleman appraised me, my slovenly attire, and my vodka and tonic, and gruffly declared, "That's a summer drink." Then he told the bartender he'd better make another Stinger.

The implication was clear: What sort of adult doesn't know when to switch from a summer drink to a winter drink? What sort of soft generation was this that needed to be told how to drink at all?

"Vodka has no taste," he continued. "It's flavorless."

"But what's in a Stinger?" I asked.

He eyed me skeptically. "Crème de menthe. Brandy. Jimmy has made yours with cognac."

I had no idea what he was talking about. I assumed cognac had something to do with rich old guys and pipes and velvet jackets and slippers and maybe sitting in a plush chair and reading a huge book with gilt edges and some title like *The History of the Decline and Fall of the Roman Empire*. I knew cognac was expensive, but what could it possibly be made from? Maybe the sweat of French people? Or perhaps cognac was sort of like those fur coats that patchouli-smelling college kids like me were protesting, the ones made from the soft, soft fur of Persian lamb fetuses? In any case, I sure as hell had never witnessed anyone drinking a cognac. And I expressed this to my would-be mentor by scrunching up my nose and saying, "Cognac?" The gentleman gave me a look that suggested he was witnessing the decline and fall of contemporary civilization before his very eyes.

It's been a very long time since I ordered a vodka and tonic. I've made a very long journey from my youth in the South Jersey suburbs to becoming the sort of man who sips a three-hundred-dollar cognac in the morning and calls it work. But it wasn't as if, one day, I switched from vodka tonics to strange foreign libations. I moved slowly, through the years, from vodka to gin, and then on to whiskey. I learned to love bourbon and rye and Irish whiskey. It hasn't always been easy. When I started my job, I had to admit a dirty secret, a skeleton in the closet: I'd never really been a huge fan of single-malt Scotch whisky. I realize this does not rise to the level of, say, shooting a man in Reno just to watch him die. But since I was a spirits writer, it caused me some discomfort. I worked my way through lighter, so-called chick Scotches, and then slowly into peat monsters that received the macho seal of approval from Scotch snobs. Eventually, single malts took their place of pride in my liquor cabinet.

But beyond whiskey, I still wanted to know more. That quest is where this book takes its shape. When it comes to flavor, I am drawn to the Old World. I like liquor with hard-to-define tastes: the bitter complexity of Italian *amari*, the ancient herbs of Chartreuse, the primal maltiness of Dutch genever. And I'm also drawn to the wilder, untamed parts of the New World: the agave bite of real tequila; the earthy, rustic edge to Brazilian cachaça; the strange, dry conundrum of Peruvian pisco. I don't know why—I guess it's the same reason I like stinky cheeses, funky wines, wild game, or yeasty beers. I'm of a similar mind to A. J. Liebling, who wrote in his classic food memoir, *Between Meals*, "I like tastes that know their own minds." Certainly, whatever it is—this impulse, this search for flavor—is in response to the relatively bland tastes that defined my upbringing.

There is much more going on in the glass when we sit down to drink a particularly profound spirit: a smoky 1928 rum from Fidel Castro's cellar, a cognac that was bottled before the nineteenth-century phylloxera plague destroyed acres of Europe's vineyards, one of the only vintage Calvados to have survived the German occupation of Normandy. And it's about more than just being rare and obscure for the sake of being rare and obscure.

Perhaps what I'm describing is the exact opposite of what's become the most widely consumed spirit in the United States: vodka. About a year into my job, I looked around and something struck me: people slowly had begun discovering, and getting really interested in, spirits. Readers sent me emails with lots of questions, and it became clear that although many people were game to learn, there were major chunks of cultural knowledge about spirits that had not been passed down. Just like me on that long-ago day with the dapper gentleman and his Stinger, people really didn't know very much about what they drank. So, despite an increased awareness of spirits, people still mostly drank vodka.

Liebling already saw vodka's surge coming in the late 1950s, as it began to usurp whiskey and gin. He, predictably, deplored the vodka trend, writing in *Between Meals*, "The standard of perfection for vodka (no color, no taste, no smell) was expounded to me long ago . . . and it accounts perfectly for the drink's rising popularity with those who like their alcohol in conjunction with the reassuring tastes of infancy—tomato juice, orange juice, and chicken broth. It is the ideal intoxicant for the drinker who wants no reminder of how hurt Mother would be if she knew what he was doing."

That was 1959. The twenty-first-century American consumer is not content to rest with the standard vodka available then. We've become an insatiable audience for new ways to buy pretty much the same old thing, and vodka has grown into an industry with more than fifteen billion dollars in annual sales. Not a week passes that I don't get an email from some public relations professional extolling the virtues of a new superpremium vodka from A Very Special Place (Latvia, Kyrgyzstan, Idaho) or infused with some wild new taste (energy drink, açaí berries, bacon) or associated with a celebrity (P. Diddy, Dan Aykroyd, Donald Trump) or tied to a political cause (Absolut Global Cooling, anyone?).

"Does the world need another vodka?" is a question that surely has been pondered by those of us who've seen liquor store shelves sagging under the sheer volume of premium vodkas on the market. I can only assume that the development of new vodkas—each in a fancy bottle and with a romantic story—will go on until the world ends in fire or ice. In fact, I have a recurring dream in which the true first sign of the Apocalypse is actually a press release for a vodka that has been quintuple-distilled from the tears of flaxen-haired angels and flavored with the ambrosia of Mount Olympus. And it's promoted by Miley Cyrus.

This is not to say there is anything pernicious or immoral or wrong about liking vodka. Plenty of good, decent people do, and some of these people I count among my friends. Some of them are even dedicated, enlightened foodies—people who pray at the altar of Slow Food and shudder at the thought of inauthentic cuisine. But when you come by their homes, they will still serve you a drink made with an overpriced vodka and perhaps also an artificial fruit mixer. I always accept their hospitality. Likewise, I try not to be like my hectoring mentor at the bar with his Stinger. Most of the time I am successful. But inside, deep down, what I really want to do is grab people by their lapels—or elbows or throats or whatever it is one metaphorically grabs. And what I want to tell them is this: Try something new. Try something strange. Expose yourself to flavors you've never considered before. Taste something—anything—that makes you stop for a moment and pay attention and experience. Hopefully, that is what this tale of my own boozy journey inspires.

CHAPTER 1

THE OMBIBULOUS ME

THEY TALK OF MY DRINKING BUT NEVER MY THIRST.

—*Scottish proverb*

T HE FIRST LIQUOR I EVER EXPERIENCED, as a teenager, was sambuca—the anise liqueur often served after dinner in Italian restaurants, with three coffee beans for good luck. The only reason for this is because, in our house, a lonely bottle of sambuca sat at the back of our kitchen pantry, hidden behind the hodgepodge bottles of Chivas Regal, Canadian Club, and VO. My parents didn't drink whiskey—they were the type of baby boomers who as young adults had eschewed spirits and cocktails for the pleasures of wine—and so they likely kept those bottles on hand solely for guests who liked whiskey. As for why sambuca lurked in a dark corner of our shelf, I have never discovered an explanation. We are not Italian-Americans. It's not as if my parents were jet-setting in Portofino (more like Ocean City, New Jersey). And we'd never hosted a foreign exchange student. Perhaps it was a gift from a guest, someone who believed that my parents might enjoy a bracing, licorice-tasting after-dinner spirit? In that case, it was one of the most misguided gifts of all time.

However, since this bottle of sambuca sat totally untouched and unmonitored, it ended up being the perfect liquor for a sixteen-year-old boy and his friends. My parents were occasionally out to dinner, and so after the police had broken up a keg party in the woods or on the eleventh hole of the local golf course and we were suddenly out of Milwaukee's Best, my friends and I would find ourselves rummaging deep in my family's pantry for our now-favorite Italian digestivo.

If we'd had any choice, I doubt sambuca would have been at the top of the list. After all, most American kids grow up calling red Twizzlers "licorice" and picking around the black jelly beans in the jar. My friends thought sambuca was gross, and we mainly drank it in shots. But I kind of liked it. Or at least I pretended to like it. I don't mean to suggest that I had esoteric tastes as a teenager. In reality, I was a rube who subsisted on Gatorade and Ho Hos, gagged on mustard, and scraped the onions or mushrooms off any dish served with them. But I had seen *La Dolce Vita* on VCR tape, and I took on an air of sambuca connoisseurship as if I'd just returned from café life on the Via Veneto, splashing in the Trevi Fountain with Anita Ekberg, and now had a Vespa parked in the garage next to our riding mower.

The reason was quite simple: L., a certain Valkyrie-like girl who'd recently moved to our neighborhood and started hanging out with us. Her mother had an accent, and everyone said they were "European." They had a last name that seemed vaguely Scandinavian or, as some in the neighborhood called it, "sort of Aryan." But who knows where they came from. Regardless, the stunning blond-haired, blue-eyed L. was clearly different from most of the Jersey girls who went to high school with me. I was smitten, and had spent an entire summer trying to convince her to fall in love with me, but had remained squarely in the friend zone.

Still, I was on the lookout for ways to impress her. One autumn night, a group of us fled a busted party on the golf course. "Sambuca, anyone?" I suggested. Among our friends, L. and I walked to my house, cozily arm-in-arm in the crisp fall air. On that night, I decided to make my move.

The sambuca bottle had one of those plastic pourer spouts. After so much usage—since we didn't really know how to use it properly and never wiped it off—a sugary crust began to form, making it increasingly hard to pour. As luck would have it, on that very night the crust had finally grown impenetrable; I couldn't even coax a trickle of sambuca from the spout. "What's the deal?" my friends wanted to know. "We want shots!" L. joined the chorus. Panicked, seeing my moment slipping away from me, I began hacking away at the crust with a butter knife. When that didn't work, I grabbed a pencil from the kitchen counter and jammed it, forcefully, into the spout. The pencil immediately broke in two, and the top part somehow ended up floating inside the sambuca bottle.

My friends erupted in laughter. L. did, too. I was eventually able to pour the shots, but by then—humiliated in the way only a love-struck teenage boy can be—I'd lost my nerve and pride. When, later, I embarrassingly, tearfully, professed my undying affection to L., she gently patted me on the head and told me I was "a good friend."

The only other thing I remember from that night is my mother dragging me to my bedroom by the ear, yelling at me. Apparently, my parents found me passed out in the kitchen in my boxers, and I would be grounded for quite some time. Fortunately (or unfortunately), my brother had earlier stashed the sambuca bottle safely in its regular hiding spot. Years later, well after I'd graduated from college, my mother was clearing out the pantry and found it. She remained puzzled as to why there was a broken pencil floating inside a half-empty bottle.

Soon after, L. began dating a guy in his twenties with a classic Mustang who drove around town with photos of L. in his hubcaps as a sign of affection—pretty much a deal maker in 1980s suburban New Jersey. Of course, I was crushed. This was my first true romantic heartbreak, and its sting was so acute that I can vividly recall the feeling more than twenty years later. What could I do? I was still a boy, and no match for a dangerous older man with a Mustang. Stealing that sambuca, gagging down the overwhelming 80-proof anise liqueur—this was about as edgy as I got in those days.

It's a curious thing about memorable flavors. They always come back.

When I began writing my column, one of the first big spirits stories I covered was the legalization of absinthe. Until 2007, the mythic, louche liqueur of nineteenth-century Parisian decadence was classified as a dangerous, potentially hallucinogenic, and banned substance by the U.S. government. The reason it had always been verboten was because of a chemical called thujone, the active ingredient in wormwood. Wormwood is the mysterious plant that makes absinthe *absinthe*—the Green Fairy, with its legends of hallucination and belle époque debauchery embraced by writers and artists such as Verlaine, Baudelaire, Toulouse-Lautrec, and Modigliani. By the turn of the twentieth century, absinthe was so popular that the French were drinking thirty-six billion liters of absinthe versus only five billion liters of wine. But then in 1905, some crazy guy in Switzerland named Jean Lanfray, drunk on absinthe, murdered his family—which led to a public outcry against the spirit. One by one, Western nations began banning absinthe. Some historians suggest it was actually the powerful French wine industry, concerned about its eroding market, that helped trump up the Lanfray murder and lobbied for the Green Fairy's prohibition. Regardless, by 1912 absinthe was illegal in the United States.

But here's the thing: absinthe was never banned by name. In the United States, the law expressly prohibits any spirit that contains over ten parts per million of thujone. It took nearly a century, but in the late 2000s, someone suddenly had the bright idea to apply a little modern chemistry to the issue. A New Orleans–born chemist named Ted Breaux was creating a new absinthe called Lucid, and he began testing bottles from the late nineteenth century to show that properly made absinthe contained very little thujone. He proved that just about all absinthe, both historical and contemporary, had less than ten parts per million of thujone. The whole thujone scare appeared to be overblown, and the ban existed mainly because, until 2007, there had been no way to prove absinthe's innocence. The U.S. Alcohol and Tobacco Tax and Trade Bureau did similar tests and came to the same conclusion. The ban had been misapplied. Voila! Americans were now free to drink absinthe.

Over the next twelve months, absinthe seemed very much in demand, dovetailing with another new fad for classic, speakeasy-era cocktails. The *New York Times*, in December 2007, announced "A Liquor of Legend Makes a Comeback." Nearly every lifestyle publication followed suit, championing the obscure, notorious spirit's return. By the end of 2008, at least a half dozen premium absinthe brands had come on the market, most selling for more than sixty dollars a bottle, including one called Mansinthe created by Marilyn Manson. You knew the inevitable backlash was only a matter of time, but even jaded observers had to be surprised at just how swiftly the cognoscenti gave the official Thumbs Down on poor old absinthe.

The first *New York Times* Sunday Styles section of 2009 declared absinthe "uncool," with Styles reporter Eric Konigsberg calling it "falsely subversive" and likening absinthe to such fleeting cultural fads as cigar bars, soul patches, women's lower-back tattoos, brushed-nickel kitchen fixtures, and "blogging about one's bikini grooming." He wrote, "Once the naughty aura of the forbidden fruit is removed, all that remains is a grasp at unearned sophistication."

The *San Francisco Chronicle*'s Food section was more blunt, calling absinthe "out" in its 2009 New Year's predictions. Harsher still: "We liked it much better when it was illegal. Somehow the notion of being illicit overrides the flavor of NyQuil dripping down your throat."

As I observed this phenomenon, I thought, "Well, duh." Americans mostly don't like the taste of licorice. Absinthe is flavored with anise, giving it a strong licorice taste. These two basic truths pretty much ensured that the spirit would never be enduringly popular in the United States. So presenting the sleight-of-hand notion that absinthe was ever "cool" before being reported as "uncool"—essentially hyping absinthe, then

twelve months later calling it overhyped—is breathtakingly shallow even
by the usual standards of lifestyle journalism. It smacks of high school.

But maybe this makes sense. There's always been a whiff of adoles-
cence when it comes to Americans and absinthe, a teenage sort of long-
ing to experience something thrilling and subversive—drama followed
by the callow need to point out, Holden Caulfield–like, just how phoney
it all is.

I can empathize. I first tasted absinthe while on a magazine assign-
ment in the late 1990s, in Barcelona at a dive called Bar Marsella. "An
absinthe or two at Bar Marsella" was firmly established as one of the
Lonely Planet guide's "highlights" of the city, and the crowd was a typical
mishmash of backpackerish tourists from around the globe. Sure, some
Moroccan guys tried to sell me hash outside. Sure, the bartender physi-
cally tossed two pickpockets out the door. And sure, that bartender
was a dodgy, middle-aged American guy named Scotty, a six-foot-two,
well-over-two-hundred-pound, red-haired man who wore pink shirts,
who referred to himself as "Super Queer," who claimed to be a former
child actor, and who refused to tell me his last name because "as far as
you're concerned, I don't have a last name." Yet for the most part, Bar
Marsella was "sketchy" only in a safe, air-quotes sort of way. During my
twenties, I'd vaguely imagined myself as some sort of romantic flâneur,
a Eurotrash-loving vagabond hanging out in seedy bars, like Rimbaud.
In reality, my first sip of absinthe took place when I was a marginally
employed twenty-nine-year-old writing an article for an airline in-flight
magazine. The letdown was unavoidable.

Had I paid better attention in high school English class, I would
have read of this type of anise-flavored disappointment from an earlier
chronicler of subversive lifestyle trends, one Ernest Hemingway—once
again in "Hills Like White Elephants," as the quarreling couple finally
taste their glasses of anís.

> "It tastes like licorice," the girl said and put the glass down.
> "That's the way with everything."

"Yes," said the girl. "Everything tastes of licorice. Especially all the things you've waited so long for, like absinthe."

It may be true. That's not to say that the actual absinthe, in the glass, was bad. It was enjoyable, particularly when you drizzled the water over the sugar cube and through the slotted spoon. But by that point in my life, I'd already experienced enough licorice-tasting firewaters to have an idea of what to expect. Absinthe, in reality, just seemed like a stronger, more bitter, more herbal version of the sambuca I'd snuck out of my parents' liquor cabinet. And by comparison, my old act of stealing the sambuca had its own small but genuine element of subversiveness. No matter how much I wanted to feel edgy or illicit sitting in a seedy bar in Barcelona years later, how could legally purchased absinthe ever compare to stolen sambuca? Even Rimbaud had moved beyond his absinthe-drinking flâneur stage by the age of nineteen: having shocked the bourgeoisie quite enough for one lifetime, he never wrote another line of poetry.

Viewed this way, the idea that you could ever hope to sustain the imagination of adults with a sixty-dollar bottle of absinthe becomes absurd. Sure, many will purchase a bottle and try it—once—out of curiosity: Will it make me hallucinate? Will I become a decadent anarchist and write Symbolist poetry? Will I cut my own ear off, like Van Gogh? When none of that happens and they realize they don't really like licorice, they'll shove the bottle into the back of their liquor cabinet, where it will languish for the next decade or so. My advice to these people's future children: if the absinthe bottle has a pourer spout, don't try to unclog it with a pencil.

Perhaps we experience drinks very much like we experience the popular songs of our youth. An ounce and a half of booze, a three-minute song— ephemeral for sure, yet in the right context you may remember it your whole life. We know that no new song—regardless of how well made it is—will ever matter as much the one we heard as a teenager with a broken heart. Similarly, maybe no drink matters quite like the first ones we procure, with our own guile and wits, for ourselves. Only later, as we trudge into adulthood, do we realize that many of the things we wait for our whole lives do indeed taste of licorice. I believe this is why so many Americans end up drinking what they enjoyed in high school or college. Disappointed, people fall back on the visceral experience of memory. Of course memories are important, but as I've gone deeper into the world of spirits, I've been determined to keep new visceral experiences front and center.

Taste is so subjective, so fickle, and a source of so much insecurity. Anyone who's in the business of sipping or chewing (or, for that matter, looking at paintings or listening to music or watching television) and then passing judgment will inevitably have the experience of his or her taste being called into question: "Why should we trust you?" After a particularly intense stretch of tastings during the first year of my job—my palate seemingly on overload—I found myself asking this very question. Of myself.

So I decided to pay a visit to a guy who'd been doing this a lot longer than I have: F. Paul Pacult, publisher of the influential quarterly newsletter *Spirit Journal*. Over two decades, Pacult has emerged as a sort of Robert Parker of the spirits industry. The latest edition of his booze compendium, *Kindred Spirits 2*, the follow-up to his seminal 1997 guide, reviews more than twenty-four hundred spirits and rates them on a one-to-five-star scale. I had not met Pacult before, though I've regularly consulted my dog-eared copy of the first *Kindred Spirits* over the past ten years.

As I drove up to meet him in Wallkill, in New York's Hudson Valley, I worried I'd find the ultimate spirits snob—someone who might unmask me as a fraud. I arrived at Pacult's beautiful home in the morning; he met me graciously at the door. Pacult, with his round glasses, trim mustache, and proclivity toward turtleneck shirts, looks more like a high school music teacher than a spirits guru, with a sort of Ned Flanders–esque demeanor—warmhearted with a subtle tinge of smugness. We sat on his patio, drinking ice water, and looking out at his big, green yard. Pacult is nothing if not a cheerleader for fine spirits. "Americans are growing up again," he said. "We've kind of been children when it comes to our drinks."

Pacult believes we're currently entering a "golden age of spirits" and that spirits are poised at a similar place in the public's consciousness as wine was in the early 1980s. "I think it's been a natural progression," he said. "As our collective palate has grown, suddenly we needed more challenge. And spirits are a bigger challenge. From a critical standpoint, spirits, especially when you're tasting ones that have 40 percent alcohol or more, are not easy things to break down."

After finishing our ice water, we went up to his office, where his wife Sue had laid out our morning tasting on white paper. That day, we were to taste three cognacs from Martell: Cordon Bleu ($85); XO ($129); and Creation Grand Extra ($299). Pacult only tastes in the morning, usually beginning around 8:30, and will never taste more than eight spirits in a session. He uses a spittoon and rarely swallows. This surprised me—up until that point, spitting had run completely counter to my own tasting strategies.

As he opened a template for his next issue of *Spirits Journal* on the computer, he said, "It would be the easiest thing in the world to become a complete lush. But I'm remarkably abstemious. It's crucial to our industry, because spirits are already more negatively viewed. At the drop of a hat, temperance and Prohibition could all be back again. In America, things can tip just like that."

We sat together in desk chairs in front of the computer and went through his methodology. First, appearance. We held our glasses up to the light. "Now, this to me is a burnished orange. Topaz," Pacult said of the Cordon Bleu. "This has impeccable purity." Pacult writes his newsletters as he tastes, and he said these immediate reactions generally stand as his reviews. For Cordon Bleu, he typed, "topaz" and "impeccable purity."

Next, he held up the XO. "Oh my, is that sediment?" He frowned. "Oh, my, my, my. That's a shame. I love Martell, but it is what it is." He typed, "Pretty chestnut color is marred somewhat by floating debris." Pacult was similarly crestfallen at a bit of sediment in the Creation

Grand Extra. Only upon a third inspection could I see a speck of sediment. "Look," he said, "no one would ever notice this except for a maniac like me."

Smell came next, the sense that Pacult insisted is the most important in experiencing spirits. We started again with the Cordon Bleu. "Mmm. First whiff gives me nuts," he said. "Next, I smell dried flowers, almost like in a yearbook." He typed, "Sophisticated scent, mature."

We smelled the XO and Pacult said he got "pears, grapes, and an oily, buttery scent" on this first whiff. And then "cherries, dried strawberry, white chocolate, and prunes." He typed, "Mature yet owns the promise of youthfulness."

By now, I was playing along, and said that I was smelling dates. "Dates!" Pacult shouted and typed, "My friend Jason who's tasting with me says 'dates.'"

Finally, we got to actually tasting the three cognacs. Pacult took the glass of Cordon Bleu, sipped, rolled it around in his mouth a little, and spit. I took a sip and swallowed. He rubbed his hands together, moaning in ecstasy. "Sexy, sexy stuff. I have to say, I would bathe in Cordon Bleu if I could afford it." He typed, "Slow, languid . . . with a prune/raisin flavor that's silky and rich."

Next was the XO. "This spirit is a little prickly," he said. "I like that. This is not Mountain Dew. This is supposed to have a little kickback." He took another sip, rolled it on his tongue, and spit. "It's never hot, though. Or even the slightest bit rough." He typed, "Round, luxurious, and slightly coffeelike in its bittersweet approach at midpalate."

He looked up from the computer and began swirling the third glass. "I think I like the Cordon Bleu better. But jeez, what are we talking about here?"

Finally, we tasted the Creation Grand Extra. After I took my swallow, I ventured a meek opinion, in the form of a question. "Do I taste bitter chocolate here?"

"Yes," Pacult answered. "You know, I taste, like . . . a cocoa pod." He typed, "Concludes extended, but dry and cocoa bean–like. Superbly satisfying at every step."

As Pacult saved the newsletter file and started cleaning up, he told me that the Cordon Bleu would receive five stars, and that the XO and Creation Grand Extra would receive four or five stars, even with the offending sediment. How was he so immediately sure, I wanted to know. It's just one man's opinion, he said. Of course, this man estimates he's tasted more than twenty thousand spirits over his career. "I don't think I really hit my stride as a taster until about fifteen years into this, tasting every day," he said. "The only reason I can do this at all is that I've built up a library of impressions. Fifteen years of data is in my head. Anyone can do this, provided you're willing to put in the time."

After the tasting, we sat out on the patio while I drank another glass of ice water, then I bid him adieu. I wasn't exactly drunk—I'd been very careful, since I had several hours' drive home. But I was really hungry. The only thing I could find on the way to the highway was a McDonald's, and so I followed my expensive cognac tasting with a five-piece Chicken Select with barbecue sauce and a large fries. As I ate inside my car, in the parking lot, I did the math on how much catching up I'd have to do before I'd be able to duplicate Paul Pacult's memory library of twenty thousand spirits. I am nowhere near an abstemious person, and so I shuddered to imagine that I actually might die before I even came close to drinking twenty thousand spirits.

No, no, no, I thought. I'd have to find a different way of going about this. It's all fine and well that Pacult can confidently make a split-second distinction between a four-star spirit and five-star spirit. But what does it mean to most people that a spirit is "prickly" or "silky and rich" or that it tastes of "Danish and black raisins"? If I tell people that a cognac is "mature yet owns the promise of youthfulness," will they now understand what I mean? Do I understand what that means? No, this was no way to change people's hearts and minds and introduce them to the wide world of flavors. This was too much like the language of wine, and so many critics had already ruined the enjoyment of wine. I wasn't going to be an accomplice in that sort of thing when it came to spirits.

No, I needed to go out into the world and taste. I needed to continue the journey that began so long ago in my parents' kitchen pantry.

A Round of Drinks:
Old-Time Tastes

It seems patently unfair—rude, in fact—to have started talking about booze without actually fixing any drinks. So allow me to break this narrative for a moment, step behind the bar, and offer you, dear reader, both a cocktail and a few thoughts. If you're going to make it through two hundred–plus pages with me, you'll probably be needing a few more cocktails. Consider these chapter-ending interludes as sort of like big, boozy endnotes. (And if you happen to need a bit more cocktail-making advice, on anything from stocking your bar to glassware to the proper way to garnish with a citrus peel twist, be sure to turn to the appendix.)

Since the Stinger is the first real cocktail I ever enjoyed, with that dapper gentleman in the hotel bar, it is the first drink I will pour. Years after that day, I learned that the Stinger is traditionally served straight up and not on the rocks. This means, of course, that my mentor was wrong. But no matter. I still take my Stinger on ice.

Sometimes, I'll even add a dash of absinthe to the mix. I mean, now that I've spent my sixty dollars on a bottle (and realized that Toulouse-Lautrec and I do not share the same taste in spirits), I've looked for ways to utilize it. Anyway, with a dash of absinthe it's called a Stinger Royale. That's how Reginald Vanderbilt liked his, which is probably why the Stinger has always been considered a high-society drink.

A 1923 profile of Vanderbilt (quoted by historian David Wondrich in his entertaining book *Imbibe!*) describes the Stinger as "a short drink with a long reach, a subtle blending of ardent nectars, a boon to friendship, a dispeller of care." I would add that the Stinger, with or without absinthe, is the perfect drink for after dinner, after lunch, or after breakfast. It always amazes me how much I like this drink, because it uses one of the most cloying and loathed liqueurs in the bar: crème de menthe (always white, never the yucky green stuff). The cognac, however, is key.

STINGER ROYALE

Serves 1

> **2 ounces cognac**
> **½ ounce white crème de menthe**
> **1 dash absinthe**
> **Lemon peel twist, for garnish**

Fill a shaker two-thirds full with ice. Add the cognac, crème de menthe, and absinthe. Shake well, then strain into either a chilled cocktail glass (if you like being correct) or into an old-fashioned glass with 3 or 4 ice cubes (if you like a nicer drink). Garnish with the lemon peel twist.

Cognac remains a mystery to most, even though it had its run of popularity in the mid-2000s, driven primarily by hip-hop culture. Remember Busta Rhymes's "Pass the Courvoisier"? Remember cognac being referred to as 'Nyak? Remember Crunk Juice, that blend of cognac and energy drinks like Red Bull that rappers like Lil Jon were always raving about? (I don't blame you if you tried to forget about Crunk Juice.)

Even during cognac's pop cultural moment, most people still couldn't tell you what it was. Quite simply, it's a brandy produced in the Cognac, France, Appellation d'Origine Contrôlée (AOC) following a three-hundred-year-old tradition that calls for at least 90 percent Ugni Blanc, Folle Blanche, or Colombard wine grapes to be distilled in copper pots. So, what's an AOC? It's a designation that ensures a wine or spirit (or certain other foodstuffs) adheres to quality standards in agricultural and production processes, but most importantly has its origin in a specific geographic area. Basically, a brandy produced outside the cognac AOC, or by a different method, cannot be called cognac.

Most cognacs are created by blending numerous vintages and ages. The alphabet stew of cognac classifications—VS, VSOP, XO—seems confusing, but trust me, it really isn't. VS means "very special," with the youngest eau-de-vie in the blend no less than two years old. VSOP means "very superior old pale," with the youngest eau-de-vie at least four years old. XO means "extra old," with the youngest eau-de-vie at least six years old. Yes, the really good stuff can be prohibitively priced. Most of the cognac sold in the United States is either VS or VSOP. A decent VSOP will set you back forty to fifty dollars—and this is what I'd recommend in a Stinger.

I'd also recommend a VSOP cognac in another old-school drink, the Sazerac, created in Antoine Peychaud's pharmacy in early-nineteenth-century New Orleans. The Sazerac (named after a then-popular brand of cognac) may actually be the origin of the word *cocktail*—Peychaud served it in an egg cup called a *coquetier*, and legend has it that a mispronunciation of this word stuck. It is also now the official drink of New Orleans, made so by a vote of the Louisiana legislature in June 2008. These days, most people use rye whiskey in a Sazerac, but I like the original nineteenth-century version, with cognac. And, of course, always use Peychaud's bitters.

SAZERAC

Serves 1

1 sugar cube
3 dashes Peychaud's bitters
1 1/2 ounces cognac or rye whiskey
1/4 ounce absinthe
Lemon peel twist, for garnish

Take two old-fashioned glasses. Pack one with ice to chill it. Combine the sugar cube and bitters in the other, with a splash of water; muddle until the sugar dissolves. Add the cognac and an ice cube or two; stir to mix well.

Discard the ice from the packed old-fashioned glass; add the absinthe and swirl just to coat the chilled glass, pouring out any that remains. Strain the cognac mixture into the chilled glass. Twist the lemon peel over the drink, rub it around the rim of the glass, then use it as a garnish.

Finally, perhaps my favorite use of cognac and absinthe—as well as a spirit called Dubonnet—is in the Phoebe Snow, named after one of the most famous advertising mascots of the twentieth century. Phoebe Snow was a fictional woman in flowing white who extolled the virtues of the "clean" anthracite rail travel on the Lackawanna Railroad: "Says Phoebe Snow/about to go/upon a trip to Buffalo/'My gown stays white/ from morn til night/upon the Road of Anthracite.'" Why someone named this particular drink—which is brownish red—after Phoebe Snow is anyone's guess. With its French ingredients, perhaps it's what one bartender imagined a sophisticated lady, dressed in white, would sip in a dining car on the Lackawanna Railroad.

PHOEBE SNOW

Serves 1

> 1½ ounces cognac
> 1½ ounces Dubonnet
> ½ teaspoon absinthe
> 1 dash Angostura bitters

Fill a mixing glass halfway with ice. Add the cognac, Dubonnet, absinthe, and bitters. Stir vigorously, and then strain into a chilled cocktail glass.

So what exactly is Dubonnet? Obscure spirits become obscure for many obscure reasons. But there may be no bottle more enigmatic than this fortified wine. Its strange journey from popularity to obscurity begins with malaria; involves the French Foreign Legion, the Queen of England, and Pia Zadora; and ends with it languishing on the dusty bottom shelves of your local liquor store, usually next to the vermouth.

Luckily for us, malaria hasn't been endemic in the United States in decades. If it were, we might be better acquainted with Dubonnet and its category of wine-and-cinchona-bark-based aperitifs called *quinquinas*.

Long before the days of modern medicine, a cinchona bark extract called quinine was the only weapon against the deadly mosquito-borne parasite that caused malaria. And so, by the nineteenth century, pharmacists were continually mixing up ways to mask the bitter taste of quinine in a drink. British colonials began drinking gin mixed with quinine-rich tonic water in South Asia and Africa for prophylactic reasons.

During the French conquest of North Africa in the 1830s, the government offered incentives to anyone who could create a recipe that would help make quinine more palatable to the soldiers. Not long afterward, Dubonnet was born, created in 1846 by a Parisian chemist named Joseph Dubonnet. Its "infusion of sensual flavors" (according to the bottle) "won world-wide acclaim after Madame Dubonnet began serving it to family and friends." An image of Madame's cat remains the brand's logo. Dubonnet's distinct port-like flavor is spiced with cinnamon, coffee beans, citrus peel, and herbs (a secret formula, of course), but the quinine is what creates its slightly bitter edge.

Dubonnet reportedly is a preferred tipple of Queen Elizabeth II and was favored by the late Queen Mother. "I think that I will take two small bottles of Dubonnet and gin with me this morning, in case it is needed," the Queen Mother once wrote to her butler in preparation for an outdoor lunch (this handwritten note was sold at auction for £16,000).

Dubonnet even had a sort of moment in the late 1970s and early 1980s when Pia Zadora starred as the "Dubonnet Girl" in television commercials. Those might be among the cheesiest liquor ads of all time: Zadora plays sensually with ribbon and peers out between gauzy curtains while her Continental lover approaches by motorcycle—wearing a helmet, tuxedo, and white scarf—for their rendezvous. Excellent, really, if you're a connoisseur of Eurotrash, as I am. It may help you forget for a moment that, these days, Dubonnet is actually made and bottled in Bardstown, Kentucky.

Dubonnet comes in either Rouge or Blonde, and let me be clear about one thing: the white is to be avoided at all costs. It has an unpleasant aftertaste and a god-awful cat-pee smell (perhaps channeling Madame Dubonnet's feline?). Dubonnet Rouge, on the other hand, makes an excellent mixer, particularly with gin. It doesn't have a million applications, but the few it does have stand out and make it worthwhile. Case in point: The Dubonnet Cocktail (the Queen Mother's drink) is a mix of equal parts gin and Dubonnet that's simple and wonderful, an early-twentieth-century classic. Add a dash of orange bitters to the mix, and it might give the martini a run for its money. It's the perfect drink to share with the Queen. Or with Pia Zadora. Or if you happen to be sent off to the French Foreign Legion. Or if you're relaxing at home and want to be super-certain that you remain malaria free.

CHAPTER 2

FLAVOR AND ITS DISCONTENTS

ALL OF LIFE IS A DISPUTE OVER TASTE AND TASTING.

—*Friedrich Nietzsche*

W HEN WE TALK ABOUT FLAVOR, we must make a simple distinction. First, there are actual tastes that grow out of a place, a tradition, an artisan method; then there is Flavor™, which is conceived in a conference room, developed in a lab, and validated by focus groups.

With that in mind, I feel the need to say a few words about the explosion of flavored vodkas. Well, maybe just two words: totally ridiculous. No, that is perhaps too harsh, too strident, and ungenerous. So maybe a few more. I mean, I can understand the impulse behind, say, a basic citrus vodka, and maybe even vanilla. But is there any earthly justification for the existence of a lychee-flavored vodka? Or coconut vodka? Watermelon vodka? Green grape vodka *and* red grape vodka? Cherry *and* black cherry vodka? Huckleberry vodka? Kaffir lime vodka? Blood orange vodka? Pink lemonade vodka? Organic cucumber vodka? Sweet tea vodka? Cola vodka? Root beer vodka? Sake-infused vodka? Protein powder–infused vodka? Dutch caramel vodka? Espresso vodka? Double espresso vodka? Triple espresso vodka? So-called mojito mint vodka? Bubble gum vodka? Yes, every one of these vodka flavors has sat on a liquor store shelf, and this list represents only the tip of the iceberg. In 2003, there were about two hundred flavored vodkas on the market. Today, there are more than five hundred.

The liquor store has swiftly come to resemble those Jelly Belly stores that sprung up when I was a kid in the 1980s. I can remember the first time my brother Tyler and I were let loose, on a family vacation, to scoop our own half pounds of jelly beans from dozens of varieties. You were allowed to taste all the beans as you scooped, and we went nuts, bingeing our way into a sugar overdose. "Cotton candy! Dr. Pepper! Green apple! Chocolate pudding! A&W root beer! Piña colada!"

"Can you believe this jelly bean tastes like buttered popcorn?"

"Taste this one! It's like cheesecake!"

"Toasted marshmallow!"

There was certainly no pretense of *real* flavor. The idea of *authenticity* was rendered utterly irrelevant—I mean, all the flavors came from freaking identically shaped beans! They were a food engineering marvel and it was absolutely awesome . . . at least when I was, um, eleven. You know what else I liked when I was eleven? Garbage Pail Kids, Mr. T, parachute pants, snapping Jenny Bellamente's training bra strap, and building forts in the woods. These days, I go to the liquor store for a slightly different experience. (Although ironically, in the summer of 2010, Jelly Belly introduced several "adult" flavors as part of their new Cocktail Classics line: Mojito, Peach Bellini, and Pomegranate Cosmo among them.)

Flavored vodkas follow the same flavor fads that sports drinks, fruit snacks, and sugar cereals follow. A flavorist for Givaudan, the world's largest manufacturer of flavors, explained the development of these trends in a 2009 article in the New Yorker: "You are trying to sell a flavor. It's not like you are getting judged on how close you are to the real fruit. At the end of the day, you are getting judged on how good the flavor tastes."

With that sort of calculation, it's no surprise that flavor trends seem to work a little like high school. One day, the cool kids—usually the people with suspicious job titles like "flavorist" or "cool hunter" or "trendspotter"—wake up and decide that, say, pomegranate will be the next big flavor. There's usually talk of antioxidants or benefits to the urinary tract, but everyone knows the popularity is really all about the crimson-purple color. Suddenly, everywhere you turn, they're putting pomegranate into everything. How did we ever live without the sweet-and-sour nectar of the pomegranate? So you welcome the pomegranate into your life. Then, without warning, you're told that pomegranate is so, like, last year. Pear is the new pomegranate. Hadn't you heard?

Yeah, well, me neither. When I first began writing about spirits—basically before I learned to ignore 99 percent of the emails I received—I got this from the Pear Bureau Northwest: "Pears Make a Splash as Fresh Drink Trend for 2007."

Okay, so pears were the New Black. This, of course, made total sense . . . if I just could overlook the fact that pears have been cultivated and enjoyed by humans since about 5000 BCE. But I kept receiving the same message. In another breathless news release, a spokesperson for Absolut vodka declared pear to be "the next big flavor." Said this spokesperson, "We constantly have flavorists on the hunt for all the new scents, flavors, and tastes, and pear was 'ripe' for us." Not surprisingly, Absolut was, at precisely the same moment, launching a new flavored vodka, Absolut Pears. Within weeks, Grey Goose unveiled its own pear vodka, La Poire.

Now, anyone who understands lifestyle journalism knows that three of anything is a certifiable trend, and so by early 2007 we were getting dangerously close to the tipping point on pear vodka. When I tasted the two new pear vodkas, what struck me immediately was how differently each company interpreted pear flavor. Grey Goose had a delicate, sort-of-natural-ish pear bouquet. But the mild flavor was so subtle as to be nearly lost in the mouth. Absolut Pears had a strong candy scent and an assertive, "fruity" taste that no pear in nature could possibly convey.

So what was one supposed to do with pear vodka anyway? That is a very good question—one that I ask myself every time I see those two three-quarters-full bottles that sit in the back of my liquor cabinet. No one else seemed to know, either. This post on the industry site Webtender was typical: "I work at a rather nice upscale restaurant in Manhattan and our bartender recently ordered Absolute [sic] Pear. After we all tasted it in several drinks we decided to make a few drinks based around it for our signature drink list. We aren't having much luck." Or this, regarding La Poire, on the website Chowhound: "I don't get it, personally. I'd rather drink poire eaux-de-vie." Or harsher still: "I tried it straight and would've rather of [sic] drank warm piss through a dirty sock."

I kept waiting, but a year or so went by, no third pear vodka ever appeared, and the pear vodka trend came and went with a whimper. But no matter. By then, people had moved on to sweet tea or bubble gum or some other ridiculousness. People, people, people.

By "people," of course, I mean the vast majority of spirits consumers. The largest liquor companies in the world haven't launched more than five hundred flavored vodkas because no one wanted to drink them. Of course, whenever a vast majority pursues any kind of macrotrend, there will always be a backlash from a smaller group who vehemently resists the mainstream. Which means that, as usual, we're right back in high school. In the world of spirits, these vodka rejecters might be called cocktail connoisseurs or aficionados. But since high school continues to be a useful metaphor here, let's just call these people what they are: cocktail geeks. I must confess that I usually sit at the cocktail geeks' lunch table.

What the cocktail geeks' rejection of the most popular spirit wrought was the alternative trend of the so-called classic cocktail, culled from the dusty pages of antique drinks guides like Jerry Thomas' 1862 Bar-Tender's Guide, or Harry Johnson's 1882 New and Improved Bartender's Manual, or William T. "Cocktail Bill" Boothby's 1908 The World's Drinks and How to Mix Them. These classic cocktails called for more challenging, forgotten spirits like rye whiskey, applejack, maraschino liqueur, Old Tom gin, and crème de violette—spirits with more assertive, unclassifiable flavors that can be a shock to a modern palate weaned on the likes of Jelly Bellys.

The classic cocktail trend led to the rise of faux speakeasy bars, which began in places like New York and San Francisco but soon enough trickled down to most other cities. Certain conventions of the faux speakeasy quickly became universal (and soon thereafter risked cliché). There's usually no sign, and often some kind of "secret" entrance: through a phone booth in a hot dog shop (PDT, aka Please Don't Tell, in New York); through a side entrance of an Irish fish-and-chips shop marked by a blue light (PX in Alexandria, Virginia); below street level through a black unmarked door under a sign that reads "Liquids" (Franklin Mortgage & Investment Co. in Philadelphia). The speakeasy bartender's uniform is an old-timey vest and tie and maybe sleeve garters; beards and tattoos and maybe a man-bun; and possibly a waxed mustache, depending on how much pre-Prohibition role-playing is going on. Some ironically retro rules ("Gentlemen must remove their hats"; "No roughhousing, horseplay, tomfoolery, or high jinks") will usually be listed on the menu. Other, nonironic rules, like "You can't stand at the bar" or "You need to be on the list" will be enforced by a hipster in skinny jeans at the door. Most importantly, at the faux speakeasy you will find almost no cocktails with vodka. Your cocktails will be handcrafted and wonderful, but they will also sport double-digit price tags.

Now, I love many of the bartenders who work in faux speakeasies across the country. Many are my friends, and speakeasy bartenders such as Jim Meehan at PDT, Todd Thrasher at PX, Derek Brown at the Columbia Room in D.C., and the guys at Bourbon and Branch in San Francisco make some of the best cocktails you can find. Their obsession with the pre-Prohibition era is genuine and logical. The cocktails of that era are revered for a reason. Prohibition basically destroyed the craft of bartending, making the profession illegal and forcing bartenders into other lines of work. And make no mistake: bartenders prior to Prohibition were viewed as craftsmen, akin to pastry chefs or cheese makers or chocolatiers. Whether the puritans among us like it or not, cocktails are traditional American foodways. But Prohibition irrevocably broke the cultural chain of bartending knowledge. Everything horrible about contemporary drinking could reasonably, if indirectly, be blamed on that broken chain. Day-Glo premade mixes: Blame it on Prohibition. Bartenders forgetting bitters in your Manhattan: Prohibition. The rise of those flavored vodkas: Yes, blame that on Prohibition, too.

Still, at a certain point, I have to roll my eyes. Faux speakeasies can very much resemble real, historic speakeasies, except for one thing: real speakeasies, operating from 1919 to 1933, were totally illegal and run by gangsters like Al Capone. That disreputable nature—the inherent seediness—of the operation was part of its allure. With the faux speakeasy, no one is worried about the Feds busting up the place; they're merely concerned with keeping out the, you know, riffraff—that "uncool" crowd who might order Coors Light. The faux speakeasy clearly grows out of a nostalgia for the glamorous seediness of Prohibition. "Seediness has a very deep appeal," Graham Greene famously wrote. "It seems to satisfy, temporarily, the sense of nostalgia for something lost; it seems to represent a stage further back." So if seediness itself is a form of nostalgia, then is the faux speakeasy an example of nostalgia for . . . nostalgia? This is the kind of thinking that leads one to drink way too many cocktails.

I believe something snapped for me during the run-up to Repeal Day in the fall of 2008. In the classic cocktail world, there is no day more feted than December 5, the anniversary of the repeal of Prohibition—it has become a sort of pseudoholiday. To help celebrate the seventy-fifth anniversary of Repeal Day, I received a press release from the Distilled Spirits Council of the United States with "tips for hosting a Repeal Day party at home." Here were the tips:

1. Ask guests to dress in 1930s attire.
2. Make sure your guests "speak easy" in order to gain admittance to the event. Suggest a password for admittance to the event.
3. Hire a band or singer that specializes in music from the "Roaring 20s" or download period-specific jazz.
4. Provide a Great Gatsby dining experience by recreating specialized dishes from archived menus of the Waldorf-Astoria and the 21 Club in New York City.
5. Offer cocktails of the era.

Was it any surprise that the speakeasy trend quickly became so overdone that journalists and bloggers started referring to any new "top-secret" bar that evoked the Prohibition era as a "speakcheesy"?

Right around the time the term *speakcheesy* was coined, Washington, D.C., got its first faux speakeasy project, called Hummingbird to Mars. The name comes from a statement by Senator Morris Sheppard, an infamous Dry from Texas whose proudest accomplishment was that he helped write the Eighteenth Amendment, which ushered in Prohibition. Sheppard famously boasted, "There is as much chance of repealing the Eighteenth Amendment as there is for a hummingbird to fly to the planet Mars with the Washington Monument tied to its tail."

Hummingbird to Mars operated "clandestinely" on Sunday and Monday nights above a popular bar called Bourbon in the popular Adams Morgan nightlife district. As with any super-hush-hush speakeasy, media were tipped off to its opening well in advance. I arrived at Bourbon, rang a bell, and was let upstairs to a smaller private room. After the doorman dutifully made certain I was on the list, I received a delicious glass of classic Fisherman's Punch (rum, cognac, lemon and lime juices, honey syrup, and grated nutmeg). The bartenders were gussied up in vests and sleeve garters, mixing superb classics such as the Corpse Reviver #2 (gin, Cointreau, Lillet Blanc, and absinthe) and the Blood and Sand (blended Scotch, Cherry Heering, orange juice, and sweet vermouth), and variations on the classic Sling (applejack, sloe gin, lemon juice, bitters, and simple syrup).

And then I was given this note, in an envelope:

Welcome to Hummingbird to Mars and thank you for finding us. By accepting a reservation you must agree to certain terms and any infraction will cause you to be unwelcome at our establishment.

1. If you are a member of the press/blogger/other media type person you are not permitted to write about our location or our operation in any way, shape, or form.
2. You are not allowed to disclose our address to anyone.

3. You may not take any photographs of the inside or outside of our bars.

4. Cell phone use will not be permitted within the establishment.

I sipped my drink for a moment. It was very tasty. But then I thought about this note, these rules. I looked around the bar, which was about half full with twenty or so people—all of whom obviously knew someone who knew someone. It was great that the bartenders wanted to expose people to new spirits and cocktails they'd never find in typical bars, but this whole faux speakeasy thing began to feel way too exclusionary to me. This suddenly felt like the wrong way to reclaim some golden pre-Prohibition era of drinking. And so I just stopped wanting to play along. Here's what I did: I sent a text message to a friend (along with a photo of the bar) that read, "You should come over to [Popular Bar Named After a Whiskey Made in Kentucky], in Adams Morgan. We're upstairs." Then, the following week, I published this episode in my column in the *Washington Post*, essentially "outing" Hummingbird to Mars.

Had it been 1928, of course, I might have been shot by Al Capone's henchmen with tommy guns. But since it was 2008, I was simply called a jerk and a dick and a douchebag in various comment sections on the Internet and told to "enjoy [my] mudslides at T.G.I. Friday's." I was slightly surprised by this in-crowd's defensiveness and virulence. My big outing had been done as a joke—I mean, how serious could Hummingbird to Mars have been about the secrecy if they'd emailed the media? Anyway, it was still reservation only; it's not as if hordes were going to crash the gate and demand bad drinks. But soon enough, Hummingbird to Mars closed down. Rather than deal with a wider audience, the cocktail geeks just decided to take their ball and go home. Which, I hate to say it, basically proved my thesis.

As silly as the faux speakeasy can be, we must credit the classic cocktail movement with numerous major advancements. A prime example: creating a backlash against the Very Dry Martini. Is there any cocktail that invites more bloviation than the Very Dry Martini? Yeah, yeah, yeah, I know how you take your martini, gramps: no vermouth. I should just whisper the word *vermouth* while I mix it, right? I should simply wave a capped bottle of vermouth over the shaker? Never heard that one before! You'd rather just drink this tumbler of gin and bow in the direction of France? Yes, sir! You are correct, sir! Ugh. The joke's on you, because you're not really drinking a martini anyway. You're just drinking a cold glass of gin.

There was a lot of talk early in the Obama administration that the era of American Exceptionalism was coming to a close. If that ends up being the case, I sincerely hope the post–World War II era dry martini goes away with it. The Greatest Generation may have been great for many reasons. But can we finally, at long last, be honest about one crucial thing? Their taste in martinis is awful.

I've had a number of discussions about the martini with cocktail historian David Wondrich, the amazingly bearded drinks columnist for *Esquire* and the high priest of the classic cocktail movement. Wondrich's bearing in the world is that of a benevolent wizard, and few know more about the social history of drinking. His history of early American cocktails, *Imbibe!*, published in 2008, is perhaps the best book on drinks ever written. I count him as a guru, and I sometimes consult him on issues like this. He, unsurprisingly, takes a dim view on the midcentury Very Dry Martini. "That generation was really aggressive at working the macho angle," he says. "People were afraid to say that they liked vermouth in their drink." Thus, the rise of martinis with a gin-to-vermouth ratio ranging from 7:1 all the way up to 15:1.

Of course, if you look at mid-twentieth-century luminaries who championed a nearly vermouthless martini—such as Hemingway, Churchill, and Bogart—a certain truth emerges. Robert Hess, another classic cocktail apostle who blogs at the popular DrinkBoy.com, has called it like it is: "The authors of many of these convoluted methodologies were borderline, if not full-blown alcoholics . . . They knew exactly how to best increase the amount of personal alcohol consumption." Hess published this revelation in a scholarly journal called *Mixologist:*

The Journal of the American Cocktail. (Yes, this is a real publication. I told you we've entered hard-core geekdom here!)

Bernard De Voto (the crotchety midcentury *Harper's* columnist and Pulitzer Prize winner) declared a dry martini the "supreme American gift to world culture." But De Voto also made a lot of other silly declarations, including the idea that there "are only two cocktails"—a dry martini and "a slug of whiskey"—and that the Manhattan was "an offense against piety" and that any man who drinks one has "no spiritual dignity." Well, at least no one reads De Voto anymore.

Come to think of it, in nearly every other realm of arts and culture, the grumpy old white male has been excised from the canon, except when it comes to the Very Dry Martini. I still get emails from readers who suggest that vermouth is the handiwork of the devil. Well, I say we've been bullied far too long by conservative martini drinkers into believing there's only one way to make a martini, and that way is Very Dry. "It's pretty much undrinkable," Wondrich says. "It's not a pleasant drink. It's no wonder people turned to vodka."

Which brings me to this animal called a vodka martini, which was introduced by the baby boomers and then wholeheartedly embraced by my own generation. There simply is no such thing as a vodka *martini*. The martini is certainly more of a broad concept than a specific recipe, but the one constant must be gin and vermouth. Beyond correctness, vodka and vermouth is just a terrible match. So call this drink whatever you'd like, but it is not a martini.

We can pretty much blame the vodka martini on Ian Fleming, who introduced it in the first James Bond novel, *Casino Royale*—along with the ridiculous concept of shaking and not stirring a martini. Look, I don't care how good Daniel Craig looks in his square-cut Speedo, or how much you love Sean Connery's rakish suavity: a martini should always be stirred. That's the only way you can achieve that silky smooth texture and dry martini clearness. In his classic 1948 bar guide, *The Fine Art of Mixing Drinks*, David Embury has a terse footnote: "If you shake the Martini, it becomes a Bradford." For those attempting to work the macho angle, by the way, a shaken martini is a weaker drink.

Because change is in the air, here's an idea: Let's put to rest both the mid-twentieth-century Very Dry Martini and the vodka martini. Let's pass a resolution that stipulates every dry martini should consist of a gin-to-vermouth ratio of at least 4:1 (okay, 5:1 in some cases) and offer incentives for those that move toward 2:1 or equal parts. (Even De Voto advocated a 3.7:1 ratio.) And while we're at it, let's sign an executive order banning the torturous use of jokes about vermouth.

"The martini evolves," Wondrich says. "It has evolved since it was born." Since it's now so stunted and mutated, perhaps it's best to go back to the beginning and start the evolution all over again. That's what Wondrich and other classic cocktail people have done.

Let's revisit what the martini was like before Prohibition. At the beginning there was actually a lot of vermouth in a martini. In fact, it was sweet vermouth from Italy. The Martini brand of sweet vermouth (for decades sold in the States under the name Martini & Rossi) was available since at least the early 1860s. There's a lot of debate and a lot of crazy theories in cocktail geek circles about the mysterious origins of the name *martini*. Here's my two cents: it probably came about because people called for a specific brand of vermouth—um, say, *Martini*—to mix with their gin. It's probably no different than dudes who call for a Ketel One martini or Maker's Manhattan at a bar today.

In the 1880s and 1890s, the martini and its cousins the Martine, the Martinez, and the Turf Club were basically differing ratios of gin and vermouth, with numerous variations involving dashing in bitters (orange or aromatic), sugar syrup, curaçao, maraschino liqueur, or even absinthe. One of my favorite martini cousins from that era is called the Fourth Degree, which is two parts gin and one part Italian vermouth with dashes of absinthe and aromatic bitters. One key difference in those early days was the gin. The predominant martini ingredient was Old Tom, a sweeter style of gin with more intense botanicals and less of the medicinal aftertaste. The famed Tom Collins actually derives its name from the fact that Old Tom gin was its original ingredient.

Beginning in the 1900s, there was a turn toward dry vermouth and dry martinis, and this is the first time we see *dry* becoming a code word for sophistication. In *Imbibe!*, Wondrich quotes an 1897 newspaper interview with a New York bartender: "When a customer comes in and orders a sweet drink . . . I know at once he's from the country."

During Prohibition, of course, the martini took a bad turn. Vermouth from Europe became scarce, as did certain liqueurs and bitters and Old Tom gin, and people started going for maximum alcohol. "Who was bootlegging vermouth?" says Wondrich. But there was plenty of gin—you could make it in your bathtub.

We now live in an era of huge advancements in the world of gin, bitters, and vermouth. Today, we are lucky that many of the original nineteenth-century ingredients have been resurrected. There are now more styles of bitters—from aromatic to Peychaud's, from orange to lemon, from cherry to celery—widely available. Hayman Distillers, in London, has reintroduced Old Tom gin to the United States for the first time in almost a century.

In the world of vermouth, most notable is the appearance in the States of high-end Dolin, imported from France and based on an 1821 recipe (and costing eighteen dollars to the usual seven dollars for Martini & Rossi or Cinzano). Even gold-standard dry vermouth Noilly Prat has returned to its roots and now sells its original European recipe in the States—the Noilly Prat we've enjoyed for years was a *special* (read: dumbed-down) recipe for Americans. I like the European-style Noilly Prat—it's got a lot more flavor—but, of course, this change has been a lightning rod for criticism. When it was launched, the conservative *Wall Street Journal* called the new-recipe Noilly Prat "evil" and a "fussy imposter" and said that a martini made with it was "a mess." I completely disagree—it's just more of that Very Dry Martini bullying.

Most of the general public, of course, has ignored the various quasi-academic, pseudophilosophical discussions regarding classic cocktails. Perhaps this ignorance has been bliss. Certainly I've wanted to slit my own wrists once or twice after debating and dissecting the finer points of a martini or Manhattan. But surely those who've never ventured beyond vodka have also missed out on something.

Not too long ago, I was sitting at the bar of Franklin Mortgage & Investment Co., a faux speakeasy in Philadelphia that's named after a historic bootlegging front. The Franklin follows almost all the standard conventions, including the entrance being below street level. There is actually a hint of real seediness though, since it took over the space of a previous bar that was known for a being a reliable place to buy ecstasy and cocaine. What I love about the Franklin is what I love about any speakeasy—its bartenders make great drinks the right way.

On this night, I was chatting with the bartenders and I was drinking a Carroll Gardens, a mix of rye whiskey, sweet vermouth, an Italian amaro, and maraschino liqueur. This is one of no fewer than half a dozen variations of the Manhattan on their cocktail menu, all named after different neighborhoods and cities—the Brooklyn, the Bronx, the Newark, the Kensington (in north Philadelphia).

The place was getting crowded, and as I sipped, two big guys pushed their way to the bar. They wore suits, but these guys were of a familiar type in Philadelphia—hair gel, tans, definitely major gym time and some protein powder in the recent past. I don't want to label, but if we're calling the cocktail crowd geeks, then we might reasonably call these guys meatheads. Both were scoping the crowd. Instead of the male bartenders in the vests, they made a beeline to Katie, the lone female shaking drinks behind the bar. "Get me two Grey Goose martinis," said the shorter of the two. "Very dry."

"Oh, I don't have that," Katie said. She smiled.

"What vodka do you have?"

"We don't have any vodka."

The guy looked genuinely perplexed. For a moment, I sort of felt bad for him. "You don't have any vodka? Are you shittin' me?"

"No, we don't have any vodka."

He turned around to his friend and scrunched up his face. "What kind of fucking place is this?" He turned back to the bartender. "Are you fucking with me? You don't have vodka?"

"No, I'm sorry," she said, smiling even more widely. She handed the pair a leather-bound, ten-page cocktail menu. "Take a look, and I can recommend something if you'd like. What other spirits do you like?" The two studied the menu for a moment as if it were written in Estonian.

The guy who'd ordered turned to me, exasperated, and asked, "What are you drinking? That any good?"

Okay, I thought. Here we go. Here's the perfect chance to turn someone on to something new—a new taste, a new flavor. So I said, "You know a Manhattan, right?" He nodded his head in cautious affirmation, suggesting he had some faint notion of a drink called a Manhattan. "Well, this is sort of like a Manhattan except this is a mix of rye whiskey . . ."

"Ugh," he cut me off. "Rye whiskey, fuck that."

"Well, maybe you could try your martini with gin then?" I said, hopefully.

"No way. I hate gin!"

His taller friend slapped him on the shoulder and finally spoke. "Fuck this place," he said. "Let's get out of here. No wonder there's no fucking girls in this fucking place."

A Round of Drinks:
Beyond Martinis and Manhattans

H. L. Mencken famously called the martini "the only American invention as perfect as the sonnet." The sonnet, as anyone who took freshman English may remember, is a poem with a specific meter, a structure of exactly fourteen lines and a strict rhyme scheme. This being the age of free verse, no one writes sonnets anymore. Which is just as well, since almost no one reads poetry anymore.

I've been tasting a lot of silly drinks lately, and I believe we have entered the age of free verse in cocktails. Creativity is to be admired, and it's certainly exciting to fancy oneself a "bar chef" or a "mixologist" or even a *"molecular* mixologist." But as I said to several mixologists when I began this job, "Let's make a deal: I promise not to pretend I'm going to win a Pulitzer Prize for writing about booze. And in exchange, this is what we will call people who make drinks for a living: bartenders."

Sometimes I think we're all losing our minds. Here are some ingredients I've seen on recent cocktail menus: rose hips, yuzu juice, truffle oil, tarragon soda, Szechuan peppercorns, tonka bean syrup, cherrywood-smoked white pepper meringue, dehydrated lotus roots, cotton candy floss. Mencken would not be amused.

A lot of contemporary cocktails bring to mind Robert Frost's assertion that writing free verse poetry is like playing tennis without a net. Or, in the words of one wise friend, befuddled by an upscale cocktail menu, "Dude, every once in a while can I just get something to drink?"

That same friend asked me to tell him honestly—as a normal human being—what my favorite cocktail is. I thought about a drink with ingredients that don't require a visit to an expensive gourmet shop, an act of Congress to import, or the hiring of a private detective to track down.

That's easy, I said. No contest. The Manhattan.

With apologies to Mencken, the Manhattan is more complex than the martini and more flavorful. Like a strong poetic structure, the Manhattan's recipe is more of a starting point than a rote list of ingredients. It is both universal and highly personal. The Manhattan encourages modifications, riffs, virtuoso performances.

And it is deceptively simple. In its most basic form, the Manhattan is two parts whiskey, one part vermouth, a few dashes of bitters, and a garnish. But that is simply an outline. As any art school student is told, you have to know the rules before you know how to break them. Consider the following as you customize:

- Will you use bourbon or rye? The original nineteenth-century Manhattan was meant for rye, which is brasher and spicier, but I just as often reach for smoother, sweeter bourbon.

- What vermouth will you use? The basic choice is an Italian vermouth, or sweet vermouth, such as Martini & Rossi or Cinzano. But there are so many excellent Manhattans that replace vermouth with a bitter Italian amaro such as Averna, Cynar, Punt e Mes, or Ramazzotti. Likewise, you can experiment with other types of vermouth. A Perfect Manhattan calls for a little dry vermouth. A Bianco Manhattan calls for bianco vermouth, which, with its vanilla and floral notes, is totally different than dry vermouth.

- Do not omit the bitters. I cannot stress this enough. The most common cause of a bad Manhattan is a poor bartender who leaves out the bitters. Most often I go for a couple of dashes of Angostura bitters, but there are excellent versions that call for orange bitters, Peychaud's bitters, and others.

- Will you garnish the drink with a maraschino cherry, a lemon twist, or both? I would suggest making a batch of homemade preserved cherries (page 217) or using real marasca cherries from Luxardo, rather than relying on the typical, fluorescent, artificial-red orbs.

- One last item: A Manhattan is always stirred. That is nonnegotiable.

BLACK MANHATTAN

Serves 1

> 2 ounces rye whiskey
> ³/₄ ounce Averna
> 1 dash Angostura bitters
> 1 dash orange bitters
> Preserved or maraschino cherry, for garnish (page 217)

Fill a mixing glass two-thirds full with ice. Add the rye whiskey, Averna, and both bitters. Stir vigorously for 30 seconds, then strain into a cocktail glass. Garnish with the cherry.

Adapted from a recipe of Bourbon & Branch, San Francisco

RED HOOK

Serves 1

2 ounces rye whiskey
¹/₂ ounce Punt e Mes
¹/₄ ounce maraschino liqueur, preferably Luxardo
Preserved or maraschino cherry, for garnish (page 217)

Fill a mixing glass two-thirds full with ice. Add the rye whiskey, Punt e Mes, and maraschino liqueur. Stir vigorously for 30 seconds, then strain into a cocktail glass. Garnish with the cherry.

Adapted from a recipe by Enzo Enrico of Milk & Honey, New York

NOTE: If you substitute ¹/₂ ounce of yellow Chartreuse for the maraschino liqueur, you will have what is called a Greenpoint. If you substitute ¹/₂ ounce of Cynar and ³/₄ ounce of sweet vermouth for the Punt e Mes and the maraschino liqueur, you'll have a Little Italy.

BIANCO MANHATTAN

Serves 1

This is the only Manhattan variation in which I'd skip the bitters.

1¹/₂ ounces bourbon
1¹/₂ ounces bianco vermouth
Lemon peel twist, for garnish

Fill a mixing glass two-thirds full with ice. Add the bourbon and vermouth. Stir vigorously for 30 seconds, then strain into a cocktail glass. Garnish with the lemon peel twist.

Now, I realize the world seems to cleave into Martini People and Manhattan People. But really, isn't there enough division in the world already? If you actually consider both cocktails—about the ratios of base spirit to vermouth, the dashes of bitters, the effects of stirring and shaking—there are way more similarities than differences between the two.

So, my having professed my love of Manhattans does not mean I am not also a fan of the martini. I am, and if I'm making one I will use a ratio of three parts of juniper-forward gin, such as Beefeater's or Tanqueray, to one part Noilly Prat vermouth. I also like a dash of orange bitters and I garnish with a lemon peel twist. I am also a fan of martinis that would have been standard at the turn of the twentieth century, which call for equal parts vermouth and Old Tom gin—a more robust, *slightly* sweeter gin that has undergone a recent revival after a century of obscurity.

I count Washington, D.C.'s star bartender, Derek Brown, as a friend—even though he was one of the principals behind the Hummingbird to Mars speakeasy that I outed, and thus was resolutely not speaking to me for a while. Since then, he's moved on to other great bars like the Gibson and the Passenger.

In making his dry martinis, Brown goes for a 1:1 ratio of dry gin to dry vermouth, with a dash of orange bitters and a lemon twist. He is a big proponent of high-end vermouths like Dolin, which is imported from France and based on an 1821 recipe, and Carpano Antica, which may be the original vermouth, created in eighteenth-century Italy. (These are also about three times pricier than Martini & Rossi or Cinzano.)

Brown also uses Old Tom gin in resurrecting a nineteenth-century martini variation called the Martinez—which some theorists believe is the original martini, hailing from Martinez, California. I disagree with this crazy theory, but the Martinez does shed light on the link between martinis and Manhattans. In O. H. Byron's 1884 *Modern Bartenders' Guide,* these are the directions for making a Martinez: "Same as Manhattan, only you substitute gin for whisky."

While Brown has nailed the cocktail's historical accuracy, he also insists that the martini is not a historical document. "It's intellectually interesting," he says. "But on a certain level who cares? Does it or does it not make a good cocktail?" That answer would be yes.

MARTINEZ

Serves 1

1 ¹/₂ ounces Old Tom gin
1 ¹/₂ ounces sweet vermouth
1 teaspoon maraschino liqueur
2 dashes orange bitters
Orange peel twist, for garnish

Fill a mixing glass halfway with ice. Add the gin, vermouth, maraschino liqueur, and bitters. Stir vigorously for at least 30 seconds, then strain into a chilled cocktail glass. Garnish with the orange peel twist.

Recipe by Derek Brown of the Passenger and the Columbia Room, Washington, D.C.

One final note: You'll notice that both the Martinez and the Red Hook call for maraschino liqueur, and some of you may be wondering what that is. Never confuse, and never replace, maraschino liqueur with the juice from a jar of maraschino cherries or with other cherry spirits. The sharply sweet and fragrant Luxardo maraschino liqueur—in its telltale straw-covered bottle—is widely available, and it's what you want to seek out. The original Luxardo distillery, with its recipe dating to 1821, operated in Zara, on the Dalmatian coast of what is now Croatia, until it was destroyed during World War II. Giorgio Luxardo emigrated to Italy and rebuilt the company in 1946 at its current site, near Padua. Giorgio's descendants still make the same product. Their maraschino liqueur is distilled from a special variety of sour cherries called Marasca Luxardo, which are grown near the Luxardo family's distillery. The cherries are infused with distillate and aged for three years in Finnish ash casks, which adds no color to the clear liqueur.

As recently as a century ago, maraschino liqueur was used to preserve marasca cherries. But today, maraschino liqueur has nothing to do with the generic, glowing spheres you find in jars in American supermarkets. When I met Franco Luxardo in Italy, he had a laugh as he recalled first encountering the ersatz "maraschino" cherries while in the United States as an exchange student in the 1950s. "I remember being surprised by this strange, bright red cherry they served me," he said.

CHAPTER 3

LIQUOR STORE ARCHAEOLOGY

**THE PROBLEM WITH THE WORLD IS THAT
EVERYONE IS A FEW DRINKS BEHIND.**

—*Humphrey Bogart*

MY BROTHER TYLER AND I—long past our forays at the Jelly Belly store—used to play a game we called Liquor Store Archaeology. The aim was to make a pith-helmeted-like visit to older, neglected liquor stores—the sort of family-owned shops that perhaps were once prosperous and now do business mainly in pint-size flasks or liters of cheap wine or beer by the can. Inside, we'd scour the dark bottom shelves and dank back corners of the place, looking for forgotten bottles that had been languishing, perhaps for decades. That's one of the special things about booze. Unlike just about every product in the world, distilled spirits almost never have to be rotated. More often than not, we turned up something rare or just plain strange. Our finds spanned the world: caraway-flavored kümmel from Germany, a wasabi-flavored schnapps, a brandy from Armenia called Ararat, a honey liqueur bottled with a real honeycomb.

It became rather competitive for a while, and it was funny to find the sorts of strange spirits that had been earlier generations' versions of flavored vodka. I thought I had taken a slight lead in the game when I discovered a sweet, peachy aperitif called Panache—with a hippie-ish, 1970s faux–Art Nouveau label—that was made by Domaine Chandon but now is impossible to find. Then Tyler countered with a liqueur from Sicily called Mandarino del Castello. The label says it's made from mandarin peels, and the oversaturated photo of the hilltop castle and too-blue Mediterranean sky suggests the mid-1960s, but about Mandarino del Castello we can find no information.

I figured I'd won when I unearthed a bottle of Cordial Campari. Though made by the same company, Cordial Campari is not to be confused with the more famous red Italian aperitivo. Cordial Campari is a clear, after-dinner liqueur with a taste of raspberries. I'd heard tales of Cordial Campari and seen it in a couple of old-man bars in Italy. It had been popular with the glamorous crowd that hung out on Rome's Via Veneto in the 1950s and 1960s, but it's never been widely available in the United States. Campari ceased production entirely in 2003. The bottle I found is probably decades old. It may have even been valuable—though probably not anymore, since my friends and I broke into the bottle during a party, and it's now sitting half empty in my cabinet.

It was Tyler, though, who appeared to be the clear victor when he turned up something called, rather disturbingly, Peanut Lolita: a thick, peanut-flavored liqueur that once was produced by Continental Distilling in Linfield, Pennsylvania. The logo and fonts on the label suggest the early 1960s, but according to what little information we could unearth, Peanut Lolita was still around in the mid-1970s, when infamous presidential brother Billy Carter "often made drunken appearances" with the liqueur's spokesmodel (this according to an essay by Christopher S. Kelley in *Life in the White House: A Social History of the First Family and the President's House*). Due to the liqueur's overwhelming whiskey-and-peanut taste and grainy texture—not to mention its unfortunate name—

it is unlikely to make a comeback anytime soon. We may now own the only two bottles of Peanut Lolita left in existence. Tyler tried his best to create a semirespectable drink with the stuff: he layered ice-cold Peanut Lolita and raspberry-flavored Chambord in a shot glass and called it a PB&J. Tyler's bottle is three-quarters full, and probably will remain so for some time. After tasting his, I've never opened my own.

The unique frustration of Liquor Store Archaeology (though I guess this was also part of its appeal) lay in its zenlike experience. What we found was never what we were looking for. The harder we looked for something, the more likely it was that we'd never find it. This became especially frustrating as I began to hear tales of more and more lost spirits being revived. Other than in boutique bottle shops in big cities, it was nearly impossible for several years to find all the rediscovered gins and rye whiskeys and vermouths and bitters that cocktail world insiders were buzzing about. With liquor store shelves taken over by the booze equivalent of suburban McMansions, there seemed even less room left for these idiosyncratic tastes. Though we'd been using the word *archaeology* facetiously, at a certain point it really did feel like we were trying to recover fragments of an ancient Rome or Athens from beneath the layers of newer, shinier cities.

We also had to be on the lookout for frauds during our archaeological digs. I became excited one day when I found a bottle of sloe gin, which I hadn't seen in many years. For me, sloe gin evokes a youthful summer night long ago at a particular watering hole on the Jersey Shore that served pitchers of sloe gin fizzes and Alabama Slammers (that frightening mix of sloe gin, amaretto, and Southern Comfort), leading to a make-out session with a hair-sprayed Jersey girl in a Camaro in the Wawa parking lot. Ah, sloe gin, like Proust's madeleine for a once-mulleted boy like me.

It was only later, when I was speaking with an affable British chap named Simon Ford, the so-called "brand ambassador" for Plymouth gin, that I learned my sloe gin of memory—as well as the dusty bottle I'd found—was not the real thing, but a poor imitation. "Full of artificial flavoring and artificial coloring," he told me, with disapproval. "The kind that gathers dust in dive bars." The syrupy facsimile sloe gin was the kind of thing you'd find in embarrassing drinks such as the Sloe Comfortable Screw (sloe gin, Southern Comfort, and orange juice), or the Sloe Comfortable Screw Against the Wall (which adds Galliano), or the Panty Dropper (a horrifying concoction of sloe gin, Kahlua, and half-and-half).

Real sloe gin comes not from some factory in the Garden State, but from England. It's made from (who knew?) sloe berries (the sour, almost inedibly bitter fruit of the blackthorn, a relative of the plum) which are macerated for several months in real gin. In England, it is made mostly in family kitchens in autumn and carried in flasks during hunting season. "Sloe gin, to the English, is a little bit like limoncello is to the Italians," said Ford. "In the countryside, everyone makes their own." So for Ford, the tart, ruby-colored spirit reminds him of walking through the idyllic English countryside, picking ripe sloe berries from hedgerows with his grandmother, and sipping her homemade elixir on a cold day by a warm fire.

About ten years ago, Plymouth dusted off its dormant 1883 recipe for sloe gin and started producing very small batches of it. Sloe berries are in short supply, and it takes more than two pounds of them to make one bottle of the gin. By late 2008, Plymouth, at Ford's urging, finally managed to produce enough to export a small amount over to us.

It's fascinating how one liquor can inspire such different nostalgic connections for different people. For me, a sip of a Sloe Gin Fizz does take me all the way back to the Jersey Shore—even though it's not made with the same sloe gin I'm remembering. I must say, it's bittersweet and a bit disconcerting to realize that one's coming-of-age memories are based on a lie. But this Proustian experience flows both ways. "I taste my grandmother's sloe gin now, and it's disgusting," Ford told me. "But I don't tell her. I always tell her it's better than the one we do."

When it comes to Liquor Store Archaeology, the winner by a landslide would have to be a man named Eric Seed. "The Indiana Jones of lost spirits" is how Seed is often described in food-and-drink media. As an importer of the rare and the obscure from around the world, Seed's fingerprints are all over so many forgotten-but-now-revived spirits that it's hard to think of anyone who's been as influential in the renaissance of fine cocktails.

Seed's company, Haus Alpenz, is the one that imports Hayman's Old Tom gin, the missing link in recreating the original martini. As people gained new appreciation for vermouth, he began importing the highly regarded Dolin brand from France. He found a source for Batavia arrack, distilled from sugarcane and red rice on the Indonesian island of Java; it had been a staple in the punches of colonial America but had long ago disappeared. In Barbados, Seed located falernum, a spiced rum that had been essential to the mid-twentieth-century tiki drink craze but since vanished. When Seed can't find what he's searching for, he'll commission a distiller to recreate a spirit from old recipes—as he's done with pimento dram, a traditional Jamaican allspice liqueur. "The customers I sell to," Seed has told me, "take a very dim view of vodka."

As globetrotting as he is, Seed's "Indiana Jones" moniker is pretty funny, kind of like calling a fat guy "Tiny" or a fuzzy kitten "Killer." That's because Seed is the complete opposite of Harrison Ford's swashbuckling, lady-killing rogue archaeologist. Seed is cerebral and mild-mannered, a bespectacled forty-year-old husband and father who lives in the Minneapolis suburb of Edina. Unlike Indiana Jones, Seed seems happiest when he's lecturing like a tenured professor of booze. Wayne Curtis, drinks columnist of the *Atlantic*, described Seed as "the only person I've heard use the term *Hanseatic League* since I was in high school."

My friend Emily and I once shared a taxi ride to the airport with Seed, and he held forth for the entire thirty minutes on the history of vermouth; the species of alpine botanicals that grow near Chambéry, France; the genealogy of the Dolin family; and a comparison of French *amers* versus Italian amari. (Emily, who was very hungover, later joked that she nearly jumped out of the speeding taxi.)

The first time I met Eric Seed was in 2007 at Tales of the Cocktail, the famed spirits industry event that happens every year in New Orleans. Tales of the Cocktail is a blend of academic conference, trade show, and, as one prominent bar owner put it, "Star Trek convention for cocktail geeks." Unlike your typical professional or scholarly conference, however, you get about three cocktails per session along with the PowerPoint presentations. Free booze continues to flow in all-day tasting rooms, happy hours, dinners, and after-parties. Needless to say, just about every serious bartender and boozehound in America attends.

At Tales of the Cocktail, one moment you'll be tasting a new product like a gin from France distilled from green grape flowers or sampling a liqueur made from "baby Vietnamese ginger" or comparing four different kinds of absinthe. The next moment, you'll attend a panel discussion with a title like "Citrus: In History and Application" or "Aromatics and Their Uses in Cocktails" or "Spice and Ice: The Art of Spicy Cocktails" or "Tiki Drinks—From A to Zombie." Then you'll attend a panel called "Molecular Mixology," being served a Ramos Gin marshmallow or a Sazerac gummy bear, and you'll hear something scolding and manifestoish like, "I hope people in this community will think a little bit more about how you shake." And then a few hours later, in another panel called "On the Rocks: The Importance of Ice," someone else might declare, "We've all been preaching ice. We all realize what a travesty ice has become in the American bar."

During the week, you might attend a presentation on "Big Trends" where someone talks about "bartender proactivity" in getting people to try new spirits. Perhaps someone suggests how important it is for a spirit to have something called an "equity delivery vehicle." Tequila, for instance, is fortunate to have the popular margarita as its equity delivery vehicle. Perhaps, it will be suggested, pisco and cachaça need better equity delivery vehicles to expand their appeal? "What's new in fruits right now?" the moderator will ask. "In Europe, we're over fruit," will come the reply from a British bartender. There will possibly be talk of a movement to eliminate tedious muddling in high-volume bars. And it will be agreed that mezcal, rye whiskey, and grapefruit juice are all hugely popular.

At various points during Tales of the Cocktail, the issue of vodka will be addressed. Someone will say something solemn like, "We needed to kill vodka in order to create a place for ourselves." Later, a famous bar owner—a leading figure in the so-called mixology renaissance—will cause audible gasps by telling the cocktail geeks to lighten up a bit. "If someone wants a vodka drink, give 'em a vodka drink. Are we fascists? Vodka tonics pay the rent."

Then, later on, you'll be tasting an aged rum next to someone wearing a fedora, a kilt, or a seersucker suit and bow tie.

In the midst of my first visit to this craziness, I attended a panel called "Lost Ingredients: Obtaining (or Making) Rare Ingredients for Even Rarer Cocktails." Eric Seed was among the experts on this panel. We all got to taste falernum, Swedish punch, Amer Picon, and what the presenter referred to as the "holy trinity of lost spirits": absinthe (this was several months before legalization), pimento dram, and violet-flavored Crème Yvette (out of production for a half century). For some people in the room, that tasting clearly was a life-changing experience. I cannot say I wasn't one of them.

For years, the holy grail of our Liquor Store Archaeology game had been Crème Yvette, which was a purple-hued violet-and-vanilla liqueur, a variation on the traditional crème de violette liqueurs found in Europe. Crème de violette and Crème Yvette pop up as ingredients over and over again in old recipe books. Even as late as the 1940s and 1950s, bartending guides suggested that a particular brand called Crème Yvette was part of any well-stocked home bar. But by the late 1960s, Crème Yvette had simply disappeared. The Charles Jacquin et Cie distillery, in Philadelphia, was Crème Yvette's final place of production. Since that's near where I'm from, I searched for years, with false hope, wasting hours in dicey Philly bottle shops and neon-lit "package goods" stores in Jersey strip malls. But I never found Crème Yvette.

And then, just like that, in a conference room at the Hotel Monteleone, a guy named Rob Cooper, the scion of the family who owns Charles Jacquin, was pouring little plastic cups of the spirit for all of us. "From one of the only two bottles left in existence," said Cooper, who promised that—if he had anything to do with it—he would return Crème Yvette to the market. It would be 2010 before that came to pass.

However, that same afternoon at the same panel, the Indiana Jones of spirits beat Cooper to the punch, casually mentioning that he would very shortly be bringing out a crème de violette made by a distillery in Austria. The next day, Eric Seed and I had a drink, and then he invited me up to his hotel room. Don't get the wrong idea. At Tales of the Cocktail, the big liquor brands host lavish tasting rooms and parties with bands and DJs and tons of free booze and swag—and sometimes even burlesque dancers and scantily clad women painted blue (such was the case at one Hendrick's gin party, for instance). Smaller companies, like Seed's Haus Alpenz, can't afford those sorts of things. Which is why a bartender from Boston with a shaved head and I found ourselves sitting on opposite hotel beds while Seed sat at the desk and opened what he called his "medicine bag," full of tiny bottles of his various products.

First, we tasted the two products that Seed had originally begun importing in 2006—*kletzenlikör*, a traditional Austrian pear cream liqueur, and *zirbenschnaps*, a liqueur made from the fruit of the native Arolla stone pine, both made in Austria by Josef Hofer, a two-hundred-year-old family-owned distillery. Seed had discovered these spirits during a college semester abroad in Vienna and thought they might be popular at ski resorts like Aspen. The spirits never quite caught on. Of the kletzenlikör, which sells under the name Lauria, Eric Felten wrote in the *Wall Street Journal*, "The texture is off-putting. One expects a cream liqueur to be creamy. Instead, Lauria, thick with a pulpy pear purée, is gritty and gloppy." The zirbenschnaps, which sells under the name Zirbenz, tasted like . . . well, pine. Not in an unpleasant way, but it was certainly a unique, acquired taste. Gary Regan advised, in the *San Francisco Chronicle*, to use Zirbenz "sparingly in cocktails, lest it take over the drink completely." Both Zirbenz and Lauria are lovely spirits, but they have very little application for most bartenders. And I can tell you from spending my formative years as something of a ski bum . . . the après-ski crowd was likely looking for something else. Like maybe a shooter of some kind.

After the Zirbenz and Lauria, we tasted Seed's upcoming launches, including an apricot liqueur, a walnut liqueur, and then—the thing we'd come to the hotel room for—the crème de violette. Now, with a larger glass of the lavender-hued stuff and more time to contemplate it, I could tell that Seed was on to something. The bald bartender from Boston and I agreed that this would be his breakout product. Indeed, several years after that day in New Orleans, events have proved us right. Today, crème de violette is one of Haus Alpenz's top sellers, and you will see it on the back bar of most serious cocktail bars.

Here I must pause to raise the reasonable questions that you might well be asking yourself right now: Why? Why had a taste of it brought a conference room of cocktail geeks nearly to tears? What was the big deal with crème de violette? On its face, crème de violette, with its fancy-soap aroma of spring violets ("It smells like your grandma's underwear drawer," according to one friend), should have been no more successful than a liqueur made of pear puree. Seed's apricot and walnut liqueurs were bolder and tastier, seemingly more in line with modern tastes. If you were simply looking for obscurity, what could be more obscure than a liqueur made from fruit harvested from a frickin' wild stone pine tree that grows in the high Alps! Maybe it was simply nostalgia for a pre-Prohibition taste? But almost none of these people had been of legal drinking in the 1960s, so how could it be actual nostalgia for something they had never before tasted?

During that first trip to Tales of the Cocktail, my outlook on Liquor Store Archaeology changed significantly. For one thing, I was quickly learning that finding interesting spirits would require slightly more effort than a jaunt to my local liquor store.

After we'd sampled everything in Seed's room, I shook hands with him, then took the elevator back downstairs. In the Hotel Monteleone's lobby, a local jazz band was jamming, trumpets blaring, and people were handing out free samples of new vodkas, one called Absolut New Orleans, and another one, from the Netherlands, called Sonnema Vodka-Herb. I ran into a woman named LeNell Smothers, a liquor store owner from Brooklyn, who wore a pink cowboy hat. I'd met her late the night before, in the wild after-hours suite sponsored by Sonnema VodkaHerb, as she'd been pouring shots of Chartreuse directly into people's mouths. LeNell had promised me a taste of her new private bottling of rye whiskey, and I reminded her of this promise. She graciously pulled a hip flask out of her jeans pocket and gave me a nice big swig, right in the lobby.

LeNell wasn't the only one with a hip flask in that lobby. A friend of a friend introduced me to an Irish fellow named Phil Duff, who worked for Lucas Bols in Amsterdam. I had actually been looking for this guy for a few days because word had it that Duff was carrying around a hip flask of Dutch genever.

Genever is the original gin, dating back to the sixteenth century when a chemist in Leyden invented the spirit by adding juniper (*genever*, in Dutch) to distilled alcohol. With a traditional recipe that calls for at least 15 percent malt wine, genever—particularly *oude* (old) genever— has a funky, earthy quality that is unlike any of the London dry gins that most of us know. It's a flavor that seems to predate the modern world. In the nineteenth and early twentieth centuries, genever or "Holland gin" was the preferred gin in the United States. By 1880, six times more genever was imported than all other gins combined, and it was one of only four base spirits mixed for cocktails. After Prohibition, however, the London dry styles took over, and imports of genever slowed to a trickle, until finally it was nearly impossible to find the stuff in America.

I told Duff that I had spent one very memorable day drinking genever in Amsterdam, and since then I'd pissed away many hours searching for the stuff at home. Duff smiled and said he knew what I meant, produced the flask, and let me take a long sip . . . Wow. That funkiness and earthiness from the flask took me directly to that Amsterdam afternoon.

Yes, I realize I'm probably violating some sort of literary law by including two Proustian moments in one chapter, but I don't care. Proust was writing about a cookie, and not liquor. As Liebling joked in *Between Meals*, "The man ate a tea biscuit, the taste evoked memories . . . In light of what Proust wrote with so mild a stimulus, it is the world's loss that he did not have a heartier appetite."

Perhaps surprisingly, my afternoon in Amsterdam didn't involve magic mushrooms or space cakes or spending any quality time with the ladies of the Red Light District. Instead, during that afternoon, I learned the traditional Dutch way of drinking genever in several of the city's *proeflokaal* (or tasting rooms) and its brown cafés (so-called because of the dark wood and years of cigarette smoke). The Dutch have a word for the atmosphere in these places: *gezellig*, which can mean "cozy" or "quaint," but also connotes togetherness and seeing a friend after a long absence. *Gezellig* is pretty much untranslatable, much like the joys that spirits bring. (In fact, one could say that this sip of genever from the flask in the hotel lobby was rather *gezellig*.)

I happened to be in the Netherlands to write a travel article for a luxury car company's magazine. I didn't need to be anywhere for any interviews until Monday, however, and the car company generously sprung for an all-expense-paid weekend in a beautiful hotel in a renovated canal house. As I checked in, Woody Harrelson and his stoner buddies were checking out.

As luck would have it, I found out that my old friend T., a photographer from Denmark, was in town to shoot Amsterdam's brand-new Muziekgebouw—"the music hall of the twenty-first century"—but had nothing better to do that afternoon but join me in a bender. I'd met T. years before, when both of us were traveling aimlessly in Iceland, me avoiding work on another failed novel, and she waiting to hear that she would not be accepted by the Royal Art Academy and taking a break from a boyfriend (whom I later deduced was an ecstasy dealer in Copenhagen). Though we don't see each other often, the two of us have spent dozens upon dozens of hours across from each other drinking at some smoky table in a café or bar. T. is my one friend who, like me, embraces both gezellig—there's a similarly untranslatable concept in Danish called *hygge*—and seediness.

Amsterdam, let's face it, can be pretty seedy. Wonderfully so. Genever was the perfect drink for that afternoon. Genever, especially oude genever, tastes like the incarnation of seediness itself—a primeval taste, truly from a stage further back. The bald bartender with the handlebar mustache at a proeflokaal with sawdust on the floor called Wynand Fockink (yes, *Fockink* is pronounced like you think) poured genever out of earthenware bottles that looked like they'd been excavated from ancient ruins. He filled the cordial glasses just above the rim; we leaned down and slurped the first sip right off the bar. Then we chased the genever with beer. The whole thing is called a *kopstoot* (head butt). T. and I slurped several times.

We moved over to De Drie Fleschjes, another dark, sawdust-on-the-floor spot. There we drank the house specialty, shots of *jonge* (young) genever, curaçao, and bitters called Boswandeling (A Walk in the Forest.) Then, we moved on to Proeflokaal de Ooievaar, where the drunk at the bar told T., very specifically—in Dutch that was expertly translated by his buddy—what sorts of dirty things he would like to do to her.

As the sun started to set, we figured we were already in the Red Light District, and so we decided, what the hell, let's go see a live sex show. Neither of us had seen a live sex show before, and so we entered a theater called Casa Rosso—"one of the most superior erotic shows in the world, with a tremendous choreography and a high-level cast." We had another kopstoot at the theater bar. The sex show may have been one of the most unerotic things I've ever seen, weirdly stylized with lots of pumped-up muscles and fake boobs and tans. "He just looks like he's doing gymnastics on top of her," T. said, and we both dissolved into hysterics. At a certain point, a naked woman came out with tassels on her nipples and danced as if she were having a seizure. We nearly screamed. Really, we were louder than the crew of British lads on stag weekend behind us. The real couples—the ones who'd actually come to the show to theoretically add some kind of spark to their lovemaking—started shooting us nasty looks. So at the intermission, we bailed.

After the sex show, we went to Jamie Oliver's restaurant Fifteen Amsterdam, where reformed juvenile delinquents cook dinner for you. This is where things took a strange turn. T., normally quiet and mellow, got into an argument with the waitress. Then she and I got into a heated debate about the nature of friendship and love and memory, which revolved around dueling reminiscences of a night in Iceland when we'd driven up to a hill above the town to make a photo of the northern lights. On that night, she'd set up her camera on a tripod and pointed it at the sky, while the car radio played Icelandic pop music, and we stood in the dark. The shot needed a long exposure, and T. left the shutter open while we waited as if we had all the time in the world. We knew we didn't, of course. Now, our debate—over dinner in Amsterdam cooked by reformed juvenile delinquents and accompanied by more genever—centered around what could have or should have happened, but didn't, that night in Iceland many years ago.

After dinner, T. got very sad about missing her boyfriend back in Denmark and for a brief moment threatened to jump into the canal. Then, as if on cue, our attention was diverted by some kid who staggered out of a coffeehouse and fell over flat, knocking down an entire line of bicycles, like dominos. Laughing now, T. decided not to jump in the canal, and we found a new bar for another genever.

Yes, this is what genever tasted like to me. Not just "earthy and funky." Not something I could encapsulate into a few tasting notes capped by a three-star versus four-star rating. It was something untranslatable. Genever tasted exactly like that day in Amsterdam, and everything surrounding that day. Genever tasted like seediness and nostalgia itself. I was smiling to myself about all this when I suddenly snapped back to the present in the hotel lobby. Duff looked slightly concerned that I might drink his entire flask. I recapped it and handed it back.

Duff told me that Bols was actively working behind the scenes to bring genever back into the United States. "It's all very Secret Squirrel at the moment," he said. "But you could always come visit us again in Amsterdam."

In fact, a few months later I did return to Amsterdam. Things had started to change a little since my last visit. The eradication of seediness had begun. There had been a crackdown on coffeehouses that sell cannabis. The government had closed a large number of the brothels in the Red Light District.

At the same time, Lucas Bols was well on its way to reintroduc-
ing genever—with an American-friendly recipe—to the U.S. market
in 2008. On the first day of my visit, I went to the House of Bols for
a genever sampling. Genever can only be made in the Netherlands (a
designation of origin from the European Union was awarded in 2007).
While it's technically true to call it "the original gin," in reality genever
often has more similarities to whiskey in taste and application than to
contemporary gins. The reason is that genever must always consist of
a small percentage of malt wine, which is a distillate of three kinds of
grain: corn, rye, and wheat. There are three basic genevers: oude, jonge,
and *corenwyn*. Genever labeled oude, or old, is not necessarily aged,
but rather is made according to the traditional, old recipe from the sixteenth century calling for at least 15 percent malt wine. Jonge, or young,
genever is the most popular spirit in the Netherlands, and it follows a
younger recipe dating from the early twentieth century, with less malt
wine. A more neutral spirit, it still maintains some of the flavorful maltiness of the oude. Corenwyn, literally corn wine, is a cask-aged genever
that must contain at least 51 percent malt wine. The spirit's best expression, corenwyn shares many of the characteristics of fine aged whiskey.

After the tasting, I wandered throughout the House of Bols's touris-
tic, high-tech multimedia museum. I stepped into a 280-degree projec-
tion room that—at least as Bols described it—"makes it possible for the
visitor to step literally into the world of night life." It was a very loud
world, filled with pumping house music. Along one rainbow wall was
a sensory exercise to practice my smelling: thirty-six puffers, each of
which had a different mystery scent—from peach to mint to strawberry
to coffee—which I was supposed to puff into my face and try to guess.
One big surprise was the emphasis Bols seems to place on what's officially called "flair bartending," or what most people would describe as
"bartending like Tom Cruise did it in *Cocktail*." Bols apparently takes the
whole flair bartending thing very seriously and reengineered its liqueur
bottles specifically for optimal flair bartending, developing "a bottle that
is scientifically proven to offer significant cocktail making performance
improvements of up to 33 percent," according to one exhibit. They sell

practice flair bottles, made of rubber, in the gift shop. And you can make a video of yourself flipping bottles and email it to friends.

I hadn't really thought about flair bartending for many years. It's been, after all, more than two decades since Cruise portrayed an acrobatic, poetry-reciting bartender. In fact, allow me to quote one of his poems from the film:

I am the last barman poet. / I see America drinking the fabulous cocktails I make. / Americans getting stinky on something I stir or shake. / The Sex on the Beach / The schnapps made from peach / The Velvet Hammer / The Alabama Slammer. / I make things with juice and froth. / The Pink Squirrel / The Three-Toed Sloth. / I make drinks so sweet and snazzy. / The Iced Tea / The Kamakazi / The Orgasm / The Death Spasm / The Singapore Sling / The Dingaling. / America, you've just been devoted to every flavor I got. / But if you want to got loaded / Why don't you just order a shot? / Bar is open.

Some might say that this poem (and the entire film itself) pinpoints precisely the nadir of bartending in the twentieth century. Just look at the list of drinks. Long Island Iced Tea? Alabama Slammer? Orgasm? Maybe the classic-cocktail crowd should lobby for a remake: Tom Cruise could be replaced by a hipster who comes to work at a popular speakeasy in Brooklyn.

Inspired, I bought two practice flair bottles from the gift shop in hopes of auditioning for the potential remake (possibly as the grizzled older bartender who takes the young upstart under his wing). Once home, I immediately spilled a lot of liquor on my kitchen floor, and then put the bottles away, never to be practiced with again.

A couple of days after visiting Bols, I took a train to the historic distilling town of Schiedam, near Rotterdam. As late as 1880, Schiedam boasted about four hundred distilleries, with dozens of windmills in operation to produce the malt for its famous genever. But as worldwide demand for genever diminished over the course of the twentieth century, Schiedam ebbed into a quiet, pleasant town with canals, cobblestone streets, and six windmills still in operation.

At least until the remaining distillers realized they could export expensive vodka to the Americans. It wasn't a hard transition. Vodka is made from neutral spirits. And the distilleries were already making genever out of neutral spirits. So, hold the malt wine, tinker a bit, and voila! For instance, Nolet Distillery in Schiedam sells jonge genever under the label Ketel 1 for about ten dollars a liter. Now, it sells vodka under the label Ketel One (numeral spelled out) for more than thirty dollars a liter.

That's not to say there weren't unique flavors in Schiedam. For instance, I made a stop at the Jenever Museum, chronicling three hundred years of Dutch distilling tradition, where I *ate* a bowl of a custard-like spirit made with egg yolks and brandy called *advocaat*. After that, I sampled some small local brands at Jeneverie 't Spul. The bartender there certainly didn't want to hear anything about a genever specially made to Americans' taste. In fact, he deplored cocktails, the existence of which he blamed on Americans. Moreover, as I drank some of his finest aged genever, he make it clear that it was the Canadians, and not the Americans, who'd liberated Schiedam in World War II. In fact, to make the point, he showed off a portrait of the Canadian general on the wall.

I visited Dirkzwager Distillery for a classic illustration of how tradition gives way to contemporary tastes. Dirkzwager has long been the producer of a popular genever, Floryn. In 2000 it produced its first flavored vodkas, imported to the United States under the name Van Gogh. What began as a sideline has taken over. In the early 2000s, Dirkzwager bottled vodka about once every other month. Now, three of every four weeks are spent bottling flavored vodka. Van Gogh exports about twenty flavors, including wild apple, pineapple, double espresso, and, yes, mojito mint and açai-blueberry.

I spent some time in the flavor laboratory with master distiller Tim Vos, who has been making spirits for twenty-five years. "There's a big difference in taste between Americans and Europeans," he said, not surprising me. Vos, for instance, had a difficult time creating an orange-flavored vodka. He'd been using Spanish oranges as his model, and the product wasn't testing well with Americans. One day, he suddenly realized that Florida oranges have a decidedly different flavor.

Oranges are one thing, but what about açai-blueberry? "Americans like bold taste, overwhelming taste," he said, chuckling. "We don't have this taste in Europe."

During my visit, Vos told me Van Gogh's next vodka would be "absinthe-flavored," and he let me taste it, along with some other flavor ideas he has been working on, including ginger, cucumber, and grapefruit. There were also interesting mash-ups of fruits and plants: pear-geranium, violet-cherry, lavender-yuzu. After the tasting, Vos and I had lunch at a restaurant that was inside a windmill, where we drank a beer and an oude genever—a kopstoot.

Later that afternoon, I paid a call to another distiller, UTO, a few blocks away, past the windmill. UTO makes the Sonnema VodkaHerb that had been marketed heavily at Tales of the Cocktail. It's tough to edge into the U.S. vodka market. At UTO, I tasted a beautiful oude genever, Notaris, which was aged like whiskey. I also tasted Sonnema's Berenburg, a dark, bitter herbal liqueur, akin to an Italian amaro, that's extremely popular in the Netherlands. Sonnema uses a bit of the Berenburg formula of seventy-one herbs in the secret recipe for VodkaHerb.

I asked Edwin Holleman, UTO's commercial director, how well Sonnema VodkaHerb sells in Holland. "There is almost no premium vodka market here," he said. "People can buy a liter of genever for eight or nine euros. No one in Holland is going to pay twenty-nine euros for a vodka."

There's always America, I guess. Actually, after I left Schiedam, I'd developed a vague theory on the flavored-vodka thing: it's a European conspiracy foisted upon unwitting American consumers to see just how far we'll go into the realm of the absurd. I imagined a distiller (perhaps wearing a beret, or lederhosen, or wooden shoes) snickering as he chatted with his importer: "They drank mojito mint? Really? And espresso vodka? Dude, seriously? It was brown! Yeah, *that* was a good one. Okay, well, here's one that'll really give us a laugh. Let's send them bubble gum and see what happens!"

A Round of Drinks: Unearthing the Past

It's mind-boggling how many fascinating spirits disappeared during Prohibition—and equally mind-boggling how many of these have been "rediscovered" and become available in the last years of the first decade of the twenty-first century. So much more cocktail acumen—more historical insight, finer technique, cooler tools—exists in the world now than did in, say, 2007. It feels as though it took us seven decades to move from the Dark Ages of Prohibition to the Early Renaissance of Cocktails. Then, in a matter of months, we leapt from the Renaissance to the baroque and the rococo.

Remember, until 2007, many of the spirits I'm writing about simply were not available except, maybe, if you went abroad. For example, now that real sloe gin can be had in the United States for the first time in generations, creative bartenders have made the old new again. That was the case with the following cocktail, which was on the menu at the gone-but-not-forgotten Washington, D.C., speakeasy Hummingbird to Mars.

PHILLY SLING

Serves 1

> 1½ ounces applejack
> 1 ounce Plymouth sloe gin
> ¾ ounce freshly squeezed lemon juice
> ¼ ounce simple syrup (page 218)
> 2 dashes Angostura bitters

Fill a mixing glass halfway with ice. Add the applejack, sloe gin, lemon juice, simple syrup, and bitters. Stir vigorously, then strain into a chilled cocktail glass.

Recipe by Derek Brown of the Passenger and the Columbia Room, Washington, D.C.

When I first began writing about cocktails in 2007, I published a recipe for the Aviation cocktail, a classic drink from the early twentieth century and one of my favorites. At the time, I called for gin, freshly squeezed lemon juice, and maraschino liqueur, all stirred over ice and served in a cocktail glass. I also wrote that no one really knew why this drink was called the Aviation. Well, it turns out I was all wrong. It's not totally my fault. I gleaned my misinformation, and adapted my recipe, from the august body of cocktail knowledge to which I had access in May 2007. Specifically, I relied on *The Savoy Cocktail Book*—one of the bibles of its genre. My error perfectly illustrates a couple of points about the swift evolution of cocktail making that happened at the end of the 2000s. As cocktail geeks delved further into dusty, out-of-print cocktail guides, we soon learned that our Aviation was missing a key ingredient: the purple, floral liqueur called crème de violette. Adding a tiny amount of it to the gin, lemon juice, and maraschino results in a sky blue drink. So the name Aviation suddenly becomes self-explanatory. Today, of course, you can find any number of speakeasies that will serve you a historically correct Aviation. But that's a recent development—crème de violette didn't become available until 2008.

AVIATION

Serves 1

> 1 ¹/₂ ounces gin
> ³/₄ ounce freshly squeezed lemon juice
> ¹/₂ ounce maraschino liqueur
> ¹/₄ ounce crème de violette or Crème Yvette

Fill a mixing glass halfway with ice. Add the gin, lemon juice, maraschino liqueur, and crème de violette. Stir vigorously, then strain into a chilled cocktail glass.

Maraschino, absinthe, and curaçao were among the first liqueurs to make their way into cocktails in nineteenth-century America. Much of the time, they were paired with genever. The Bols genever we have in the United States is a special formula created specifically for the American market, but it mimics very closely a traditional oude genever style, and those who may have enjoyed a taste of it in Amsterdam will recognize it as the real thing. Beyond Bols, real Dutch genever is not widely available in the United States. Some brands, such as Boomsma and Zuidam, are here but hard to find.

When you track down your genever, try this classic adapted from the legendary nineteenth-century bartender Jerry Thomas's 1876 bar guide. In those days, there were three standard cocktails for brandy, whiskey, or genever: Plain, Fancy, or Improved. *Fancy* meant you got a dash of curaçao. *Improved* meant you got dashes of both absinthe and maraschino liqueur.

IMPROVED GIN COCKTAIL

Serves 1

>2 ounces genever
>1 teaspoon simple syrup (page 218)
>1/2 teaspoon maraschino liqueur
>2 dashes Angostura bitters
>1 dash absinthe
>Lemon peel twist, for garnish

Fill a mixing glass halfway with ice. Add the genever, simple syrup, maraschino liqueur, bitters, and absinthe. Stir vigorously for 30 seconds, then strain into a cocktail glass. Twist the lemon peel over the drink, rub it around the rim of the glass, then use it as a garnish.

Another Round of Drinks: Fizzes and Collins

If I told you that mixing a drink required you to squeeze the juice from a lemon into a glass and add a tablespoonful of sugar or some simple syrup, it wouldn't seem so difficult, right? It would be somewhat less complicated than, say, driving a car while chatting on your cell phone? Or, if you worked as a bartender, perhaps less complicated than, say, drawing a Miller Lite from a tap while chatting up an attractive bar patron about her new lower-back tattoo?

Well, then, allow me to be blunt: I harbor a major dislike of bars that sidestep that simple maneuver by using commercial sour mixes made from concentrate or powder. Most of us have by now shaken that mid-twentieth-century love of artificial and processed foods and drinks. We don't see a lot of Tang being served these days, or Salisbury steak TV dinners in aluminum trays, or squeeze-tube Velveeta, and I think most of us have given up the Jetsons fantasy that we'll someday get all our flavor and nutrients from a little pill served by a robot. Why, then, during this supposed golden renaissance of cocktail making does commercial sour mix persist?

This mix usually sneaks up on you, like a mullet seen from the front. And you usually spot it too late, once you've settled onto the bar stool. It's a hot day, and you're maybe thinking about a Tom Collins, and suddenly you hear someone down the bar order an Amaretto Sour or a Long Island Iced Tea, and out of the corner of your eye you see the bartender reach for the artificial sour mix in all its glowing-yellow, high-fructose glory. And then you start thinking a whiskey neat might be the safe way to go.

It's because of commercial sour mix that certain basic drinks—even though everyone has heard of them—rarely are served the right way. Prime among those are two hot-weather favorites, the Collins and the Fizz. The two are very similar. Both use a base spirit, fresh lemon juice, and a little bit of sugar or simple syrup, and are topped with soda water or sparkling water (I like using Apollinaris brand, with its flavorful minerality and small bubbles). Very simple, very cool, very delicious. The key differences are that a Collins uses slightly more gin and is built in an ice-filled Collins glass, while a Fizz is shaken (sometimes with egg white) and strained into either an ice-filled Collins glass or an iceless highball glass.

The Tom Collins is the simpler of the two, and it is always clear. It originally was made with Old Tom gin, and its cousins were soon to follow: Mike Collins (Irish whiskey), Jack Collins (applejack), Pedro Collins (rum), Pierre Collins (cognac), and, of course, John Collins.

JOHN COLLINS

Serves 1

> **3 ounces genever**
> **1¹/₂ ounces freshly squeezed lemon juice**
> **¹/₂ ounce simple syrup (page 218)**
> **Sparkling mineral water**
> **Lemon slice, for garnish**

Fill a Collins glass with ice. Add the genever, lemon juice, and simple syrup. Top with the mineral water and stir gently. Garnish with the lemon slice.

The Fizz is also one of the great underappreciated cocktails—a palette on which to experiment. There are so many variations to play with, beginning with the basic Gin Fizz. A Fizz with egg white is called a Silver Fizz, one with egg yolk a Golden Fizz, and one with whole egg a Royal Fizz. A Crimson Fizz adds crushed strawberries, while a Green Fizz adds a teaspoon of crème de menthe. A Diamond Fizz eschews water for sparkling wine. An Apple Blossom is a Silver Fizz made with applejack. The Brandy Fizz replaces gin with brandy; a Sea Fizz replaces it with absinthe. A Purple Fizz uses sloe gin and grapefruit juice; a Pineapple Fizz calls for white rum and pineapple juice.

"What's the difference, if any, between a Tom Collins and a Gin Fizz?" asks David A. Embury in his 1948 cocktail geek bible, *The Fine Art of Mixing Drinks*. "I insist a Fizz should actually fizz." Embury suggests keeping in mind a basic formula: sweet (sugar, syrup, or liqueur), sour (lemon or lime juice), strong (the liquor), and weak (the sparkling water and ice). "If you keep these principles firmly in mind," he writes, "you can ad lib ad infinitum."

Here are my two very favorite Fizzes.

SLOE GIN FIZZ

Serves 1

> 2 ounces Plymouth sloe gin
> 1 ounce freshly squeezed lemon juice
> 1 teaspoon simple syrup (page 218)
> Sparkling mineral water
> Orange slice, for garnish

Fill a shaker two-thirds full with ice. Add the sloe gin, lemon juice, and simple syrup. Shake well, then strain into a chilled highball glass filled with ice and top with the mineral water. Garnish with the orange slice.

NOTE: I occasionally like to substitute 2 dashes of Angostura bitters for the simple syrup if I want a slightly less sweet drink.

VIOLET FIZZ

Serves 1

> 1 1/2 ounces gin
> 1 ounce freshly squeezed lemon juice
> 1/2 ounce crème de violette or Crème Yvette
> 1 tablespoon egg white
> Sparkling mineral water

Fill a cocktail shaker halfway with ice. Add the gin, lemon juice, crème de violette, and egg white. Shake vigorously for at least 1 minute. The egg white should get frothy. Strain into an ice-filled Collins glass and top with the mineral water.

NOTE: If you have a sweet tooth and absolutely must, you may add $^1/_2$ teaspoon of sugar.

CHAPTER 4

ROMANCE: THEY POUR IT ON

TRUTH IS BEAUTIFUL, WITHOUT DOUBT; BUT SO ARE LIES.

—*Ralph Waldo Emerson*

I WAS IN COLLEGE in the early 1990s, when drinking shots of Jägermeister was in the early stages of popularity. You'd go into your local bar and a bevy of so-called "Jägerettes" in hot pants and tank tops would be pouring this weird brown liqueur with a fierce herbal-cinnamon-licorice kick. It came in rectangular green bottles bearing an almost biblical image of a cross shining over an elk's horns. It was like nothing else we had ever been served. If you happened to be a student at the University of Vermont in the early 1990s, as I was, you too may have sucked down many a Jägermeister—generally the last drink of the night in a certain basement bar in downtown Burlington—before stumbling upstairs and into the snowy night en route to Nectar's for fries and gravy, which you had to eat steaming hot on the walk home before the gravy congealed in the subzero night air.

Anyway, rumors quickly spread about the obscure German booze with secret ingredients. Some said it contained elk's blood. Others said that what we were getting in America was a watered-down version of the original. Or that the real stuff—available only in Germany—contained special herbs (maybe opiates?) that gave it an even more special kick.

When my friend S. and I were backpacking in Europe one summer—in our Phish T-shirts and Birkenstocks—the first thing we did upon crossing the border into Germany was to buy a bottle of Jägermeister. We sat on a bunk in the hostel, took sips from the bottle, and looked at each other. "Do you think it's different?" I asked.

"I don't know," she said. "I think so. I think I feel different."

"Yeah," I said. "I think I feel different, too."

We also believed the rumors that the gold flakes in another popular liqueur, the cinnamon Goldschläger, would make microscopic cuts in your throat and stomach when you drank it, thus allowing the alcohol to directly enter the bloodstream for maximum intoxication. What's more, S. and I believed we could travel through four countries as enlightened hippie-platonic travel companions, sharing a bed, and there would be no drama. Ah, the naïveté of youth!

Until I started writing about spirits for a living, I always wanted to believe the corporate storytelling that accompanies so much booze in the marketplace. The genre is well established: miraculous tales of rustic peasants gathering some obscure ingredient, a secret recipe from the Middle Ages zealously guarded by monks who have taken a vow of silence, the stern family patriarch carefully sampling every barrel before bottling. Who doesn't want to believe these stories? There is, as we all know, so little magic left in the world.

"Quintessential liquor industry puffery!" That's what Rob Cooper called it, in his booming voice. We were talking on the phone, only about two months into my job at the *Post*. "I guess you could say it's romantic and that it allows the consumer to dream. Or whatever. But it's just a lie.

They need to have a compelling story of some sort. A lot of companies probably feel that pressure." Cooper added, "I'm over the whole puffery thing."

Now, this was a somewhat contradictory statement. If you remember, Cooper is the man who promised a room full of people at Tales of the Cocktail that he would bring Crème Yvette—nostalgic, lavender-hued, part of the "holy trinity of lost spirits"—back to market. During this particular phone conversation, Cooper and I were discussing another new liqueur he was launching: a spirit called St-Germain that is allegedly made of elderflowers from the Alps. St-Germain's compelling, romantic story sounded like a doozy. A classic of the genre.

According to the lavish marketing material when it launched, St-Germain uses only fresh, wild elderflowers picked high in the French Alps. Immediately after harvest, the flowers undergo a "highly secret" maceration process that extracts flavor "without bruising the flowers." It is "a carefully orchestrated sequence of events, which must be completed during the short three- to four-day span when the blossoms peak."

So, with only a few fleeting days to gather all the elderflowers needed for an entire year's production, one might reasonably wonder: what method, what technology, do they employ to harvest the elderflower crop? According to the company's tale, "*bohémien*" farmers—adorably quaint and wearing berets, no less—handpick the elderflowers. "After gently ushering the wild blooms into sacks and descending the hillside, the man who gathers blossoms for your cocktail will then mount a bicycle and carefully ride the umbels of starry white flowers to the market," read the marketing material, which included photos of a mustachioed man in a beret, his bicycle loaded down with satchels of white flowers.

Said St-Germain, "You could not write a better story if you were François Truffaut." Indeed.

Other spirits industry insiders, on the other hand, remained a little more skeptical. When I recounted the St-Germain story to Frank Coleman, a lobbyist for the Distilled Spirits Council of the United States, he rolled his eyes and said, "Guys on bikes? Yeah, right."

Maybe I was still naive, but I sincerely wanted this story to be true, and I asked Cooper if I could meet his *"bohémiens"* on bicycles. The annual elderflower harvest happens in early May, and I would to be in Europe then, so I offered to drive down from Geneva into the Haute-Savoie region to check out the elderflower harvest.

After some back-and-forth, Cooper flatly rejected the idea. "I will not divulge the name of the town where the elderflowers are grown," he said. "I want to protect this brand." And in regards to his secret maceration process, he said, "I'm not going to show you. I'm not going to show anyone. Ever."

The elderflowers grow on public land, Cooper said, and he worried that a huge multinational liquor company—say, Diageo or Pernod Ricard or Bacardi—would swoop in on the action if it learned the location. I questioned that business model. What if the elderflowers didn't bloom one year, or what if he lost availability? People in the Alps certainly pick elderflowers and use them in cooking and making drinks. You may even be able to find some kind of elderflower spirit made in someone's barn. But that's a long way from supplying fresh elderflowers for a liqueur that's having an expensive, nationwide U.S. rollout, supported by ads in nearly every food and beverage magazine.

I pressed further. I offered to keep the town anonymous. I told him that I'd visited numerous distilleries and had never once completely figured out secret methods or recipes. Still, Cooper would not budge.

Instead, he offered to send a mysterious-sounding man named "Yves" to meet me at my hotel in Geneva. From there, I would be driven into the Haute-Savoie, to a destination he would not disclose. It all sounded very James Bond. "Are you going to blindfold me or throw a sack over my head, too?" I asked.

Cooper chuckled. "Maybe we should!"

Even then, I would still be forbidden to see St-Germain's team of guys on bicycles, and he would not show me his production facility. What exactly would he do? It was unclear. "Yves" and I would apparently drive around the mountains, have lunch, and then return to Geneva. I declined.

A few months later, at Tales of the Cocktail in New Orleans, Cooper hosted a tasting room for St-Germain. During his PowerPoint presentation, he showed the same photos of the same mustachioed man in a beret, harvesting and stuffing his bicycle basket with elderflowers. During the Q&A segment, as the photos flashed in an endless loop, a woman raised her hand and said, "Is this a true story? Because I am from France, and I have lived in France my whole life, and I have never heard of anything like this."

Cooper promised that day, and pretty much every time I've seen him since, that one day he'll invite members of the press to meet his elderflower pickers in berets. Three years on, that has never happened. So the story of Frenchmen on bikes, handpicking fresh elderflowers in the Alps for St-Germain liqueur remains a good tale. The liquor itself, on the other hand, has become so ubiquitous in contemporary cocktail recipes that some refer to the elderflower liqueur as "bartender's ketchup."

About a year after St-Germain launched, in 2008, I finally did make it to the French Alps during elderflower season, when I visited, on a sunny alpine Sunday, the Chartreuse distillery in the small town of Voiron, near Grenoble.

Chartreuse is about as old-school as liquor gets. In fact, Chartreuse's story may be the granddaddy of romantic liquor industry tales. The liqueur is famously made from a secret blend of 130 herbs, flowers, and spices dating back to a alchemical manuscript titled *An Elixir of Long Life* that was given to the Carthusian monks in 1605 by a French military officer. The full recipe is known only to two Carthusians—each of whom knows only half of the formula, and both of whom have taken a vow of silence. The story goes that these two monks occasionally leave the solitude of their cells—in a monastery at the top of a mountain—in order to distill and barrel the liqueur. And, when they're through, the monks return to their cells and their quiet life of prayer and meditation.

I didn't get to meet any of the monks, of course, what with them having the vow of silence and living in solitude at the top of a mountain and all. I did, however, meet a public relations director named Florence Donnier-Blanc. I also met a number of young women working in the tasting room, who wore (yes, it's true) chartreuse-colored business suits.

On my tour of the "longest liqueur cellar in the world" (and who knew that *length* of cellar was important?), I was assured that the monks still keep a close eye on the process. But most questions went unanswered. How long does Chartreuse age in the barrels? "We don't know," Donnier-Blanc said. "The monks decide when they're ready." Are there really 130 ingredients? "We suppose," Donnier-Blanc said, "but we have no way of knowing for sure."

In Voiron, they sell a version of the original Élixir Végétal, based on the original recipe, which comes in a wooden bottle and is 71 percent alcohol by volume. It's said to be a medicinal curative. "The Élixir really works," Donnier-Blanc said. "My mother gave it to us when we had a bad stomach. You can rub it on a bee sting, and in twenty minutes, it's gone."

The monks cannot export their Élixir Végétal to the United States, however, because the FDA mandates that ingredients have to be described in full on labels, meaning the Carthusian secret would be irrevocably revealed. EU rules already require that Chartreuse list gluten-containing ingredients, causing some consternation in Voiron.

Chartreuse is one of the few liqueurs that are aged, and the extra-aged VEP (*Vieillissement Exceptionnellement Prolongé*) bottles can sell for upward of two hundred dollars. The rarest, most expensive bottles of Chartreuse in the world are those that were made before and during a period of exile. In 1903, the French government tried to nationalize the distillery, and the monks, unwilling to give up the secret, moved to Tarragona, Spain. "The quality of nineteenth-century Chartreuse has never been equaled, and of course it is one of the very few liqueurs that benefits from aging," according to the United Kingdom–based rare spirits dealer Finest & Rarest. Today, the mythic "Tarragona" bottles of Chartreuse fetch €800 or more. Most Americans have to make do with the standard green (at 55 percent alcohol by volume) and the yellow (at

40 percent alcohol by volume). Both offer complexity—herbal, floral, vegetal, peppery, sweet—that's hard to pin down, and both suggest tastes that predate the modern world. Neither is predictable or boring, and I always find new elements when I taste them, though the yellow is definitely more rounded and honeyed.

After my tour of the distillery, I really wanted to walk up to the Grand Chartreuse monastery. Claire, one of the tour guides, volunteered to accompany me—and she seemed pretty happy to slip out of the chartreuse uniform and into normal clothes. As Claire and I hiked, she told me Chartreuse was having a tiny surge in popularity at her university in Grenoble. The maker often sponsors parties thrown by the students. But the students certainly were not sipping it as a *digestif*, as their grandparents did: "Among young people, Chartreuse is almost always served in cocktails, never by itself." And what's the most popular spirit among kids her age? "Vodka, of course," she said.

The hike up to the monastery on that afternoon was beautiful, and we passed families, troops of boy scouts, teenage lovers, and even a few old men wearing berets. It made me so happy to be in the mountains again, and then in the same moment, it made me kind of sad and nostalgic. When I was in Vermont, I always imagined I'd live in a place like this, someplace where there was excellent skiing, and mountain herbs from which secret elixirs were made, and perhaps alpine girls who wore chartreuse to work. Claire cheerily pointed out wild herbs like gentian and génépi, surely part of the secret recipe. We saw some elderflowers, and I asked Claire, "Do little men with mustaches and berets ride bikes into the mountains to harvest these?"

She looked at me like I was crazy, so I launched into the story of St-Germain. "Do Americans really believe this?" asked Claire, her laughter echoing through the Alps. She continued to laugh for several more minutes, until we drew close to the monastery and the sign that noted we were entering a "Zone De Silence."

Nearly twenty years after the summer of my backpacking trip with S., I had the opportunity to tour the inner sanctum of the Jägermeister plant in Wolfenbüttel, Germany, a cozy town of half-timbered homes about an hour from Hanover (meaning it's pretty much in the middle of nowhere). In fact, when I asked whether it was worth sticking around Wolfenbüttel for a day of sightseeing, the reply from the Jägermeister people was "Unfortunately there's nothing more to see in this area." Jägermeister corporate headquarters sits outside the center of Wolfen-büttel, and when you arrive, you are met by a rug that says, in bright orange, "Achtung WILD!"

The continued popularity of Jägermeister is undeniable. More than 2.8 million cases are sold in the States annually, part of more than 6 million cases total sold worldwide. Jägermeister is the best-selling liqueur in the States, according to the industry analyst Beverage Information Group. Yet because of its viral popularity, and also because Jägermeister is most commonly consumed in shots by young people, the liqueur has a mixed reputation among the spirits cognoscenti. There's its association with heavy metal bands such as Metallica and Slayer; its mingling with Red Bull in the infamous Jäger Bomb; the big, branded tap machines that bring chilled shots to the masses. Whatever the reason, Jägermeister is rarely discussed in serious spirits and cocktail circles.

In the first edition of his ratings compendium, *Kindred Spirits* (1997), critic Paul Pacult, the Robert Parker of spirits, gave Jägermeister three out of five stars and said its herbal quality "is so profound that it's like walking into a Chinese herbalist's shop." He offered this summa-tion: "a charming and quaffable shooter; but that's about it." Curiously, in Pacult's 2008 second edition, Jägermeister is not even reviewed.

I've remained a fan of Jägermeister, though surely this has more to do with warm memories of college nights than with the flavor itself. These days, I rarely find myself in a situation that calls for shots of it. Which makes sense, since the prime demographic, according to Dietmar Franke, Jägermeister's business development director for the United States, is drinkers aged twenty-one to thirty-one: "the age bracket when you are out every evening."

Franke, as if out of central casting, looks like a benevolent version of the Burgermeister Meisterburger from the Claymation Christmas classic "Santa Claus Is Coming to Town." You could totally picture this guy in lederhosen. He'd certainly slurped down a few Jägermeisters in his day. Franke thought it was hilarious that I wanted to know the secret ingredients. At one point, when I asked where the toilet was, he said, "If you find a secret in there, you're welcome to publish it."

"We are not an oversophisticated drink," Franke said. "It's an easy, uncomplicated product. Just make sure it's ice-cold, and have a group of friends with you." In case buyers are unclear about the ice-cold part, it says "Serve Cold—Keep on Ice" in big, bold letters right on the label. "The recipe has never been changed for the American palate. In this case, the American palate matches up just fine."

Franke and I were sipping Jägermeister and tonics at the Jägermeister guesthouse, overlooking a clay tennis court, and, as usual, several members of the public relations department were with us. In this case, there were two young German women and one young American woman who'd come over from New York. Now, one might wonder, why all the public relations support for one slightly inebriated spirits writer? Well, I'd been told I was the very first journalist who would be allowed into Jägermeister's vaunted secret herb room. In fact, before I secured permission, I had to fill out a multipart questionnaire requesting, among other thing my "positions on the spirits industry." It seemed a somehow appropriately German interrogation.

Here are some things I learned during my tour. Jägermeister is produced by macerating, rather than distilling, its ingredients of herbs, spices, roots, and fruits in pure, neutral spirits, then aging for a year in huge ten-thousand-liter oak barrels. Jägermeister spends more than $500,000 on barrels every year. Liquid sugar, 135 grams per bottle, is added to the macerate late in the process. Meaning that even though Jägermeister is often referred to as a bitter, it is actually a liqueur because of its high sugar content. This sugar, I think, is a key part of Jägermeister's particular appeal in the States; without its sweetness, there would likely be way too much licorice and herbs for the American palate.

All of those facts were fine and dandy—and wandering among the huge barrels was pretty cool. But what I really came for was a visit to the herb room. I was hoping it would shed some light on the fifty-six-ingredient secret recipe. As we entered the building, I could smell a huge number of aromas, and then we stepped inside the room. For all the buildup in my head, the room very much resembled other sterile labs where people in white coats develop secret flavors. The main item of interest in the herb room was a huge display of fifty-six samples of secret herbs and spices, each labeled with its name. Right away, like a good journalist, I whipped out my notebook and began copying down the list. As I did, I could tell that the German public relations people were becoming agitated, and one disappeared from the room. "They're getting nervous," said the American PR woman. "You're causing problems." The German PR person sternly handed me a sheet of paper listing the five herbs that are "officially" disclosed: cloves, ginger, chamomile flowers, cinnamon bark, and saffron.

Well, I'm not usually one to stick to "official" lists, and so—much to the certain dismay of my German handlers—I will tell you that there is also licorice root, lavender, rose hips, hyssop, mace, turmeric, cardamom, coriander, star anise, clove, lemon, and orange, as well as many of the herbs and spices usually found in bitters. Of course, just knowing those ingredients, but not the amount and preparation of them, doesn't make it likely that you or I can recreate Jägermeister in our kitchens at home.

It was in the herb room that I learned definitively, sadly, that the rumors of deer's blood and opiates are completely unfounded. Telling you this, dear drinker, somehow feels like telling you that Santa Claus does not exist. It felt as though a small part of my youth shriveled up and died. Alas, we soldier on.

Jägermeister was developed in 1934 and for most of its history in Germany, it was an after-dinner digestif. It was a drink enjoyed by middle-aged men who might have worked in the Playmobil or Volkswagen factories, after their meal of pilsner and pork knuckle. I'm fascinated by how Americans have turned that tradition on its head by making it a shooter.

You can thank Sidney Frank for that. Frank is the spirits industry legend best known for convincing Americans to spend thirty dollars on a superpremium vodka made in France. That vodka (Grey Goose—you may have heard of it) was eventually sold to Bacardi for two billion dollars in 2004, only a year or so before Frank's death at eighty-six. One of his last projects was actually an energy drink called Crunk!!!, in partnership with the rapper Lil Jon. Frank's first big success, however, was acquiring the rights to import Jägermeister in the 1970s, and then building the brand throughout the 1980s. It was Frank who invented the idea of sending attractive, scantily clad young women into bars late at night to convince horny young men to drink shots of product. In a way, guys like Rob Cooper and Eric Seed are following in the footsteps of Sidney Frank—the key difference is they're putting their marketing faith in bartenders in high-end cocktail bars and not women in hot pants (although the possibilities for demo girls for Crème Yvette boggle the mind).

By now, the idea of the Jägermeister shot is so ingrained in least two generations of American drinkers that the liqueur has pretty much lost any tie to Germany. Jägermeister could really be from anywhere. In fact, we've exported our way of drinking Jägermeister back to Germany, where you'll see young Germans sucking down Jäger shots. I certainly did at a popular spot in Wolfenbüttel called Laguna Beach Club—a sort of beer garden in the landlocked town, where they'd trucked in sand and set up a volleyball court.

Jägermeister sales chiefly rely on shot consumption by young drinkers, and this presents the company with a tricky marketing situation—one in which *responsibility* is the buzzword. We discussed this responsibility over shots of Jägermeister at lunch. "To promote shots is not to promote overconsumption," insisted Alexandra von Tschirschky, Jägermeister's head of public relations. "Maybe just have one or two shots."

"Well," said Franke, with a chuckle, "maybe three."

Stop me if you've heard this one. An old liqueur from old Europe, made with a secret old formula and traditionally enjoyed by old men, somehow makes its way into the U.S. market and becomes wildly popular among the college and postcollege crowd, who knock back shot after shot of the stuff. In fact, this odd European liqueur inexplicably becomes the shot of a generation.

In the not-so-distant future, we may be telling that story about another strange spirit, called Tuaca. This one is not bitter herb and cinnamon, but a citrus-vanilla liqueur from Tuscany that is reputed to have been created during the Renaissance for Lorenzo de Medici. There are those who believe that Tuaca may soon become the new Jägermeister. It's certainly already extremely popular in Western states such as Colorado. Which prompts the question, What is it with strange liqueurs and ski areas anyway?

Tuaca's popularity means that the sweet liqueur is already mixed with Red Bull in a Tuaca Bomb and with tequila in a Tuaca-rita. There is also, as with Jägermeister, a Tuaca shot-chilling machine. I recently was sitting in the kind of place where the patrons—young, flannel-clad, and bearded—were drinking Pabst Blue Ribbon, with their fixed-gear bikes parked out front, and I was surprised to see the chalkboard advertising three-dollar shots of Tuaca, right alongside the Jägermeister. "When did Tuaca get so popular?" I asked the bartender.

He stared at me blankly and said, "When it got to be three dollars a shot."

It's not just drunk college students who've noted Tuaca's appeal. I, for one, enjoy it. And Nigella Lawson, on whom I have a deep and abiding crush, has written, "I can't help reaching for the Tuaca . . . Think panettone in liqueur form." I don't really understand the panettone comparison, but Nigella—well, she can pretty much tell me anything she wants and I'll go with it. It's true that nearly everything tastes good with a little vanilla, and golden-brown Tuaca is no exception. But the vanilla is balanced with brandy and notes of orange and nutmeg.

Tuaca still has a long way to go to overtake Jägermeister, of course, but its growth trajectory is strikingly similar. U.S. sales of Tuaca more than doubled between 2001 and 2009, from 60,000 cases to more than 140,000 cases. As I write this, in 2010, Jägermeister has long been the best-selling brand in the cordial/liqueur category, but in 1985, it was only selling about 140,000 cases.

On a trip to Italy in late summer 2009, I decided to pay a visit to the Tuaca distillery in Livorno, on the coast of Tuscany. Tuscany! Could you dream up a more romantic spot for a liqueur to come from? Tuscany is, of course, the biggest fantasy destination for American Italophiles. Think rolling vineyards and olive groves, charming peasants, fiascoes of Chianti, hilltop villas, al fresco dinners of figs and prosciutto taken leisurely at long tables filled with beautiful people, Frances Mayes renovating her dream home in *Under the Tuscan Sun*, Liv Tyler's sexual awakening in *Stealing Beauty*.

All of that adds up to a fairly saccharine vision of Tuscany. So I have to admit I was hopeful when everyone, including my guidebooks and the Tuaca people, called Livorno "the ugliest city in Tuscany," with few recommended tourist sights. Most visitors simply pass through on the way to the ferryboats that leave from the port. Livorno to me immediately felt like a real, workaday Italian city, and I loved it. The evening before my visit to Tuaca, I sipped *aperitivi* at a few of the waterfront bars, and then as the sun set, I wandered along the quiet canals to a restaurant where I ate a striking, briny-sweet sea urchin spaghettini, and squash blossoms stuffed with bacalao. The restaurant itself was raucous, and the crowd that dined along with me that night included a local Harley-Davidson club with a dozen motorcyclists dressed in leather, a loud group of thirty-something women on girls' night out, and a family who brought their tiny dog. The owner joined me at my table, and when I couldn't get a taxi, the waitress offered me a ride to my hotel on the back of her scooter.

One thing I noted during my evening out in Livorno, however, was that none of the bars had a bottle of Tuaca. When I asked for Tuaca in the restaurant, they acted as if I'd requested something impossibly foreign or exotic. I've spent a great deal of time in Italy, and it made me realize, thinking back, how rarely I've seen of bottle of Tuaca anywhere in the country.

This was not unusual, I was told when I arrived at the Tuaca distillery in the morning. "Tuaca is much more well-known in the United States than in Italy," said Stefano Amico, the operations manager. "Two years ago, they tried to distribute Tuaca in Italy, but it was not successful. In Italy, we are practically selling only to the old men who know Tuaca from long ago."

Tuaca was actually purchased in 2002 by American liquor giant Brown-Forman (which owns Jack Daniels and Finlandia vodka, among dozens of other brands). Prior to that, Tuaca had been owned by the Tuonis and the Canepas, two Jewish families that found refuge in Livorno during World War II. The name, originally Tuoca, was derived by combining the two names. American GIs got a taste for the stuff while stationed in Livorno during the war, and an entrepreneur began importing it to the States in the 1950s. That's when the spelling *Tuoca* was changed to *Tuaca*, because Americans had a hard time pronouncing it. "Tuaca looks a bit like a Mexican name to me," Amico said.

Now, 98 percent of the bottles produced in Livorno are shipped to the United States. If that's the case, I asked, then why doesn't Brown-Forman move production to the States? Amico chuckled uncomfortably. "Well," he said, "we certainly hope that doesn't happen."

Then, Amico thought for a moment, and added, "The reason Tuaca is made here is that all of their marketing is based on 'Made in Italy.' This is the important reason. The Italian style of life, Italian food and drink, Italian fashion. People know that Italians have good taste in these things." (In fact, the "Made in Italy" thing will soon become even more of a facade, since a Brown-Forman executive told me in May 2010 that they would move Tuaca production to the United States.)

On the distillery tour, I was struck by how automated the place was. Amico, who'd previously been an economics professor at the University of Pisa, was clearly pleased with efficiency. "We have a robot," Amico said. "As you can see, there's practically no manual intervention at all. It only takes twelve people to run this plant. We are one of the most profitable brands at Brown-Forman."

"But the blending is done manually, right?" I asked.

"No, it's not," he said. "The only thing they do manually is to cut the bags of sugar open and pour it."

He showed me where the brandy is blended with neutral spirits and sugar "and our natural flavors, which of course I cannot disclose."

In its marketing, Tuaca makes a big deal out of tracing the recipe's ancestry back to the Renaissance and the Medicis. In fact, the Medici crest is on the bottle. I asked Amico if that's the same formula the Tuoni and Canepa families used. Is it true that the recipe really dates back to the Medicis? "I cannot tell you because I have lost the tracks of history," Amico said.

What we do know is that when Tuaca was launched in 1938, it was originally called Cognac al Latte, or "Milk Cognac"; this was, of course, in the days before Cognac was an AOC-protected name. In the beginning, Tuaca clocked in at 42 percent alcohol by volume, or 84 proof. Now, it's sold in the United States at a much more accessible 70 proof. "Tuaca has an easy taste. It's not difficult to drink. I've never found someone who doesn't like it," Amico said. "I tasted the old Tuaca, at 84 proof. It could be that it was even a little more tasty, but the current recipe is easier to drink. So probably you can drink more of the current one."

I noted that Jägermeister is also sold at 70 proof, and I wondered if that was coincidence or whether Brown-Forman saw Tuaca as a competitor to Jägermeister. "Yes," Amico said. "For some reason, the benchmark in this category is Jägermeister. But I really don't understand why Jägermeister is the benchmark."

After our tour, we went to lunch at a restaurant overlooking the port. We were joined by a dozen Brown-Forman distributors who were visiting from the United States, mostly New York. During a wine-soaked lunch, I sat next to a guy named George Sideris, who'd been in the spirits business for more than thirty years, and who'd handled Tuaca when it was originally distributed by Seagram's. "I remember it before they dropped the proof," he said. "Man, when it was 84 proof, it was like turpentine." Back in the 1970s, the main Tuaca cocktail being promoted was a winter warmer called Hot Apple Pie. "It was supposed to be an after-skiing drink," Sideris said. "Tuaca was also popular in the gay community in San Francisco. There was a drink called a Bear Hug, and they served it in a glass with a little bear on the stem. If one guy was interested in someone, he would send over a Bear Hug. And if the other guy accepted the drink, that meant he was interested."

At the other end of the table, one of the younger distributors was saying loudly, "Tuaca, man. I probably drank a case of Tuaca my freshman year at college!"

A Round of Drinks:
Secret Old Recipes

How do you know that you're in a real cocktail bar? I've found that there are always a couple of bottles sitting on the back bar that will serve as a sort of secret handshake or knowing wink. One is maraschino liqueur, which I described in chapter 2. The other is Chartreuse, usually the 110-proof green version. If you spy those two, you can be pretty certain you're in a bar that takes its cocktails seriously. In fact, when I see a speakeasy menu these days, I am shocked if I don't see any drinks using either of those two spirits.

Perhaps the finest use of both liqueurs is in the Last Word. This is a Prohibition-era cocktail invented at the Detroit Athletic Club and resurrected a few years back by Murray Stenson at Seattle's classic-cocktail haven, the Zig Zag Café. Its fame has spread as far and wide as the classic-cocktail movement itself, spawning numerous variations. A bit sweet, a bit sour, a bit herbal, a bit pungent, with huge, bold flavors, the Last Word is definitely not a poolside drink, and probably not for the Cosmo crowd. It's a thinking person's drink. A drink with a swagger.

THE LAST WORD

Serves 1

> ³/₄ ounce gin
> ³/₄ ounce freshly squeezed lime juice
> ³/₄ ounce green Chartreuse
> ³/₄ ounce maraschino liqueur, preferably Luxardo

Fill a cocktail shaker halfway with ice. Add the gin, lime juice, Chartreuse, and maraschino liqueur. Shake well, then strain into a chilled cocktail glass.

Another great use of Chartreuse is in the Bijou, a turn-of-the-twentieth-century cousin of the martini. Just like the Last Word, the Bijou harkens to a time when bartenders were adept at mixing Continental liqueurs with their gin. This recipe exists in all the great early cocktail books. Always be sure to use green Chartreuse.

BIJOU

Serves 1

> 1 ounce green Chartreuse
> 1 ounce gin
> 1 ounce sweet vermouth
> 1 dash orange bitters
> Preserved or maraschino cherry (page 217), for garnish
> Lemon peel twist, for garnish

Fill a mixing glass two-thirds full with ice. Add the Chartreuse, gin, vermouth, and bitters. Stir vigorously, then strain into a cocktail glass. Garnish with the cherry and lemon peel twist.

A more contemporary use of Chartreuse can be found in the Chartreuse Swizzle, which is a mash-up of Old World and New World. In this case Chartreuse replaces rum in the Swizzle, a Caribbean standard.

CHARTREUSE SWIZZLE

Serves 1

> 1¼ ounces green Chartreuse
> 1 ounce pineapple juice
> ¾ ounce freshly squeezed lime juice
> ½ ounce falernum, preferably John D. Taylor's Velvet Falernum

In a Collins glass packed with crushed ice, combine the Chartreuse, pineapple and lime juices, and falernum. Swizzle with a bar spoon or swizzle stick until the outside of the glass frosts, adding more crushed ice as needed to fill the glass. Serve with a straw.

Recipe by Marcovaldo Dionysos, created for Clock Bar, San Francisco

St-Germain: Beyond the Romance

As much as I tease St-Germain about its fantastic story of men in berets on bikes harvesting the elderflowers, the liqueur itself is tasty and has many uses in great cocktails. It's become so prevalent among top bartenders that it's been called "bartender's ketchup" by some wags.

ELDERFASHIONED

Serves 1

This is an elderflowery take on the classic Old Fashioned.

2 ounces bourbon
¹/₂ ounce St-Germain elderflower liqueur
2 dashes Angostura bitters
Orange peel twist, for garnish

Fill an old-fashioned glass with ice. Add the bourbon, St-Germain, and bitters. Stir gently. Garnish with the orange peel twist.

Recipe by St-Germain

BORIS KARLOFF

Serves 1

This is an elderflowery take on a gin fizz.

³/₄ ounce gin
³/₄ ounce St-Germain elderflower liqueur
1 ounce freshly squeezed lime juice
1 tablespoon confectioners' sugar
1 egg white
1 ounce club soda
Pinch of grated lime zest, for garnish
Pinch of freshly ground black pepper, for garnish

In a shaker, combine the gin, St-Germain, lime juice, sugar, and egg white. Shake well without ice. Then fill the shaker with ice and shake well for another 30 seconds. Strain into an ice-filled Collins glass. Add the club soda and stir. Sprinkle the lime zest and pepper over the top.

Recipe by Todd Thrasher of PX, Restaurant Eve, and the Majestic, Alexandria, Virginia

Tuaca: Made in Italy, for Americans

Tuaca has much more complexity and potential as a cocktail ingredient than as a shot in a college bar. There are actually several citrus-vanilla liqueurs on the market, including Licor 43 (or Cuarenta y Tres) from Spain and Navan from France, but I like Tuaca best of the bunch. I think Navan (with a cognac base) tastes like Dimetapp, but I enjoy Licor 43 very much. In fact, I often use it interchangeably with Tuaca. Licor 43, like Tuaca, is an old spirit: it claims a heritage that stretches back two thousand years to the ancient Carthaginians and derives its name from the forty-three secret ingredients used to make it. Like Tuaca, Licor 43 is also fast becoming a trendy staple on bar menus around the country.

I find that Tuaca mixes best with whiskey. I've made several variations of a Manhattan, my favorite of which I call a Livorno, for the town where Tuaca is made.

LIVORNO

Serves 1

> 1 1/2 ounces bourbon
> 3/4 ounce Tuaca
> 2 dashes Peychaud's bitters
> Preserved or maraschino cherry (page 217), for garnish

Fill a mixing glass two-thirds full with ice. Add the bourbon, Tuaca, and bitters. Stir vigorously for 30 seconds, then strain into a cocktail glass. Garnish with the cherry.

Another Tuaca favorite mixes it with Scotch on ice, then tops it with tonic water and a squeeze of lime. Think of this Scottish-Italian tall drink as a sort of Tuscan-influenced Rusty Nail with the refreshing addition of tonic. I recommend using a lighter Scotch (not too smoky or peaty) with notes of vanilla and sherry, such as Glenfiddich or Glenkinchie.

UNDER THE TARTAN SUN

Serves 1

> 1 1/2 ounces Tuaca
> 3/4 ounce Scotch
> 3 ounces tonic water
> 1 lime wedge

Fill a highball glass with ice. Add the Tuaca and the Scotch, then top with the tonic water. Squeeze in the lime wedge, drop it into the drink, and stir lightly.

Beyond Jägermeister:
The Redheaded Slut Revisited

It has become a tradition in New Orleans to hold a jazz funeral—with a coffin and a procession through the French Quarter—for a truly bad, embarrassing cocktail that the bartenders who attend the annual Tales of the Cocktail event believe should die. The first year, they laid to rest the Appletini, that girls'-night-out stalwart based on neon-green Sour Apple Pucker schnapps. The time had come. If bartending was ever to move forward as a respectable craft, then sacrificing one of the 1990s faux-tini drinks seemed reasonable. Very few tears were shed.

The following summer presented a slightly different scenario. A funeral was held for a well-known shot with a rather off-color name, served in so many college bars: the Redheaded Slut. Consisting of equal parts cranberry juice, peach schnapps, and Jägermeister, the Redheaded Slut is meant to be taken in one gulp, usually after shouting something like "Woo hoo!" At first I thought, Yeah, good riddance, Redheaded Slut, with your nasty mix of herb, licorice, cinnamon, and cloying artificial "peach" odor. But later, I started to think its burial might have been misguided.

Please understand: I am by no means here to defend the Redheaded Slut. I think anyone who serves one of those 1980s shots-with-a-naughty-name—Sex on the Beach, Slippery Nipple, Screaming Orgasm, Dirty Girl Scout—should be forced to listen to an iPod that plays only Rick Astley's "Never Gonna Give You Up" over and over again.

When I look at recipes for this drink genre in a book I own called *Big Bad-Ass Book of Shots*, I am struck by how often the drinks are based on a very small group of ingredients: Jägermeister, peach schnapps,

Bailey's Irish Cream, Southern Comfort, cranberry juice. Sometimes more than one of them. Sometimes all of them. Clearly, more time was spent on coming up with a risqué name for most of these than on the formula for the drink itself.

But then I think, I'm not being fair. Perhaps hundreds of years from now when the history of our era in bartending is written, this type of shot will represent a primitive but significant stage of the craft. Sort of like cave paintings. In the 1980s and 1990s, most bartenders were working with what they had, without access to the sorts of obscure flavors and ingredients we now enjoy. What bar in 1984 had Old Tom gin or maraschino liqueur or crème de violette? Maybe, I thought, instead of an RIP for the Redheaded Slut, I should turn my attention to helping it evolve. So I spent a lost summer weekend trying to reengineer it.

It's not as if the shot did its job well, anyway. We all know the purpose of a shot, and Jägermeister at 70 proof and peach schnapps at 30 proof aren't exactly high-octane. I'd suggest one slug of 101-proof Wild Turkey if a real shot is what you're looking for. So my plan was to shift the Redheaded Slut from shot to proper cocktail.

I wanted to get rid of the peach schnapps, cranberry juice, and Jägermeister yet still retain some memory of the fruit, the herbs and spices, and the color, which is a sort of ginger color like . . . red hair. The first ingredient was easy. I hate peach schnapps and it happened to be peach season, so I was going to use fresh yellow peaches in whatever I made. The second ingredient was also a cinch to lose, because the cranberry juice wasn't doing much of anything in this drink except adding color. The third was trickier. I actually like Jägermeister now and then. But maybe Jägermeister as a mixer isn't always a good idea. It can overpower.

Still, Jägermeister has a flavor profile similar to the Italian amari that so many trendy "mixologists" use. And I'd read about an interesting experiment using peaches and Punt e Mes vermouth on a blog called Cocktail Notes. Punt e Mes's flavor lies somewhere between sweet vermouth and Campari. I liked it, but Punt e Mes is brown, and I wanted this drink to be red. So I mixed sweet vermouth and Campari with muddled peaches. Once I had my vermouth-Campari-peach mixture, I was in business. I combined this mixture with all sorts of spirits, but found it worked best with brandy or bourbon.

The drink still needed a new, less offensive name, however. I was stumped. My experimentation happened around the time we learned of John Hughes's death in August 2009. That weekend, I ended up watching a bunch of his great 1980s teen films. At a certain point during *Sixteen Candles*, the name of my nicer, fresher, more sophisticated—but still redheaded—drink became obvious.

THE MOLLY RINGWALD

Serves 4

> 1 large yellow peach, peeled, pitted, and cut into small chunks
> 2 1/2 ounces sweet vermouth
> 1 1/4 ounces Campari
> 3 dashes peach bitters
> 3 ounces brandy

Muddle the peach chunks in a mixing glass until most of their juice has been released. Add the vermouth, Campari, and bitters. Shake well. Strain through a fine-mesh strainer, using the muddler to press as much liquid as possible through the strainer, and transfer the mixture to a small pitcher, jar, or other glass container. You should have about 6 ounces of liquid.

Pour 1 1/2 ounces of the peach mixture into each of 4 old-fashioned glasses. Add 2 or 3 small ice cubes and 3/4 ounce of brandy to each glass. Stir well.

NOTE: If you like, you may substitute bourbon, gin, Calvados, or another spirit for the brandy.

CHAPTER 5

BITTER IS BELLA

**WHO HAS NEVER TASTED WHAT IS BITTER
DOES NOT KNOW WHAT IS SWEET.**

—*German proverb*

WHEN INTRODUCING new and strange drinks to people, I find that some libations can be a harder sell than others. Italian bitters, or *amari*, are always among the most challenging. Take, for instance, Cynar. The picture of the artichoke on the bottle does not help. Neither does the fact that the name shares four letters with the word *cyanide*. But I try to spread the good word on Cynar anyway. Here's how the conversation usually goes:

> *Friend:* What the hell is that?
> *Me:* Cynar.
> *Friend:* Cynar?
> *Me:* Yes! You must try Cynar! Do yourself a favor!

Friend: What does it taste like?

Me: Um, it's a 33-proof liqueur that's distilled from artichokes, but also lots of other herbs and stuff.

Friend: Artichokes? WTF? It's not one of those bitter Italian things you're always trying to get me to drink, is it?

Me: Well, yes. But this one is sort of bittersweet.

Friend: Is it at least pretty in a martini glass?

Me: Well, it's kind of like a dark brown. But you can maybe call it sepia or mahogany or burnt sienna if that makes it seem better.

That's when they usually make a face, just as you may be doing right now. Cynar doesn't sound very promising, does it? I won't lie. Cynar—perhaps like anchovies or modern jazz or certain sexual positions—takes a bit of effort, at first, to enjoy. But I implore you: make the effort.

Yes, I'm one of those irritating Italophiles who long ago acquired the seemingly unacquirable taste for those bitter herbal liqueurs that Italians drink before and after dinner. Over the years, I've found that nothing flummoxes the average American drinker more than an aperitivo like Campari or an amaro like Averna or Ramazzotti served as a digestivo.

Some of the unease surely stems from the concept itself. An aperitivo is meant to stimulate the appetite—literally to "open" the stomach before a meal. The higher-proof amaro (bitter) is traditionally consumed as a digestivo, or digestive aid. Let's be honest: these ideas can seem a little gross. The word *digestivo*, in particular, is one place the Italian language, generally so poetic and mellifluous when it comes to food and drink, veers sharply into the prosaic and unpretty. Few Americans really want to think about digestion, or to ponder the relationship of our before- or after-dinner beverages with our stomach enzymes.

Italians, on the other hand, are obsessed with the digestive process. For instance, beware of a drink that's too cold: it will block digestion and cause the dreaded *colpo di freddo*, which according to many Italians can cause cramps—and possibly even death! In Italy, there are many apocryphal stories of people being rushed to the hospital for taking too cold a drink on a hot summer evening. When I was living in a northern Italian village as a nineteen-year-old exchange student, my host father was always very concerned about my digestion, especially after I'd gorged myself into a food coma on my host mother's delicious cooking. His sure-fire cure (of which he partook with me) was a shot of amaro.

Once, after a lavish wedding in a restored fourteenth-century convent, an American friend, finding nothing else to drink, chugged half a bottle of Campari. A little while later, he proceeded to vomit all over one of the convent's walls, which just happened to be painted with a fresco that dated to the fourteenth century. In the morning, when the owners understandably freaked out, he said, "I think that Campari opened up my stomach." Ah, they said, of course! Only an American would drink Campari after a wedding feast! He wasn't quite forgiven for the thousand dollars of damage he'd caused, but at least he'd provided them a reason beyond simply "I am a jackass."

In fact, there does seem to be some validity to the therapeutic reputation of herbal bitters. A 2001 study published in a Swiss medical journal said they "sensorially stimulate" stomach secretions and digestive glands "at even very small concentrations." But medicinal value, of course, isn't our main concern when it comes to spirits.

Too much information about the digestive tract aside, there's also the issue of amari's bitter taste, which takes some getting used to. Humans, among other animals, developed a basic aversion to bitter so we didn't accidentally eat poisonous plants—obviously, there's a deep reason why it's so hard to develop a taste for bitters. A bartender in Washington once told me about a cocktail in which he substitutes Fernet-Branca for Campari. "I want to push people outside their comfort zone," he said with an evil chuckle. I can't think of anything better than amaro to push someone out of his or her comfort zone. I did this to my own mother not too long ago when I served her Fernet-Branca, after dinner, for the first time. She took one sip, made that bitter face, and said, "Oh my god! It tastes like Vicks VapoRub."

"Just remember," I said, "at least your digestive tract is smiling."

For me, acquiring the taste for bitter spirits happened simply and natu-
rally. I was a nineteen-year-old living and studying in northern Italy, near
Milan. Drinks with Campari and Aperol were what the *belle ragazze* who
arrived at the café on their Vespas were drinking. I hoped to be riding on
the back of one of those Vespas after happy hour. Taste acquired.

But I believe it's possible to acquire a taste later in life, too. Because the
Negroni and the Americano have slowly become cocktail menu staples,
many Americans are familiar with bright red Campari. Another of Italy's
best-loved aperitivi, Aperol, was only introduced to the United States in
2006—even though the spirit itself dates to 1919. If Cynar is Campari's
homely cousin, Aperol is sort of like its hot younger sister. Bright orange
in color and containing 11 percent alcohol (less than most wines), it's a
sweet and bitter blend of thirty herbs, spices, and fruits, like orange, rhubarb, and gentian. When Aperol came on the scene, Paul Pacult wrote in
Spirit Journal, "If there is any justice, [Aperol] should become a favored
pre-dinner quaff in aware U.S. households and restaurants."

I find this endorsement interesting, as it shows how tastes evolve
over time—even for an acknowledged expert. More than a decade earlier, Pacult had panned Campari as a two-star "Not Recommended"
spirit, saying, "Quite candidly I'm not an avid fan of bitters." Yet in 2007,
he revisited Campari in his newsletter, upgrading it from two to three
stars, and writing, "I didn't fully appreciate bitters when I first reviewed
this ubiquitous brand back in 1995. I've turned a corner since then and
have come to admire their special place in the international spirits sym-
phony." Why the change of heart, I wanted to know? No one would argue
that Campari's nineteenth-century recipe has changed, so when I met
Pacult, I pressed him on this revised opinion. "That was me, my palate,
changing," he admitted. "The first go-round with Campari, I really didn't
understand the bitter subcategory. I've learned a lot more since then."

By now the cocktail geek crowd has embraced amari, experimenting
wildly with many different brands (note how many of the variations of
Manhattans I described in chapter 2 called for them). Anyone who wants
to show off how much of a cocktail person he or she is will probably
make you a drink with, say, rye whiskey and at least one amaro. Diners

are enjoying more bitter flavors—think radicchio and dandelion greens and extra-dark chocolate. But as for bitter drinks . . . well, certainly not everyone has got the memo yet. The Italians also haven't got the memo that certain of us really enjoy these spirits, either, because so much of what they produce never leaves Italy. I've tried my damnedest to fix both issues.

On one of my recent trips to Milan, I stopped off at the distiller Illva Saronno, based in the town of Saronno, an otherwise forgettable stop on the forty-five-minute train that connects Milan's Malpensa Airport with the city center. Illva Saronno's main product is the superpopular Disaronno brand of amaretto, which is probably the most widely sold Italian liqueur in the United States. Surely, you remember the cheesy "Disaronno on the rocks" ads, wherein the woman licks her ice cube for the bartender? Well, anyway, I wasn't there for the amaretto, which I usually find too cloyingly sweet. Instead, I was really visiting Saronno to talk about perhaps my favorite Italian aperitivo, Zucca. Specifically, I was there to make a special plea to the Illva Saronno people to start importing it to the United States. Zucca is a *rabarbaro*, a subset of amaro that is infused predominantly with Chinese rhubarb, among other herbs. I learned to love Zucca at the famous Caffe Zucca in Milan's Galleria on the Piazza Duomo—which was actually the same café where Gaspare Campari introduced his famed red bitters in the 1860s.

First, I listened to the obligatory pitch on Disaronno (which is distributed by Bacardi). "We *are* the category," said Ludovica Reina, whose family has owned the company for generations. She also told me the secret recipe was written by her grandmother by hand and she's only been allowed a peek. "People think it's almonds, but it's not just almonds in the recipe." (Perhaps apricot pits, I thought? The same thing used to make the local amaretto cookies?) If you're looking for a romantic story, you can't beat amaretto's: In 1525, Leonardo da Vinci's assistant, Bernardino Luini, was painting a fresco of the Madonna in Saronno's church and found his inspiration in a young widow who became his model and lover. As a token of her affection, she steeped apricot kernels in brandy and presented the concoction to the artist.

Finally, we were joined by Lorenzo Vavassori, a regional marketing director who oversees the United States. That's when I mentioned that many of the high-end cocktail bars in America were mixing with Italian spirits. "Just look at cocktail menus in New York and San Francisco," I said. "Campari, Aperol, Punt e Mes, Cynar . . ."

"Cynar?" Vavassori looked at me, and then furtively at Reina. The look was clear: are you putting me on? "This is surprising to me," he said. "It's something I'm interested in investigating."

"I really, really think you should bring Zucca into the United States!" I said, perhaps a little too exuberantly. "I know you'd have a lot of bartenders clamoring for it."

Vavassori laughed and was now thoroughly convinced I was joking with him. Exporting Zucca to the United States was definitely not in the strategic plan. "Maybe I need to take you to my meetings with Bacardi," he said.

After my unsuccessful plea to the Disaronno people, it was time to head to Milan. While I waited for a taxi, I drank a Zucca with sparkling water in Illva Saronno's company bar. So what does Zucca taste like? It's a weird yet entirely pleasant mix of earthy and delicate, vanilla and bitter, yam and coffee—to toss out some pretentious, winelike descriptors. What Zucca really tastes like, to me, is Milan itself.

I arrived in Milan just before happy hour. That's what Milanese call it: "happy hour," untranslated, in English. This, however, is where the similarities to our hallowed American institution end. For starters, look at what's in the rail: Campari, Aperol, bianco vermouth, Punt e Mes, and bottles of prosecco on ice. It's not exactly the high-octane stuff most American bargoers are used to.

Take a gander at the crowd. This is not a shot-and-beer crowd or a Captain-and-Coke crowd. Look at those coiffed men with red pants and brown belts, or crisp blue suits and brown shoes, or sweaters draped around their necks, all nursing bitter, orange-colored drinks. They spill outside the bar, onto the sidewalk, into the street, chatting up the lithe, tan, sunglassed women who drive Vespas in their high heels and puff on cigarettes, causing you to rethink your whole position on smoking. No one seems to be in any hurry, and happy hour usually stretches well into the evening. Finally, look at the prices. Milanese happy hour does not involve two-for-one Coronas. The prices actually go up a few euros during happy hour, when an Americano averages about eight euros. And, wait, you can't pay the bartender directly. Be sure to go to the cashier— she's the really bored woman dressed in Prada over there behind the counter—and get a receipt. Now you may have your aperitivo.

Once you have your Negroni Sbagliato or Aperol Spritz in hand, that's when you realize what you're paying for—the "complimentary" snacks. In Milan, at places like Radetzky or Bar Brera or Bhangrabar, they don't just toss out a bowl of nuts or a tray of lukewarm hot wings. There are perfect little tramezzini and panini, made with the finest speck and bresaola and culatello and prosciutto. There are wheels of Parmigiano-Reggiano, squares of polenta covered in Gorgonzola, and three kinds of olives. There are caper berries, slices of melon, and artichoke hearts. There are platters of risotto, tortelli di zucca in butter-sage sauce, and black linguini made with squid ink.

I spent a lot of time at happy hour years ago as a student in Italy. I'd join the crowds hopping from bar to bar and piece together an amazing meal on my meager budget. I've continued to mingle in the crowded happy hours on my return visits, but I've never been able to solve this one great mystery: with so much great food, how do the fashionable Milanese still fit into their chic clothes? In Italy, happy hour is an everyday ritual that illuminates two innately Italian traits at once: it involves an opportunity to enjoy excellent food and drink; and it provides a wonderful chance to be on display, to see and be seen in beautiful public spaces. In the fashion and culinary capital of Milan, this takes on interesting dimensions.

On that late afternoon in Milan, I found myself drinking an Americano cocktail (Campari, sweet vermouth, and a lemon twist, on the rocks) within the inner sanctum of the Dolce & Gabbana men's store, sitting at a sleek black bar operated by Martini, the vermouth producer, with black leather sofas and a blood-red dragon on the dark mosaic floor and ambient techno music playing. When I entered from the Corso Venezia, one of Milan's toniest shopping streets, the clerks eyed me and my shabby attire suspiciously. When I told them I'd come for happy hour, they dismissively waved me back to the Martini Bar past leather belts worth more than my entire wardrobe.

The Dolce & Gabbana store is in the middle of the Quadrilatero district, also known as the Golden Quadrangle, an area filled with posh designer stores. This is a dangerous neighborhood in which to begin happy hour, especially while the stores are still open. For instance, I'm generally shopping averse. At home, I buy all the clothes I need for the year—mainly T-shirts and flip-flops—in about an hour and a half. But when I'm in Milan, something strange happens. In the Miuccia Prada store, I might watch a Japanese teenager matter-of-factly buy a handbag for $17,000, and I start thinking about what I might buy. I once caught myself considering buying a pair of red pants that cost more than $300. Which meant it was time to move on to the next drink in a different neighborhood.

I walked toward the Basilica of Sant'Ambrogio to one of my old favorites, Bar Magenta, a high-ceilinged, wood-paneled Milan institution for more than one hundred years and one of the city's best meeting places. All walks of life mingle here, from dreadlocked college kids drinking beers to professionals drinking Negronis to older men sipping vermouth on the rocks. At happy hour, there are always several types of housemade pasta available, and a guy behind the counter slices meats like prosciutto, speck, bresaola, and culatello. Then, at a certain point, I always try to end up on the Corso di Porta Ticinese, the main thoroughfare of Milan's most bohemian neighborhood. The centerpiece of the neighborhood is the piazza of the Basilica of San Lorenzo. Here, hundreds of people congregate on warm evenings, drinking Campari and Aperol cocktails, prosecco, or beer. Most of the action takes place at Exploit, which sits directly under the so-called Diesel Wall, a gigantic fashion company billboard masquerading as art. The entrance to Exploit is deceivingly tranquil—under an awning, obscured by hedges. Inside, however, it's a mob scene during happy hour. People crowd around the bar where waiters feverishly serve complimentary mini-pizzas, vegetable tortes, and panini. The best thing to do is get your aperitivo, fill up a plate, retreat outside to a sunny place in the piazza, and do what everyone else is doing: people watch. There are no tables outside, but people are sprawled everywhere, leaning against planters, sitting along the Roman walls, or standing in groups. As the evening wears on beyond happy hour, much of the crowd remains in the piazza, drinking, strumming guitars, or kicking a soccer ball with the illuminated ruins of Roman columns as a dramatic backdrop.

Wayne Curtis, the drinks columnist for the *Atlantic*, has described the first sip of Fernet-Branca as "akin to waking up in a foreign country and finding a crowd of people arguing in agitated, thorny voices outside your hotel window. It's an event that's at once alarming and slightly thrilling."

I was thinking of that description in my hotel room on the morning of my visit to the Fernet-Branca distillery in Milan. I'd lost my phone the night before during some excessive post–happy hour revelries, and I had no alarm. I was finally awakened by a panicked call to my hotel room from the Fernet-Branca public relations person. Ragged, I quickly showered and taxied across the city, arriving at the gates of the palazzo-like building only about fifty minutes late. I felt awful. As I shook hands with the company president Niccolò Branca and mumbled my apologies, I realized that what I actually needed—truly needed—was a shot of Fernet-Branca. None was forthcoming. Instead I was handed a sterile gown and shower cap and led on a tour.

Despite my lateness and bad shape, Branca was a consummate gentleman. "Fernet-Branca is a very intelligent drink," he told me. "It's not for the situation of getting drunk. It's very healthy. Drink one or two glasses and you'll feel fresh. You won't have a hangover." Ugh, yes, and if you do have a hangover, Fernet is probably the best hair-of-the-dog ever invented.

Fernet was created in 1845 by Branca's great-great-grandfather, a self-taught herbalist. Besides settling digestion, it originally was used to treat such maladies as menstrual discomfort, colic, and cholera. It survived Prohibition in the United States because it was sold in pharmacies for medicinal purposes. "We never change the recipe," Branca said. "It's passed down from father to son. It was only given to me eight years ago."

"Now, we go into a locked room," Branca said. "Behind this door, there are secrets." Indeed, entering into this cavernous old warehouse room was like walking into a medieval spice bazaar, an alchemist's laboratory, a temple of holy herbs. Stacks of cinchona bark, pallets of bitter orange, vats of aloe and chamomile, and—to get a little biblical—myrrh. Fernet-Branca's secret recipe has more than forty ingredients in all, including Chinese rhubarb, orrisroot, cardamom, gentian, marjoram, mace, peppermint, and, of course, anise. I saw pallets and pallets of saffron, an ingredient so key to Fernet-Branca that the company reportedly controls 75 percent of the world's saffron market.

After a quick pass through the corporate museum, where I noted the slogan *Fernet é vivere*, we returned to the conference room. Branca took off his sterile gear and excused himself for a meeting, leaving me with this thought: "Fernet, it is for the person who loves the life, the person who shares it with their friends, with a beautiful woman. It's like a concert. It's much more than a drink."

That evening, after a very long afternoon nap, I ate a huge meal of saffron-tinted risotto Milanese and cotoletta alla Milanese. Afterward, with a full stomach, I decided to do an impromptu tasting of amari at my table. I wanted to see if I was getting better at snap judgments and at quickly writing tasting notes—just like Paul Pacult. First up was Fernet. To be perfectly honest, beginning your relationship with amari by drinking a shot of 80-proof Fernet-Branca is like starting to learn a language by reading its physics textbooks. The taste? How about a bracing smack in the face with a eucalyptus tree? Most other amari are much lower proof than Fernet, in the 30- to 60-proof range. Ramazzotti, for instance, is perhaps the easiest drinking, with its gentle, sweet notes of orange and cola . . . it's like the Coca-Cola of amari. Amaro Meletti, with its floral aroma and tastes of saffron and violet, is like . . . a vase full of lily-of-the-valley that still have a day or so before you have to throw them away. Amaro Montenegro, from Bologna, is an excellent starter amaro: sweeter than the others, with orange peel and cinnamon and only a touch of bitter on the finish. Amaro Montenegro was called the "liqueur of virtues" by the famed Italian poet Gabriele D'Annunzio (though it should be noted that D'Annunzio ended up becoming a figurehead of Mussolini's Fascists, so perhaps we should be wary of looking for virtues in a bottle of amaro). Finally, Averna, so dark and coffeelike and almost burnt tasting, with a hint of cloves and a musky scent that feels like, say, the nineteenth-century Sicilian equivalent of Starbucks with, say, a real-life castrato singing rather than Norah Jones or Neko Case. Or something like that.

The waiter was pretty amused by the fact that I'd ordered five amari. He kept checking on me to see if I'd really drink all five, then he finally sat down at my table and poured himself a glass of Amaro Montenegro, his personal favorite. "Why is it your favorite?" I asked.

"I don't know," he said with a shrug. "This is what my family's always taken after dinner."

About ninety minutes west of Milan by train or car, Torino, the birthplace of vermouth, flaunts an age-old happy hour scene. It's a bit of a murky history, but either Giovanni and Carlo Cinzano created the first vermouth here in 1757, or Antonio Benedetto Carpano first produced the fortified wine in 1786. Either way, vermouth was inspired by a German fortified wine that used wormwood. The word *vermouth* derives from *wermut*, the German word for wormwood. Carpano was soon followed into the vermouth business by Alessandro Martini and Luigi Rossi in 1863.

Though most people have heard of these historic brands, they are not the only vermouths to be found in Torino. In the nineteenth century, nearly every major café in Torino produced its own vermouth, and some of these formulas exist to this day. I visited the small but stately century-old Caffè Mulassano on the Piazza Castello, with its lovely marble bar. Caffè Mulassano claims it was the favored gathering place of the Royal House of Savoy. The white-jacketed waiters still serve the bar's own sweet vermouth—a recipe dating back to 1879—a red, bitter house liqueur called Liquore delle Alpi, which looks and tastes like Campari. I took my Mulassano vermouth on the rocks, per tradition in Torino, and enjoyed a complimentary plate of little panini and tramezzini sandwiches and olives.

After Mulassano, I walked a few blocks on sidewalks covered by ornate porticos to the grandest of Torino's historic cafés, the San Carlo, which opened in 1822. I entered between its gilded pilasters and under the huge, glitzy chandelier, and the tuxedoed bartender mixed me an Americano. A local guy was also sipping an Americano, while his dog slept at his feet. He told me I should check out Eataly, a new food emporium situated in the old Carpano vermouth distillery near the edge of the city. Apparently, one of the hippest new spots in Torino happened to be the supermarket. On the top floor, a museum celebrates Carpano vermouth and Punt e Mes, a vermouth to which a little bit of a Campari-like bitter is added (the name means "point and a half" in Piemontese—a point of sweetness, plus a half point of bitterness, supposedly named for a favorable rise in the stock market that benefited Carpano).

"Not many Americans like vermouth, do they?" he said. "They only put a little eyedropper in their dry martinis, yes?"

Actually, I told him, some people in the United States were finally beginning, slowly, to appreciate vermouth. "It's a bit of a trend."

"Vermouth is trendy? Ha!" he said. This, of course, was amusing to someone living in Torino, especially during happy hour, when most everyone had vermouth in their glasses.

"The biggest issue," I said, "is that people don't realize they need to refrigerate it and treat it like a wine." The man just smiled and shook his head. In most Italian bars, vermouth is poured dozens of times every evening, so storage is rarely an issue.

Given that vermouth is so entwined with Italy's happy hour scene, a vermouth pilgrimage seemed like a must. The next day, I traveled twenty minutes to the town of Pessione, where I visited the Martini distillery, housed in a sprawling whitewashed eighteenth-century villa. A greeter led me through the gate and the garden and into a stark white laboratory where a man in a white lab coat poured glasses of extra-dry, rosso, bianco, and rosé vermouths. For more than a century, until late 2010, Martini was better known in the United States under the name Martini & Rossi. The reason, of course, had been the inevitable confusion between the Martini brand and the American cocktail of the same name. Whether Americans will be any less confused remains to be seen. But in Italy, if you order a "Martini" you will receive a glass of bianco vermouth on the rocks.

"If you ask young people in Italy what their favorite Martini is, they'll say bianco," said Luciano Boero, the head of production at the plant. "For older people like me, however, Martini Rosso is the most popular."

Vermouth is 75 percent wine, and all the wine for Martini vermouth—even the rosso—is a basic white, such as Trebbiano. The wine provides only the structure and body. "To make a great vermouth, the wine must be neutral," said Alberto Oricco, an oenologist and quality-control supervisor at the plant. "It's important not to use a wine with a big flavor, because the flavor comes from the herbs."

The aromatic herbs that give Martini vermouth its flavor are mixed secretly in a lab in Geneva. While Boero knows which herbs are used, and did admit to some ingredients, even he doesn't know the exact recipe. Besides the wine and botanicals, there is also alcohol, sugar, and, in vermouth rosso, caramel added for color.

Because we sampled at room temperature, I could much more easily pick out aromas and flavors. As we tasted the pale yellow extra-dry, there was a scent of iris, lemon peels, and raspberry, and a hint of sweet wine in the taste. "We use a little Marsala wine in this blend," Boero said.

We moved on to the rosso, which is actually brown, and what we commonly call sweet vermouth. "Why is it called red? I don't know why," Boero said with a chuckle. Besides the interesting note of coriander, one of the most important ingredients is cinchona, a tree whose bark gives sweet vermouth a bitter kick. "We never use spicy herbs," Boero said, "only mountain herbs."

The ten minutes I spent tasting Martini Rosso was easily the most time I'd ever spent thinking about sweet vermouth. Even more impressive, for me, was the bianco—different from the dry—which has always been available in the United States but little known. The scent of thyme and oregano and the tastes of cloves and vanilla create a wonderful balance of sweet and savory. I could drink bianco vermouth on the rocks, with a twist of lemon, all afternoon. To me, it is no wonder that bianco is the most popular vermouth in Italy, accounting for half of Martini's production.

It's likely surprising to many, but vermouths did not appear on this earth simply as a mixer for martinis and Manhattans. Vermouths were not originally created for being mixed at all, but rather to drink alone. "I don't think Luigi Rossi ever thought to create Martini Rosso so that it could be mixed with other liquors," said Cristiana Fanciotto, Martini's spokesperson, as we sipped Americanos in the corporate bar. "He'd already created the perfect mix. There was no need to mix it with anything else."

That night, I went to happy hour at Eataly, which was built with the support of Slow Food, the international movement that started in the Piedmont region. Besides the very best Slow Food–approved artisan foodstuffs on offer, there are nine casual dining spots, each focusing on a specific type of food, such as pasta, seafood, meats and cheeses, vegetables, or pizza. The entire bottom floor is given over to wine, beer, and spirits (in the wine section, you can fill up your own liter jug with respectable table wine for two euros).

After I gorged myself during happy hour, I ended up in Eataly's wine bar. There, I saw the woman behind the bar pouring something called Giulio Cocchi Barolo Chinato. I'd only tasted Barolo Chinato once before at a dinner party in California and had never seen it since. I asked her to pour me a glass, and this time I concentrated fully on this smooth, spicy drink with just a kiss of quinine on the tongue. It was a revelation—bitter, lush, complex, like nothing else I'd tasted. The bartender suggested I go upstairs and buy a hunk of dark chocolate and come back to finish my glass. Which I did. It confirmed my sudden belief that Barolo Chinato is one of the finest after-dinner quaffs imaginable, and a better match for desserts than even port. The problem now, of course, was that I would need to track this down outside of Italy.

The bartender told me a little more about the drink. *China* in Italian means cinchona (or quinine bark). So Barolo Chinato is, literally, Barolo wine that has been *china*-ed, or infused with quinine bark and other herbs and spices, including rhubarb root, star anise, citrus peel, gentian, fennel, juniper, and cardamom seed. The spirit is produced in much the same way as its Piedmontese cousin, vermouth, but with one big difference: Vermouth generally begins with a banal white wine to which the herbs are added. Barolo Chinato begins with Barolo, Italy's greatest wine, made with the Nebbiolo grapes of the region.

There is some question as to who invented Barolo Chinato. In the nineteenth century, many pharmacists and chefs in and around Torino were experimenting with vermouths and other fortified wines. One of them, Giuseppe Cappellano, is often credited as Barolo Chinato's creator, and the Cappellano brand is available in the United States. But Barolo Chinato is also claimed by Giulio Cocchi, a Tuscan pastry chef who came to Asti and, inspired by the region's vermouth industry, soon invented his own formula in 1891.

Cocchi's was the Barolo Chinato I fell in love with, so I decided to visit its producer in Cocconato, near Asti. The brand name Giulio Cocchi is well-known in Italy for its Asti Spumante, but the company also continues to make its founder's special formula. "We like to think the Barolo Chinato concept came because he put together the world of vermouth in Piemonte with the world of the Tuscan monasteries and their use of spices and herbs," says Roberto Bava, fourth-generation winemaker with Bava Winery, which now owns Giulio Cocchi. "His formula was, and still is, very complex. One of my brothers knows the formula. It is in an old booklet, handwritten by Giulio Cocchi, and it's in a bank vault."

In the 1920s, Giulio Cocchi opened a chain of Barolo Chinato bars in cities including Milan and Torino (the one in Torino still exists) and as far away as Caracas, Venezuela. But by the 1960s and 1970s, Barolo Chinato had gone out of fashion, swept away by the tide of amari, mass-market vermouths, and aperitivi such as Punt e Mes that began to flood the Italian market. Cocchi persisted, selling its spumante, and eventually was bought by the Bava family in 1977. But its Barolo Chinato languished for decades.

That is, until the all-important chocolate-Chinato connection came to light. Bava is president of something he referred to as the "Italian Chocolate Association." Several years ago, he says, the association's members began searching for the best after-dinner drink to pair with fine chocolate, another Piedmontese specialty. After supposedly rigorous testing, Bava says, "We learned that Barolo Chinato was the absolute best match for chocolate." Regardless of how subjective that research must have been, it seems to have been a eureka moment in the history of food and drink pairings because, believe me, it is true. "Now," Bava says, "if you ask anyone in Italy, 'What do you pair with chocolate?' They will say, 'Barolo Chinato.'"

Bava says the chocolate pairing concept has saved Barolo Chinato from extinction and spurred other producers to put their versions on the market. "I'm proud of this. It's probably the only idea in this life that I will leave behind," he says, with a wink.

While we tasted, Bava brought out a bottle of an aperitif called Cocchi Aperitivo Americano, made from a white Moscato di Asti and infused with cinchona bark. I almost flipped. Barolo Chinato had been revelation enough. But Cocchi Aperitivo Americano is a missing link in the cocktail world—a true white-wine quinquina. Many of us know, and have fallen in love with, Lillet Blanc, the lovely and refreshing white wine-and-citrus aperitif. Lillet began life as Kina Lillet, which had a much higher quinine content, then changed its recipe in 1986. Much of Lillet's recent popularity can be traced to the 2006 film *Casino Royale* (based on the original 1953 novel), in which James Bond orders his famed Vesper cocktail with gin, vodka, and Kina Lillet, "shaken, not stirred." For a while after that, you couldn't find a cocktail menu that didn't have some variation of a Vesper. The only problem is that, without the quinine level of Kina Lillet, the drink is nearly impossible to reproduce. Well, Cocchi Americano might be as close to Kina Lillet as anyone is likely to find these days.

When I returned home, I was not surprised to find that Eric Seed had made a visit to Bava before I had and would become the U.S. importer of Cocchi Aperitivo Americano. In fact, the following summer I ran into him in Philadelphia at Franklin Mortgage & Investment Co., pouring samples for the bartenders. "Let's make a Vesper!" I said.

"I can't make a Vesper," said Colin, one of the bartenders. "I don't have vodka."

Since I was already drinking my way through Italy, I decided to veer northeast and head to up to the Veneto, to Bassano del Grappa, a charming city at the foothills of the Alps on the Brenta River. The town is grappa's spiritual home, and I visited two distilleries there.

But wait. You're also afraid of grappa, right? Maybe you once had a bad sip of the stuff after dinner in an Italian restaurant, or maybe, if you're of Italian descent, you had a homemade snootful at an old relative's house. Don't worry, I'm not going tell you that my first experience with grappa was exquisite or transcendent. When I was an exchange student in Italy nearly twenty years ago, many of the men in the village where I lived enjoyed a daily *caffè corretto*, meaning they "corrected" their morning espressos with a shot of grappa. Those guys were always keen to pour me a little, too, and much of it was of the white-lightning variety and burned the esophagus like kerosene.

"Many people once had that same harsh, aggressive experience, and you'll remember that experience your whole life," says Jacopo Poli, fourth-generation distiller of one of Italy's finest grappas, Poli. "But the grappas we are distilling now are at least ten times better than the grappa we drank twenty years ago."

Grappa faces the same predicament that has plagued tequila. Most people's early experiences with tequila were with poor-quality *mixtos* that left a mean hangover. Good, premium grappa, however, can be a lovely and complex spirit, just like premium tequila. Yet, as with tequila, it will be an uphill climb to convince people of that. That's why grappa distillers in Italy went ballistic in 2008 when senators in the right-wing Lega Nord party proposed legalizing homemade grappa. "It's nonsense," Poli said. "It's taken decades to get rid of the image of the clandestine still, of moonshine, of lowbrow grappa. And now they want to go back to the past?" So far, the legislation has not passed.

For a brief time, from the late 1980s through the mid-1990s, grappa experienced a minor trendiness in the United States when Italian restaurants began offering a selection of grappas, many in showy, silly blown-glass bottles. But that small wave of popularity might have created an even larger long-term problem for premium grappa.

Around that time, some of Italy's big-name winemakers, such as Antinori, Michele Chiarlo, Banfi, and others, jumped onto the grappa bandwagon, and a whole category of winery-branded grappas took off. A few are of decent quality, but many are not. Often they were created as a value add-on to restaurant wine orders (buy ten cases of our wine, and we'll give you a free case of grappa) and also as brand reinforcement on their after-dinner menu; in other words, as a marketing gimmick.

"Just because the pomace came from a good winery doesn't mean it's going to make a good grappa," Poli said. Grappa is not a brandy, as is often reported, and it's not made with wine, but rather with grape pomace: the skins, seeds, and pulp of grapes that are left after the juice has been extracted for winemaking. The pomace must be stored in an airtight container to stop the fermentation process, and it must be kept fresh, moist, and free of mold.

"Ninety-nine-point-nine percent of making a good grappa is knowing how to handle the pomace properly," said Antonio Guarda Nardini, whose family runs the Nardini Distillery, Italy's largest producer of premium grappa. The Nardini family has been handling pomace and making grappa since 1779.

Most wineries, on the other hand, use a contract distiller who puts the winery's label on a grappa, often with mixed results. Sometimes it's even unclear whether the winery's own pomace is used. Yet if you go to a liquor store today, grappas by wineries often crowd out the premium, artisan distillers.

In the glass, what separates a bad grappa from a good one? First, a bad grappa often has what could be described as a "pet shop" aroma. At a dinner on my trip, we tasted a very poor grappa, and my tablemate said, "I feel like I can hear puppies barking when I sip this." That is often the telltale sign that moldy or stale pomace has been used.

To check quality, Nardini suggests a simple test: when a grappa is served, dip your finger in it and rub the back of your hand. When you smell your hand, the aroma should be instantly fresh and at least hint at grapes. Just as important, the grappa shouldn't feel oily. There is always some oil in the pomace because of the crushed grape seeds, but good producers filter and distill in a way that minimizes it. Poorly made grappa contains a high percentage of oil. "The oil is what makes it hard to digest and gives you a headache," Nardini says. "That's the grappa that makes you say, 'Ugh, I could feel that grappa going up and down my system for three days.'" Nardini avoids problems by filtering and triple distilling, and the result is cleaner, lighter, and smoother than you'd imagine a 100-proof spirit could be.

Nardini and Poli make excellent grappas, though each comes at the spirit from a different angle. Nardini has long been considered the gold standard in Italy, and its bianco is a great place to start if you're looking for a traditional grappa. Poli, on the other hand, considers himself more of an artisan and innovator. He has begun producing grappas with fruit infusions, plus grappa made from single-grape pomace, such as Moscato or Merlot, and he experiments with different methods of barrel aging. When I visited, Poli was about to roll out grappas that had been aged in port and sherry barrels.

I'm glad I've revisited grappa, but I'll stick to the distilleries that are committed to grappa as their main spirit and not as a sideline. The next time I'm in an Italian restaurant and the waiter comes around during coffee with little glasses of grappa, I'm checking to see. If it's Poli or Nardini, or an artisan producer such as Nonino or Capovilla, I know what I'll say to my dining companions: have no fear.

A Round of Drinks:
Improving the Negroni

As I entered one summer drinking season, that cynical line from Hemingway's "Hills Like White Elephants"—the one I mentioned earlier—was rattling around in my head: "I wanted to try this new drink. That's all we do, isn't it—look at things and try new drinks?" I was full of a similar sense of ennui. Through the colder months I'd tried so many new spirits, a never-ending line of product launches ranging from the ridiculous to the sublime. Likewise, I'd tried so many new cocktails, invented almost daily by the growing horde of "mixologists," all trying to out-innovate, out-clever, or out-classic one another.

When it came time to choose a summer drink, I was so sated with The New that I decided to go back to an old standby: the Negroni. For a long time, I'd considered the Negroni to be just about the perfect cocktail. Equal parts gin, sweet vermouth, and Campari, the Negroni is so simple that even the worst bartender can't mess it up too badly. It's more forgiving than a martini and certainly sexier than, say, a gin and tonic. It was one of the first cocktails I'd taken to drinking as a young man, and I was very much looking forward to getting reacquainted with my old friend.

NEGRONI

Serves 1

> 1 ounce gin
> 1 ounce sweet vermouth
> 1 ounce Campari
> Orange peel twist, for garnish

Fill a mixing glass halfway with ice. Add the gin, vermouth, and Campari. Stir vigorously for 30 seconds, then strain into a chilled cocktail glass. Garnish with the orange peel twist.

But here's the thing. When I mixed up a batch of Negronis, my reaction, to my surprise and chagrin, was pretty much, meh. In theory, I wanted a Negroni, but in reality, the Negroni was lacking something. That distressed me. What if all the fancy-schmancy tasting I've been doing lately has irrevocably rewired my palate? What if I can never again go back to being the young, carefree person who loved nothing better than the simple pleasures of a Negroni in summertime?

My solution: I would use my hard-won cocktail wisdom and experience to reengineer, and possibly improve, the Negroni. Starting with the classic Negroni formula and then deviating from it, I would illustrate how nearly all good new cocktails evolve. In doing so, I would also reclaim my old drink and perhaps a part of my youth. Or something like that.

At first I thought the Campari was the problem. I'd been tasting a lot of different bitter spirits lately, including several obscure local Campari competitors from Italy. Perhaps Campari now seemed a little too old hat? So, to start, I stirred up a Negroni alternative called the Cyn-Cin, which substitutes Cynar for the Campari. It was excellent.

CYN-CIN

Serves 1

> 1 ounce gin
> 1 ounce sweet vermouth
> 1 ounce Cynar
> 1 dash orange bitters
> 2 orange wedges, sliced ½ inch thick

Fill a shaker halfway with ice. Add the gin, vermouth, Cynar, and bitters, along with a squeeze of juice from one of the orange wedges. Shake well, then strain into a chilled cocktail glass. Garnish with the remaining orange wedge.

But I was still restless, so I decided to switch gins. I'd been using Tanqueray, and I shifted to Hendrick's, which is softer, with rose and cucumber notes. And because I did that, I figured I'd make a drink created by my friend, bartender Charlotte Voisey. I switched out the vermouth for Lillet Blanc. I also traded Cynar for Aperol, which is Campari's sweeter, sunnier, bright orange cousin. After mixing those three, I now had an Unusual Negroni, which was also wonderful.

UNUSUAL NEGRONI

Serves 1

1 ounce Hendrick's gin
1 ounce Lillet Blanc
1 ounce Aperol
Orange peel twist, for garnish

In a mixing glass filled halfway with ice, combine the gin, Lillet Blanc, and Aperol. Stir vigorously for 30 seconds, then strain into a chilled cocktail glass. Garnish with the orange peel twist.

Recipe by Charlotte Voisey, brand ambassador for Hendrick's Gin

While I enjoyed the Unusual Negroni very much, I realized what I really wanted to do was get rid of the gin. So I brought back the sweet vermouth and the Campari, put away the gins, and pulled out a bottle of prosecco. Then, I made what is called a Negroni Sbagliato—basically a Negroni that calls for sparkling wine instead of gin. *Sbagliato* means "wrong" or "mistaken," as in, "I messed up and mistakenly put prosecco in this Negroni instead of gin."

NEGRONI SBAGLIATO

Serves 1

> 1 ounce Campari
> 1 ounce sweet vermouth
> 2 ounces prosecco or Asti Spumante
> Thin whole slice of orange, for garnish

Fill an old-fashioned glass with ice cubes. Add the vermouth and Campari, then top with the prosecco. Stir to combine. Garnish with the slice of orange.

But I still wasn't finished, so I pulled out two of my favorite base spirits, tequila and bourbon. For the tequila, the always-excellent cocktail blogger Paul Clarke, at Serious Eats, showed me the way by blogging a recipe created by Bastian Heuser, one of Germany's top bartenders. It's called the Agavoni, and it replaces the Negroni's gin with blanco or silver tequila. (Get it? Agave plus Negroni?)

AGAVONI

Serves 1

> ³/₄ ounce blanco or silver tequila
> ³/₄ ounce sweet vermouth
> ³/₄ ounce Campari
> 2 dashes orange bitters
> Grapefruit peel twist, for garnish

Fill an old fashioned-glass with ice cubes. Add the tequila, vermouth, Campari, and bitters: Stir briefly until mixed and chilled. Garnish with the grapefruit peel twist.

NOTE: Use a good, unaged 100 percent agave blanco, or silver, tequila.

Recipe by Bastian Heuser, editor at the German bar magazine, *Mixology*

But even the Agavoni took second place (by a whisker) to another Negroni alternative. I don't know whether I was channeling Hemingway, but I found this cocktail in a forgotten bartending guide, published in Paris in the 1920s, called *Barflies and Cocktails*. In it, a drink called the Boulevardier is described: equal parts bourbon, sweet vermouth, and Campari.

The Boulevardier was named after a 1920s magazine for expats living in Paris that was run by socialite Erskine Gwynne. I added a bit more bourbon to the mix, but this drink is in every way the equal of the classic Negroni. In fact, it's better. Meaning, I guess, that looking at things and trying new drinks does occasionally have its rewards.

BOULEVARDIER

Serves 1

> 1 ½ ounces bourbon
> 1 ounce sweet vermouth
> 1 ounce Campari
> Lemon peel twist, for garnish

Fill a mixing glass halfway with ice. Add the bourbon, vermouth, and Campari. Stir vigorously for 30 seconds, then strain into a chilled cocktail glass. Garnish with the lemon peel twist.

NOTE: Use a bourbon that's on the spicier side, such as Buffalo Trace, Four Roses, or Russell's Reserve.

So now that we've reengineered the Negroni, perhaps we should focus on a few of the other strange Italian spirits we've talked about. Barolo Chinato is not featured in many cocktails, but it probably should be. This recipe, created by Adam Bernbach of Proof in Washington, D.C., is an instant classic. Maybe if more cocktails this good are invented using Barolo Chinato, it will become a back-bar staple.

DARKSIDE

Serves 1

> 2 ½ ounces gin, preferably Plymouth
> 1 ounce Barolo Chinato
> 3 dashes Peychaud's bitters
> Lime peel twist, for garnish
> 1 whole star anise, for garnish

Fill a mixing glass two-thirds full with ice. Add the gin, Barolo Chinato, and bitters. Stir vigorously for 30 seconds, then strain into a cocktail glass. Garnish with the lime peel twist and star anise.

Adapted from a recipe by Adam Bernbach of Proof, Washington, D.C.

An amaro, such as Ramazzotti, Montenegro, or Meletti, is usually consumed solo after dinner as a digestive. Many in the bar and restaurant industry drink Fernet-Branca as a badge of honor. I was recently at a dinner where one famous bartender ordered it, and then everyone else felt that they had to order one. It's particularly popular in San Francisco, where locals order a shot with a ginger ale chaser. And in Argentina, the national drink might as well be Fernet and Coke.

As for mixing cocktails with amari . . . well, that's a little trickier. But you're seeing it more and more as an ingredient on cocktail menus all over the country. Averna, for instance, has been having its moment for a couple of years now. It's used in the Black Manhattan variation on page 42.

The Intercontinental takes a different, but still classic, approach. It's a unique concoction that balances the richness of cognac with Averna's herbal and bittersweet chocolate flavors plus the fruity aroma and almond notes of maraschino liqueur.

INTERCONTINENTAL

Serves 1

1 1/2 ounces cognac
1 ounce Averna
1/2 ounce maraschino liqueur
Orange peel twist, for garnish

Fill a mixing glass two-thirds full with ice. Add the cognac, Averna, and maraschino liqueur. Stir vigorously for 30 seconds, then strain into a cocktail glass. Garnish with the orange peel twist.

Recipe by Duggan McDonnell of Cantina, San Francisco

Our last elegantly balanced cocktail is a variation on both the Greyhound (vodka and grapefruit juice) and the Salty Dog (gin and grapefruit juice with a salted rim). It calls for Italy's unique Punt e Mes vermouth, made by Carpano, whose taste falls somewhere between a traditional red vermouth and a bitter.

ITALIAN GREYHOUND

Serves 1

Kosher salt, for rimming the glass
2 ounces Punt e Mes
2 ounces freshly squeezed grapefruit juice

Rim an old-fashioned glass with salt, then add 3 or 4 ice cubes. Add the Punt e Mes and grapefruit juice. Stir.

Adapted from a recipe of No. 9 Park, Boston

CHAPTER 6

WATER OF LIFE

**I SEND YOUR GRACE SOME WATER CALLED AQUA VITAE.
THIS WATER CURES ALL TYPES OF INTERNAL DISEASES FROM
WHICH A HUMAN BEING MAY SUFFER.**

— Letter from a Danish lord to the Archbishop of Trondheim, Norway, 1531

*N*EW YORKER ART CRITIC Peter Schjeldahl once compared looking at Edvard Munch's paintings to "listening to an album of a certain blues or rock song that, once upon a time, changed my life. I can't hear the songs, as I can't see the Munch images, without recalling earlier states of my soul, as if to listen or to look were, beyond nostalgia, an exercise in autobiography. Each song, each image, reminds me of myself."

I was thinking about this around 4 a.m. on a summer Saturday morning as I walked back to the Hotel Munch after an evening out in Oslo. I'd met some lovely people who'd taken me to a country music club to listen to a band called Bastard Sons of Johnny Cash, and then to a rock club where a heavy metal cover band played Bon Jovi's "Livin' on a Prayer" for its last number, with everyone singing along.

By then, it was late, or early, and I had to wake up in a few hours to meet some Norwegian spirits industry people for a tasting. As I walked home, past lines of people waiting for kebabs and hot dogs, the sky was that amazing shade of dark blue it only turns during a Nordic summer, when the sun never quite goes away.

The Hotel Munch provides clean, agreeable accommodations for budget travelers on a side street in downtown Oslo. It's a nice enough place, a step up from the dormitory at the youth hostel, though the rooms are small and a bit overheated. One hot shower will turn the poorly ventilated space into a steam bath for several hours afterward. The shower will also leave water all over the bathroom, because "shower" is a loose term referring to a curtained-off corner where water spills down into a drain on the floor. I could tell you I chose to stay at this hotel only because its namesake is an artist whose work I have always loved. Though that is true, I was also staying at the Hotel Munch because it's as cheap as downtown rooms get in this ridiculously expensive city.

That beautiful Saturday morning, at my hotel, I was scheduled to meet representatives from two small, craft-distilled Norwegian aquavit brands. I had not intended to host a tasting of premium spirits in my steamy little room at the Hotel Munch. I don't believe the thought of a premium spirits tasting has actually ever crossed the mind of anyone at the Hotel Munch. I'd planned to do our tasting at a restaurant— perhaps the same restaurant where we also planned to have lunch. But the day before, the distiller for both brands, Ole Puntervold, emailed saying, "Norway is a civilized country, so tasting should perhaps be in your room at the hotel, not in a restaurant while you are eating lunch!"

At first I thought he was kidding, but no. Two brand representatives, Henrik Holst and Sven Hauge, showed up at the hotel before noon with bottles and promotional material and aquavit glasses. We crowded into the tiny elevator, took it up to the third floor, and entered my room; the air was still muggy from the shower and redolent of the previous late night. We set up the glasses on the tiny IKEA-like table next to my skinny single bed strewn with dirty clothes. I dumped out the dregs from a paper coffee cup, which would serve as a makeshift spit bucket.

Munch, who reveled in this type of shabby bohemian milieu, probably would have been pleased.

We wiped the sweat off our brows, and Sven and I took our jackets off. Meanwhile, Henrik took up the prime position next to the window, which was the kind of northern European window that you can only open the merest crack at the top. We all chatted awkwardly, trying to avoid looking at my dirty socks and unmade bed, and then began our tasting.

"Well," said Henrik with a nervous chuckle, "I guess we can call this a David-versus-Goliath tasting." The Goliath he was referring to was Arcus, the giant Norwegian distillery that, until 2005, had for decades operated a state-run spirits monopoly. Henrik's and Sven's are two of the first spirits brands made by privately licensed distillers in Norway.

I'd actually visited Arcus the day before, and though it technically may be a Goliath, producing about fifty different aquavit brands, the people couldn't have been friendlier. I spent the morning with Frithjof Nicolaysen, Arcus's vice president of corporate affairs, who was dressed in a white lab coat and was described to me as "one of Norway's leading experts on food, wine, and spirits." Nicolaysen took me to the company's "Spice Room," which, with its wooden shelves of spice jars and big manual scales, looked like an old apothecary shop.

Norwegian aquavit must traditionally be made with potato-based spirits and infused with herbs and spices that must include a predominant profile of caraway. Why caraway? "It was the local remedy for indigestion," Nicolaysen said. "It's a northern European flavor and it was always plentiful." But caraway is only the beginning, and the spice room was full of pungent containers. Dill is also a major ingredient in aquavit, as are mustard blossom, fennel, coriander, guinea pepper, clove, and cardamom. And of course, our old friends anise and star anise. "Star anise, you know, becomes Tamiflu," Nicolaysen said. "To fight the pig flu."

Nicolaysen clearly enjoyed the olfactory experience in the spice room. "What would life be without spices?" he asked. "Many of the spices have their basis in medicine. It was much easier to drink these herbs than to chew them."

After the spice room, we toured the cask cellar. Unlike Danish and Swedish aquavit, Norwegian aquavit must mature in sherry oak casks, and Arcus has thousands of casks stored, including several earmarked for Norway's royal family. Arcus's most famous brand is Linie, which means "line" in Norwegian—in this case the equator. Linie is carried in sherry casks aboard ships that cross the equator twice before it is sold; the voyage date and ship are listed on every label. The flavor is supposedly "mellowed by its voyage." I have asked every Scandinavian I know whether this makes any difference whatsoever to the taste. This question has been met with a shrug every time.

We tasted about fifteen of the fifty bottlings, from a young, clear *taffel*, or "table," aquavit (aged in older casks that don't impart color) to a twelve-year-old bottling that tasted like a cognac. Some versions have a blast of caraway and dill on the nose, while others have fruitier notes, and the more aged versions have hints of vanilla or caramel. Aquavit in all its versions is a strange, complex, and wonderful spirit, and a good match with the traditional winter Scandinavian fare of pungent fish, sharp cheeses, and heavy meat dishes. "The food is always deciding the character of the aquavit. We don't make wine here. So this has been adapted to the Nordic kitchen," Nicolaysen said. For example, there are special holiday bottlings to pair with bacalao (dried salt cod) or rakefisk (salted, fermented trout). In fact, the rakefisk bottling, which is aged three years, has an illustration of a fish on the label with a wavy line emanating from it—the international symbol for "stinky." "This aquavit has to match a very stinky fish."

When I mentioned to Nicolaysen that I had a bottle of Linie in my freezer at home, he nearly fainted. I told him that I'd been introduced to aquavit in Denmark, and that's how my friends always drank it, ice-cold from the freezer. "Ah," he said, "that's because the Danes and Swedes don't have this tradition of aging in casks like we do. For them, aquavit is a white spirit."

He told me never to put Norwegian aquavit in the freezer. "It goes all the way to Australia and back to age . . . and then you put it in the freezer! Good god, that's a sacrilege for those of us who make it!"

I began our tasting in the Hotel Munch with Henrik's brand, Nansen Aquavit. Nansen had already launched a Norwegian-owned cognac that had gained popularity when France was testing nuclear missiles in the South Pacific in the late 1990s, which Norwegians firmly opposed. "People were saying, 'I want a cognac, but not a French cognac,'" Henrik said. In 2007, they launched an aquavit.

Nansen's flagship aquavit tasted a lot softer than many of those I'd tried previously—light, with bright citrus fruit and a bit of approachable vanilla, which comes from younger oak casks. Henrik had a marketing reason for this: "It's a tradition in families to drink aquavit at Christmas, but maybe only three people in the family really like it. Women and young people say it's too rough. They sit through Christmas dinner saying '*skål*' and pretending to like it."

I'd heard the same thing the day before at Arcus. There seemed to be a great deal of concern that people only drank aquavit at Christmas—and then mostly the older men of the family. Close to 90 percent of Norway's aquavit consumption actually happens during that season. There was talk of finding a wider audience and diversifying the aquavit market. Arcus has recently rolled out a label called Sommer Aquavit, which, like Nansen's, has lighter, brighter citrus notes. Sommer Aquavit was targeted at, of course, young drinkers: the Cosmo crowd—young women who liked vodka cocktails.

It's still unclear how successful this effort has been, though I can say that I saw an awful lot of bottles of Sommer Aquavit on deep discount at the duty-free shop in the Oslo Airport. Generally, I find that changing an ingrained tradition—such as "Aquavit Only at Christmas Dinner"—is nearly impossible. Creating a market for summertime aquavit seems as elusive as recapturing the mythic summers of one's youth.

After we tasted Nansen's second aquavit, a more traditional caraway-flavored offering, Sven (who had now fully sweated through his dress shirt) unwrapped and presented his new aquavit brand: Edvard Munch

Premium Aquavit, its label in English. He also handed me a press release: "Edvard Munch was a forerunner of the expressionist art movement. His best-known composition, *The Scream*, is part of a series, *The Frieze of Life*, in which Munch explored the themes of life, love, fear, death, and melancholy. Therefore we are proud to present this exceptional, luxury aquavit as a taste of his art." Fear and melancholy—not to mention Munch's darkly erotic love-and-death axis—being ideas that one may or may not want to ponder when drinking shots of an 80-proof spirit.

Edvard Munch Premium Aquavit is a lovely spirit. It spends twelve months in sherry casks, yet retains intense, fresh herbal aromatics and flavor. But I worried aloud about who was going to buy it, especially with its English label, and especially with the local aquavit market clearly declining among the younger generation. "Our plan is to find some partners outside of Norway," Sven said. But most people outside of Scandinavia and Germany have no idea what aquavit even is. In fact, in my experience, most people fear it, just as they fear grappa.

Perhaps in answer to my skepticism, Sven expressed even more excitement about his second spirits project: Scream Vodka, named after the famed Munch masterpiece. "It's French grain vodka, from Cognac," Sven said. "Like Grey Goose." Scream Vodka would directly target tourists at duty-free shops and and also, he hoped, at the Munch Museum itself.

Sven admitted that he really didn't have much experience in the spirits business, but he did have a long background in the music and entertainment industry. He said one of the first big acts he'd managed was Norway's winning entry in the 1985 Eurovision Song Contest, Bobbysocks. In a strange way, this career path made sense to me. I think spirits share an emotional space with pop songs. And I'm guessing the generation who listened to Bobbysocks as young people is probably the same one that's moved away from aquavit appreciation. Maybe they were drinking other things on those summer nights when they got drunk and fell in love. On my flight to Oslo, my Norwegian seatmate, a woman about my age, nearly jumped out of her seat to point out a member of a-ha, the 1980s Norwegian one-hit wonder, who'd wandered down the aisle.

Later, when she asked what I was doing in Oslo and I told her about my aquavit research, she said, "Ah, I only drink aquavit at Christmastime at my parents' house."

After Hendrik, Sven, and I finished tasting all three aquavits, I dumped the spit cup into the bathroom sink—water was still soaking the floor—and they packed up their bottles. Later that afternoon, alone and feeling some of the usual post-tasting tipsiness, I started thinking about Edvard Munch and summertime and decided to pay a visit to Oslo's Munch Museum.

The Munch Museum was the scene of a brazen art heist in 2004, when masked, armed bandits stormed in and stole both *The Scream* and another of Munch's paintings, *Madonna*. Both were eventually recovered, and now you must pass through a metal detector to see the paintings. *The Scream*, of course, is the highlight that most tourists come to see. And in the gift shop, you can buy Scream T-shirts, Scream mouse pads, and, perhaps soon, Scream Vodka. I bought a Scream tote bag because I needed something to cart all my aquavit samples home in.

But the painting I came to look at was *The Voice (Summer Night)*, which depicts a woman, with her hair let down, standing in a secret lovers' spot near the shoreline on one of those endless Scandinavian midsummer nights. Most agree that the painting depicts Munch's great love, Millie Thaulow (the wife of his benefactor's cousin), with whom, as a young man, he had an affair one fateful summer in the coastal village of Aasgaardstrand. "When love grew!" wrote Munch in diaries. "Nature gave of her beauty and you became more beautiful the summernight cast over your face and your hair—only your eyes were dark—and sparkled with a mysterious glow."

After their first tryst, Munch wrote, "something very strange happened—I felt as if there were invisible threads connecting us—I felt the invisible strands of her hair still winding around me—and thus as she disappeared completely beyond the sea—I still felt it, felt the pain where my heart was bleeding—because the threads could not be severed." Eventually, inevitably, Millie ended the affair, and that summer rendezvous haunted poor Edvard for the rest of his life.

The thing about Munch is that, no matter how dreamlike or meta-phorical or obvious or depressing he becomes, his landscapes are some-how always right. He caught the seductive yet ominous mood of those midsummer nights. He knew better than anyone that the flip side of the glorious midnight sun is the long, dark, melancholy winter to come. That even within the moment, great happiness is already swiftly moving into the past tense.

I have stood, literally, in such a landscape. It was near the end of an Icelandic summer long ago, as a bunch of friends passed around a bottle of brennivín—the rougher Icelandic cousin of aquavit—while we quickly stripped down to our underwear and jumped into a hot spring. We relaxed as bubbles of hot water floated up from between the moss-covered rocks on the bottom, all of us settled in, chin deep, steam rising around our heads, the wind whipping across an impos-sibly blue fjord. Everyone was impossibly happy, but the midnight sun was finally beginning to set and soon it would be autumn and we'd all have to go home.

I have also been there figuratively. Let's say it was a late August, many years ago, in a lifeguard stand on a midnight beach in Ocean City, New Jersey. Perhaps I was there with a girl with whom I was hopelessly in love, who would go back to college in September and never call again. There may have been a bottle of sloe gin (or was it Jägermeister, or even peach schnapps?) and "Livin' on a Prayer" was surely playing on a cas-sette tape in the boom box.

In his essay on Munch, Schjeldahl writes, "My heart pledges alle-giance to old revelations of truth—truth-to-me, truth-of-me, truths involved in the project of being a person—that seem still true. I may be humbled to reflect that I have advanced little on those lessons since receiving them years ago." I stood before the painting that afternoon in Oslo, the taste of premium aquavit in my mouth, similarly humbled, and feeling the distinct tug of those unsevered summer threads.

A Round of Drinks:
From the North

I acquired my taste for aquavit over numerous visits to Copenhagen, sipping it ice-cold in small frozen shot glasses, accompanied by *smørrebrød*, the traditional open-faced rye-bread sandwiches piled high with smoked salmon, pickled herring, or smoked eel. My Danish friends gave me a very nice bottle for my birthday a few years ago, because they know how much I've come to enjoy their traditional spirit (which they actually call *snaps*). I also enjoy the traditional toast: lifting your glass and staring silently into everyone's eyes for moment before saying *skål* and taking a sip—or draining the glass, if you're so inclined.

At home, however, I find it nearly impossible to find others who share my enthusiasm for aquavit. I'm often met with a response that frankly irritates me: "Isn't that stuff rocket fuel?" It's been the same thing with grappa. What is it about strong foreign spirits served in tiny glasses that scares so many Americans? It feels a little xenophobic to me, and I get impatient with the rocket-fuel label. I can honestly say that after years of traveling and sampling local firewaters, there are only three spirits I would file in that category: Central American *aguardiente* (literally "burning water"); a backyard-distilled, 160-proof Serbian moonshine—the memory of which still gives me night terrors; and Icelandic *brennivín* (nicknamed "black death").

And even that might be unfair to brennivín, which for me is wrapped up in happy memories of Iceland, as well as horrible ones of using it to wash down *hákarl*, the infamous rotten shark that's served at the midwinter feast, Thorrablot. I can still remember biting through rubbery layers of skin, and a sensation not unlike a rush of ammonia flying up my sinuses, then the shot of brennivín, burning like kerosene all the way down my esophagus. *Skål*, indeed.

Anyway, aquavit is like none of these rocket fuels or firewaters. Aquavit is a lovely, complex spirit, and I have made it my mission to spread its gospel. Though aquavit is usually served cold in small glasses, it's not meant to be downed as a shot, as vodka is in Russia. It's much more rounded and flavorful, and it's traditionally meant to be sipped straight with food, particularly winter-holiday Nordic cuisine.

We've been hearing a lot about the "new Scandinavian cooking" over the past several years, led in the United States by chefs such as my *Washington Post* colleague, Norwegian chef Andreas Viestad, or Swedish-born Marcus Samuelsson at Aquavit restaurant in New York. For years, Samuelsson has been serving tasting flights of house-made aquavits flavored with nontraditional ingredients such as horseradish, lemongrass, coconut, and citrus. In 2006, the restaurant's owners launched a retail aquavit. Their spirit, Aquavit New York, is flavored with fresh white cranberries, unlike the Scandinavian imports. "Traditional aquavit doesn't really fit the American palate," said Christian Gylche, a Swede who was the brand ambassador in New York.

Though styles vary throughout Scandinavia, aquavit is basically a vodka flavored with spices and herbs such as caraway, fennel, dill, coriander, and anise. Two standard brands are widely available in the States: Aalborg from Denmark and Linie from Norway. House Spirits, a craft distillery in Portland, Oregon, also recently launched the wonderful Krogstad Aquavit, which has a slightly higher star anise profile than traditional Scandinavian versions. Christian Krogstad, the distiller, said that the initial demand came from local chefs who had tasted small batches he'd been experimenting with. "We approached it with very low expectations for sales," Krogstad said. "But people have come out of the woodwork to buy it." One reason is that aquavit is one of the few spirits in the world that pairs well with food. "I like that aquavit is savory," Krogstad said. "It pairs with some foods that nothing else will pair with." For instance, oily fishes such as pickled herring, mackerel, and salmon. I also like aquavit with cheeses such as Havarti, with sausage and sauerkraut, and, of course, with rye bread.

Beyond the kitchen, bartenders have been experimenting with aquavit in cocktails, most often as a replacement for vodka. Aquavit's herbal profile seems to make sense in savory cocktails, such as the Bloody Mary, which is probably the only cocktail served in every bar all over the world. The Bloody Mary was invented by a bartender named Fernand Petiot at Harry's Bar in Paris during the 1920s. After Prohibition ended, Petiot moved to New York and served drinks at the bar in the St. Regis Hotel. Concerned that more conservative American patrons might be offended by the name, the St. Regis rechristened the drink the Red Snapper. With equal parts vodka and tomato juice and a squeeze of lemon juice, I believe the Red Snapper is the superior expression of the cocktail—nothing like the goopy tomato-gravy disasters you usually get. The "Nordic" rendition here calls for aquavit instead of vodka.

NORDIC SNAPPER

Serves 1

> **2 ounces aquavit**
> **2 ounces tomato juice**
> **¼ ounce freshly squeezed lemon juice**
> **½ teaspoon Worcestershire sauce**
> **2 dashes celery bitters**
> **Pinch of fine sea salt**
> **Pinch of freshly ground black pepper**
> **Pinch of cayenne pepper**
> **Lemon peel twist, for garnish**

Fill a cocktail shaker halfway with ice. Add the aquavit, tomato juice, lemon juice, Worcestershire sauce, celery bitters, salt, black pepper, and cayenne pepper. Shake well for at least 30 seconds, then strain into an ice-filled highball glass. Garnish with the lemon peel twist.

NOTE: Two more thoughts: Forget the celery stalk; do not forget the lemon juice.

Beyond Bloody Mary variations, however, aquavit cocktails can be hard to find. "Aside from being a kind gesture to visiting Danes, and so on, it is practically uncalled-for in mixing." That's what Charles H. Baker wrote about aquavit in his famous 1939 book, *The Gentleman's Companion: Being an Exotic Drinking Book; or Around the World with Jigger, Beaker, and Flask.*

However, I have found one aquavit cocktail I often enjoy. This surprisingly complex cocktail gets its name from the way the savory, herbal tastes of the aquavit, the botanicals of the gin, and the touch of sweet in the maraschino liqueur complement one another. It is adapted from a recipe of Hardeep Rehal, bartender at Bar Rouge in Copenhagen, who won a local contest with it. He calls for the Danish Aalborg brand, but feel free to use any high-quality aquavit, preferably a *taffel*, or clear, aquavit. I recommend Plymouth gin, which is more subtle than a juniper-forward gin like Beefeater's or Tanqueray. As always, do not confuse or replace maraschino liqueur with the juice from maraschino cherries.

COMPLEMENT COCKTAIL

Serves 1

1 1/2 ounces Plymouth gin
3/4 ounce aquavit
2 dashes maraschino liqueur
1 sprig dill, for garnish

Fill a cocktail shaker two-thirds full with ice. Add the gin, aquavit, and maraschino liqueur. Shake vigorously, then strain into a chilled cocktail glass. Garnish with the dill sprig.

Adapted from a recipe by Hardeep Rehal of Bar Rouge, Copenhagen, Denmark

CHAPTER 7

TERROIR-ISTS

... THIS THIRST FOR A KIND OF LIQUID WHICH NATURE HAS
ENVELOPED IN VEILS, THIS STRANGE DESIRE THAT ASSAILS ALL
RACES OF MANKIND, IN EVERY CLIMATE AND TEMPERATURE . . .

—*Jean-Anthelme Brillat-Savarin*

*T*ERROIR, THE TERM THAT FOR YEARS has been mispronounced and misunderstood and has caused endless arguments in the wine world, has now gained serious currency in the world of spirits. To wit, Scotch whisky now exhibits terroir. Ditto cognac. So do the various eaux-de-vie made from orchard fruit throughout the Alps. But it's not just European Union DOCs boasting of terroir. Kentucky bourbon claims it. So does tequila. Peruvian pisco? Yep: terroir.

In the simplest terms, terroir refers to the special characteristics that a geographic place imparts on an agricultural product. I knew "terroir of spirits" had absolutely gained traction when I saw spirits represented at the huge Slow Food Nation blowout in San Francisco over

Labor Day weekend in 2008. "A spirit is an agricultural product," I was told by Greg Lindgren, the curator of the Slow Food Spirits Pavilion, and co-owner of several bars in the city. "Producing spirits has always been a way for farmers to remain farmers. It's one of the best ways to diversify a farmer's economic situation." This made me happy. I grew up in a family that made its living in produce. From an early age, I worked at a farm market selling fruits and vegetables with my brothers and cousins—we got all of our locally grown peaches and corn and tomatoes and melons from Garden State farmers within about a ten-mile radius, and this was in late 1970s, before we had Michael Pollan to tell us this was a good and virtuous thing.

Of course, understanding terroir better meant actually experiencing these spirits—and their raw ingredients—at the source. Which meant more travel. Which meant more looking at things and trying new drinks.

Famous Potatoes

It's a question I've posed before, and I will pose it again now: does the world need another vodka? Maybe that doesn't rank up there with life's great philosophical puzzles, such as "What is the nature of the universe?" or "What is the sound of one hand clapping?" or even "How many licks does it take to get to the center of a Tootsie Pop?" But it's the sort of question that people in the cocktails and spirits business—not to mention lifestyle journalism—think about. In April 2009, the Wall Street Journal officially declared, "Vodka is passé." A few weeks later, the New York Times countered, "Vodka Dead? Not So Fast." This level of debate probably explains why no one asked lifestyle journalists to help solve the financial crisis, stop the swine flu pandemic, or save the ailing newspaper industry.

Given that vodka producers keep coming up with new marketing angles, I was not particularly surprised to learn that the makers of a new Swedish vodka called Karlsson's Gold claimed to be "the first luxury vodka that can sincerely boast its own terroir." Nor did it surprise me that this vodka is made exclusively from new potatoes grown on Sweden's Cape Bjäre ("the region is to potatoes what France's Bordeaux region is to grapes," according to the company). Nor that these potatoes are so delicate that they must be washed and refrigerated within four hours of harvest. Nor that they are sought after by chefs in Scandinavia's finest restaurants. Nor that the creation of the vodka was motivated by its maker's altruistic desire to keep Cape Bjäre's potato farmers on their land. Ah yes, a terroir vodka! I was not surprised by any of it.

Potatoes, in particular, were the main part of my family business. So I was excited that summer to visit Cape Bjäre, on Sweden's southeastern coast, to meet the farmers who made terroir vodka. Håkan Paulsson, one of the farmers, greeted me and poured me a shot of vodka in coffee, a traditional eye-opener called *kaffegok*. Paulsson was a no-bullshit guy, and I liked him immediately. How did you get involved in the vodka business, I wanted to know. "Well do you want a story, or a true story?" Paulsson said, with a wink. Money seemed to be the main story. There appeared to be an awful lot of golf courses in Bjäre, which is sort of like a Swedish Hamptons. I'm guessing a lot of those golf courses were once potato farms.

He showed off the various local potatoes that grow only in Bjäre, varieties neither I nor my father nor my uncle had ever heard of: Solist, Minerva, Gammel Svensk Rod (Old Swedish Red). "How would you describe the taste of these potatoes?" I asked.

"Well, how about for you? It's very difficult to describe taste," Paulsson said. "Many Swedish people have grown up eating Old Swedish Red and herring. And then they moved to the United States!"

Later, over a boozy dinner at a fishing cottage by the sea, I met one of the founders of Karlsson's Gold, multimillionaire Peter Ekelund. As the midnight sun didn't set and the vodka flowed, I was a little surprised by Ekelund's rhetorical question. "Does the world need another vodka?" he asked. "The product has gotten so boring. It's gotten too big for its own good." His response to his own question was, of course, to create another vodka that retails for forty dollars in the United States. "We wanted to do something contrarian," he said. The contrarian idea: Can a vodka actually have taste? Odd, really, how few of the dozens of vodka companies ponder that question. Most nonflavored vodkas chase some standard of purity and neutrality and boast of being thrice distilled, five times distilled, ten times distilled. Essentially, those vodkas are marketed based on their utter lack of flavor.

Karlsson's Gold, however, is an unfiltered blend of several potato varieties that's then distilled as little as possible—going through a continuous still only once and thus retaining some funky elements, some character. When I tasted with Ekelund, he brought out some experimental bottlings of single-variety, single-vintage, single-farmer potato vodka. Say, a June 2004 Minerva, or an August 2006 Solist. To say I was skeptical is an understatement. But when I tasted, the differences were significant and noteworthy. A 2004 Solist was sweet and starchy compared with a 2004 Minerva, which was redolent of apple peels, or a 2006 Gammel Svensk Rod, which was hot on the finish but full of herbal intensity.

The Karlsson's Gold approach, then, is to make a vodka that derives its taste from carefully chosen ingredients—in this case, gourmet potatoes—meaning that its gimmick is really no gimmick at all. It's almost like a potato eau-de-vie. The final blend is rich, creamy, and smooth, with notes of herbs and crisp fruit. It is a lovely spirit: vodka with flavor. "These are the ideas that change industries," Ekelund said. "The big ideas to solve problems."

That sounds like pretty grand talk from a small-potatoes vodka company that's now selling about 25,000 cases a year worldwide. Until you realize that, in the ultimate ironic twist, Ekelund and his colleagues at Karlsson's are actually the same people responsible for setting the premium vodka snowball rolling nearly three decades ago when they worked for another little Swedish company . . . called Absolut.

You remember Absolut, don't you? The brand that single-handedly reinvented vodka as a fashion accessory back in the 1980s? The one whose Andy Warhol–designed ads seem to have graced the back page of every magazine in America for decades? The one that sells eleven million cases annually worldwide and was sold to Pernod Ricard in 2008 for more than eight billion dollars? The one with the universally recognized bottle, the one whose flagship vodka tastes like . . . well, nothing? The one that opened Pandora's box by creating flavored vodkas such as Absolut Peppar, Absolut Pears, and, more recently, Absolut Mango?

In Stockholm, the day after our visit to Cape Bjäre, I met some of the other principals in Karlsson's. One was master blender Börje Karlsson, who is credited with being the father of Absolut. At a dinner where several American and Swedish bartenders were trying to mix cocktails using his vodka, Karlsson wasn't very happy. "I've spent my life making spirits to be enjoyed on their own," he said. "I make the spirit a certain way. I like to drink it that way."

"So you never drink cocktails?" I asked.

"No, never. To do so would be to destroy a good spirit. Cocktails destroy good spirits."

Karlsson added, "This way of drinking vodka is an American idea." That comment, of course, represents the familiar European whine about how Americans ruin what is good and pure in the world. Which is sometimes true, but not always. So I was pleased when one of Karlsson's Swedish colleagues pointed out the ridiculousness of that position by asking, "What about Absolut?" Yes, I told Karlsson, I think we Americans can take the blame for a lot of things, but not for, say, vodkas called Absolut Bling-Bling or Absolut Disco.

I had to agree with him about one thing. Karlsson's Gold, beautiful as it is, is not really a vodka to be mixed in a cocktail; rather, it should be chilled and sipped by itself. Or perhaps with a little cracked black pepper, or maybe a little club soda or ginger beer (though never tonic). The subtle flavors and the creaminess were lost in most of the cocktails I tried. Of course, I also really liked the kaffegok that I'd drunk with the potato farmer. According to one of the Karlsson's people, *gok* "either means 'a bird' or 'having sex'" in Swedish. Now, there's a real philosophical puzzle to ponder.

Agave Magic

Before I left for Jalisco, the only region in Mexico where tequila is made, I met David Suro-Piñera, owner of Siembra Azul tequila brand. We tasted his new añejo at his Philadelphia restaurant named, unsurprisingly, Tequila's. "You'll see for yourself," he told me. "If there's one spirit that we can say has terroir, it's definitely tequila. If you do a blind tasting between brands, you could swear that you're drinking entirely different spirits."

Now, before we get too carried away with an ode to terroir, let me be clear that understanding the basics of tequila, one of the world's finest spirits, is easier and more straightforward than with wine. To begin, you need to know two geographical areas of Jalisco: the highlands and the lowlands. Then you need to know the three basic tequila types: blanco, reposado, añejo. So talking about tequila's terroir may seem a little bit of a stretch at first. But Suro-Piñera is pretty dead-on in making the connection to winemaking. Like wine, the spirit begins in the fields, where blue agave, a desert succulent, is the equivalent of the grape.

Seeing row after row of spiky agave in Jalisco's fields for the first time was exciting, not unlike my thrill at seeing rows of grapevines as a young backpacker in Europe. In the equivalent of a grape stomping, a *jimador*, or agave farm worker, even gave me his extremely sharp *coa* so I could hack off the bristly spikes of my own agave—that is, until the jimador, whether worried for my safety or that of his work tool, asked for it back.

Differences among producers begin in the field. They can be geographic: highland agave (used by such brands as El Tesoro de Don Filipe, Milagro, Don Julio, and Patrón) is smaller and considered to be sweeter, while lowland agave (used by Sauza, Cuervo, and Herradura) is larger and considered drier. Other differences can be chalked up to growing techniques. Some producers (including Sauza) start from seed, while others plant the "babies" from established plants. Agave takes a long time—about seven years at a minimum—to mature enough for harvest, though some plants are left in the field as long as ten years. Some producers, such as Patrón, like their agave less ripe. Others, such as El

Tesoro, want very ripe agave in which the sugars have turned to red sap that looks like blood. "I love to see my agaves bleeding," says Carlos Camarena, El Tesoro's owner.

More differences are created at the distillery. Is the agave cooked whole, or chopped up? Is it steamed, or slow-cooked in an oven? Is it pulverized by a machine, or by the huge, traditional stone wheel called a *tahona*? Is that tahona run by a machine, or dragged around by donkeys (as they still do at Siete Leguas)? Is the tequila distilled slower at a low temperature and bottled or casked straight away, or distilled at a higher temperature and then diluted with water before bottling?

Finally, there is the issue of aging. *Reposado* means "rested," and, by law, reposado tequila must have rested anywhere from two months to just under one year. Some producers let their tequilas rest only a few months; others, such as El Diamante del Cielo, don't take theirs out of the barrel until the 364th day. *Añejo* means "aged," and for those tequilas, which age for one to three years, the variation is even greater. I experienced those differences firsthand on my agave pilgrimage.

A visit to Jalisco begins in a town called—what else—Tequila. After arriving there, I had an afternoon to kill and played tourist. First, I had a blanco and sangrita at one of the small kiosk bars in the town's colorful main square, poured by a boy of about nine. Then I decided to visit Mundo Cuervo, the distiller's shiny visitors' center on the square. The tour itself was not much different from those in the half dozen other distilleries I'd visit. We wore headgear (hairnets in this case, while at other spots I was given a hard hat). The fussy young woman leading the tour complained that the hairnet was messing up her do. We were shown how the agave comes in from the fields (in huge chunks that can weigh from 50 to 150 pounds) and how it's cooked. We sampled the agave pulp, which tasted an awful lot like caramelized pumpkin. We learned how the pulp fermented and how the juice was distilled twice. We tasted the blanco right out of the still at full strength, a bracing experience with the full spicy, grassy blast of agave.

At tour's end, however, we were ushered into a bar, and our tour guide said, "Now you will taste a real margarita." I watched the bartender grab a bottle of Jose Cuervo Gold, meaning that, even though Cuervo makes premium 100 percent agave spirits, I was about to be served a mixto, a tequila made of only 51 percent agave, with 49 percent additives such as sugar or neutral spirits. To add to the insult, the bartender then grabbed a bottle of Jose Cuervo's premade, Day-Glo-colored margarita mix. He poured both into a blender and pushed the button. Yes, my pilgrimage to the seminal town of Tequila was rewarded with a margarita that could easily have been made by the lunchtime bartender at a suburban Applebee's back home. No wonder—as I later learned—no one in the state of Jalisco drinks margaritas.

Now, I might be accused of harping on the worst stop of my trip, but that margarita at Mundo Cuervo highlighted the main reason tequila has not yet won the hearts and minds of the average drinker in the United States. Sure, we keep hearing reports about tequila's rise, and we see the sales of premium tequila grow every year; according to the Distilled Spirits Council of the United States, tequila imports grew more than 50 percent between 2002 and 2010. But that growth is driven mainly by enthusiasts like me, people who see the value in spending forty dollars or more for a spirit made with 100 percent blue agave. When I offer most acquaintances a shot of tequila, a large majority of them say something like, "Ugh, tequila. I just can't drink that. Not since this one bad night in college." I have that story, too. It is the last night of my freshman year in Boston, and I will be transferring to Vermont in the fall. My girlfriend, J. (who is staying in Boston), and I are celebrating our very last night together, our last hurrah. We decide to split a bottle of Cuervo Gold. In the morning, we awaken with matching trash cans on either side of the bed. Good times! Frankly, I am tired of hearing about people's bad night in college. I am also tired of people kidding themselves that it doesn't matter whether you use a low- or high-quality spirit in a cocktail.

A plea to Mexico's Tequila Regulatory Council: Can we just stop with the mixto tequila already? If the tequila industry truly wants to improve the image of its product, then it ought to ban mixto altogether. I've heard a lot of talk about the importance of changing consumer perceptions: that tequila is not just a frat-party shot; that good tequila doesn't give you hangovers; that tequila truly exists on the level of a fine, aged whiskey or brandy. All of that is true, as is the fact that fine tequilas are not cheap and that you can even splurge, as with Scotch or cognac, on high-end choices such as Gran Patrón Platinum ($189), El Tesoro Paradiso extra-añejo ($121) and Siete Leguas five-year D'Antaño (about $200, if you can even find it domestically).

But the average consumer is still not getting the message. Worse, too many people maintain an irrational fear of the spirit. Why? Because all of the nice premium brands are sitting on shelves in liquor stores next to god-awful, headache-inducing mixtos that cost a fraction of what real tequila costs. "To me, mixtos are nonsense," said El Tesoro's Camarena. "Have you ever heard of cognac made with 51 percent cognac and 49 percent sugar?" And let's not even get into Sauza's ready-to-drink Margarita-in-a-Box that was launched in 2009.

El Tesoro is my favorite tequila, and my experience of the distillery was the opposite of my tour of Cuervo's. The owner himself gave me the tour, chain-smoking as we passed a half dozen signs that read "*Prohibido fumar*." Camarena spoke of the importance of eschewing traditional yeast during the fermentation of the agave and instead letting the microflora in the open air do the work. That is how unique flavor is created, he said: "It's where the magic happens." The magic also happens in the barrel room, where Camarena experiments wildly with different wood finishes and barrel sizes. In 2010, he launched a tequila, in partnership with French distillers, that is aged in both Sauternes and cognac casks. He's lately been pushing the limit on extra-añejos, which usually age around three years, by letting some barrels age five years or more. Searching for one of his experimental barrels, Camarena flicked on his cigarette lighter. I gasped. The air in the barrel room was so redolent with evaporating tequila, I assumed we'd be blown to bits. But no. "Don't worry," he said.

Even smaller than El Tesoro, and more traditional, is Siete Leguas. There, with little fanfare, we tasted our tequila while sitting on folding chairs in a dark room, the glasses set on a paper towel. Sipping Siete

Leguas's añejo was a revelation: it was smooth and floral with hints of caramel, while still retaining the essence of the spicy, herbal agave from which it was made.

You hear a lot of aficionados declare young, unaged blancos to be the purest expression of the spirit and criticize añejos as taking on too much wood and losing the sense of the agave. The tasting at Siete Leguas convinced me that this is not always the case. "If you have a very good blanco, you'll have a good añejo," said Lucrecia González, whose family owns Siete Leguas. Now, the average tequila drinker in the States may not know the brand name Siete Leguas. But if you've been drinking premium tequila for a while, you probably know the liquid. Until about 2003, if you drank Patrón, you were drinking Siete Leguas. Eventually, Patrón got too big, and they built a brand-new, state-of-the-art distillery and headquarters called Hacienda Patrón. And they hired away Siete Leguas's master distiller, Francisco Alcaráz. They never got Siete Leguas's recipe, though.

When I visited the distillery at Hacienda Patrón, I sipped tequila with Alcaráz on the Hacienda veranda. Alcaráz is called El Diablo by some in the tequila business (particularly at rival distillers like Siete Leguas), mostly because of his excellent silent movie–villain mustache. He, like almost everyone else I met in Mexico, expressed his preference for blancos ("I like the flavor of tequila") and asserted that tequila becomes "very woody after three or four years in a barrel. It loses a lot of character."

After our tasting, Alcaráz invited me to have lunch at the hacienda. A mariachi band started setting up on the veranda, and I asked, "Is that our lunchtime entertainment?"

"Oh no," Alcaráz said, "that's just the background music." The lunchtime entertainment, actually, turned out to be a magician. Yes, a magician performed for me and a half dozen Patrón executives. Card tricks, flames shooting out of his hands, never-ending handkerchiefs billowing out of his pockets, disappearing pesos—even a couple of tricks that were really just jokes about penis size and that caused El Diablo to double over in laughter. Copious amounts of wine and tequila were poured, and for the first time in my life I felt like some kind of Renaissance duke. I imagined that, at the clap of my hands, I could both have my tequila glass filled and have this magician beheaded. "Magician! Amuse me!" Clap. "Magician, I am no longer amused!" Clap. "Be off with you!"

Thankfully, the decadent lunch came to a close with no incident. But as we sipped añejos after lunch, Alcaráz pondered whether it was a bad thing that many of the oldest tequilas take on the complex characteristics of brandy or whiskey in the barrel. "Maybe we need to take a scientific look at this," he said. "We should take the best tequila, rum, bourbon, and cognac, and see what the taste difference is. Maybe at this point, what we're all chasing is a similar luxury spirit." Ah yes, luxury. The underlying point of all this nonsense, right? Most of us, sadly, are not Renaissance dukes. We're not even counts or barons—we'd be lucky if we were the accordion player in the court mariachi band. But Patrón, let's remember, is "affordable" luxury. Its añejo sells for fifty dollars a bottle . . . just about in reach on payday. It's fascinating to me that the only place you can buy Patrón in Mexico is in an airport duty-free shop. Somebody's gotta pay for that house magician, right?

Still, it's noteworthy that El Diablo, Patrón's master distiller, is one of the few I've met who's candid about this nebulous issue of luxury. After all, it's become fashionable in cocktail geek circles to turn one's nose up at Patrón. It's too big, sort of like the Darth Vader of premium tequila, right? Too many ads, right? It can't possibly be good. Well, let's be clear about one thing: if it hadn't been for Patrón entering the market in the late 1980s, there wouldn't be a premium tequila market in the United States. You'd still be drinking Cuervo Gold. Bagging on Patrón reminds me a little of teenagers who hate a band as soon as it becomes famous.

It also, strangely enough, sounds like the sort of debate that routinely happens in the wine world. Yes, to enter the world of tequila is to slip down a rabbit hole. Which probably proves that it is much more complex than most people think.

Fruit Forward

For most Americans, "fruit" is not the word that immediately comes to mind when they hear "eau-de-vie." If eau-de-vie evokes any words, those might be: intense, burning, foreign. Or if one thinks of fruit, it's the whole pear sitting inside a curious bottle. Some home cooks may have purchased a bottle of kirschwasser long ago to attempt a real fondue. But as I have said, Americans mostly steer away from clear European spirits that are served neat in small glasses.

"These are hard-to-sell, expensive products that no one likes," jokes Stephen McCarthy of Clear Creek Distillery in Portland, Oregon, which makes some of the nicest eaux-de-vie in the United States, including one with the pear inside the bottle. "People just aren't getting the message."

I wish that were not so. Near the midpoint of my winter doldrums, in particular, I miss the abundance of seasonal fresh fruit. Maybe that's why one of my winter drinks is an eau-de-vie after dinner, just a bit of poire Williams or kirsch or a plum brandy called slivovitz. Eau-de-vie is a delight and, with its digestive properties, a fabulous way to finish a meal. Unlike liqueurs, which often have a cloying percentage of sugar and a lower alcohol content, eau-de-vie is clear, unaged brandy, generally clocking in at around 80 proof. Although many still think of eau-de-vie as Alsatian or alpine, there are a few wonderful producers in the United States.

The domestic market was basically created in the 1980s by two men: Stephen McCarthy, and Jorg Rupf of St. George Spirits in Alameda, California, which produces the amazing Aqua Perfecta brand of eau-de-vie (and also, it should be said, Hangar One vodka; gotta pay the bills, right?). Both McCarthy and Rupf came to the business in a roundabout fashion. Rupf grew up in Germany's Black Forest in a family of distillers but went into law and became Germany's youngest judge at the time. On a scholarly visit to the University of California at Berkeley, he fell in love with the local fruit and decided to stay and distill it. "Seeing the blossoming fruit in California," he says, "it was like the

Garden of Eden." McCarthy ran a successful business producing parts for hunting guns, which took him on sales trips to Europe. There he realized that the Williams pear, used to make the French eau-de-vie poire Williams, was the same as the Bartlett pear grown back home on his family's orchard in Oregon. In the mid-1980s, he sold his business and started Clear Creek.

Both men's epiphanies get at the heart of eau-de-vie: ripe fruit. For centuries, eau-de-vie was the product of peasant farmers who, after harvesting their orchards, needed a way to turn surplus fruit into profit. "These products weren't created by a marketing committee," McCarthy says. "Those farmers made eau-de-vie because they had to figure out some way to use their fruit." Eau-de-vie was a way for struggling farmers to keep their land.

"If the fruit doesn't have it, the eau-de-vie never will," said Lance Winters, Rupf's partner in St. George Spirits. In making eau-de-vie, "you're taking an aromatic and flavor profile of a moment in time and place. It's a time machine." For that reason, Rupf seeks out organic pears grown at over five thousand feet in Colorado and Montmorency cherries from Michigan's Upper Peninsula. McCarthy uses local Pacific Northwest plums and cherries for his slivovitz and kirsch, and even springtime Douglas fir buds for a complex, surprising evergreen eau-de-vie.

All of that sounds like just the sort of handcrafted, Slow Food–friendly product that foodies should be all over. But that's not the case. "The biggest hurdle is that we do not yet have a digestif culture," Rupf says. "As soon as coffee and dessert comes, so does the bill. In Europe, when you have your table, you have it for the whole night. An eau-de-vie is a wonderful culinary tradition."

One place where they do have a digestif culture, and a taste for eau-de-vie, is Austria. For several years, I'd been told by people ranging from bartenders to other distillers to Eric Seed that there was a crazy guy named Hans Reisetbauer who lived on a farm in Austria. And Hans made just about the best eau-de-vie in the world.

So during one September harvest, I finally was able to arrange a too-short, one-day layover in Linz. I took a thirty-minute taxi ride along the

Danube River to Hans's farm—the landscape so lush and green, dotted with pointy church steeples and groups of blond schoolkids waving to us as we passed, as if in a scene from *The Sound of Music*.

Hans can be described as *big*—tall, substantial belly, booming voice. And there's something rather untamed about him, too. The day I met him, he emerged unshaven, his long gray hair swept back, and shook my hand. "You know the secret of a great eau-de-vie?" he said. "You do a good job in the orchards! Then the job of fermenation and distillation is so easy and nice. Just don't fuck it up!" He took me directly out into his orchards, driving his SUV into the middle of the plum trees. Then he jumped out of the truck. "Here!" he said, grabbing a bright purple plum off a tree. "You have to taste this plum! We have 2,500 trees here and they are the best plums in the world. We planted these trees in 2004, and this is the first year they've been ready for harvest." It was a pretty delicious plum.

"Are you making slivovitz?" I asked, referring to the traditional eastern European plum brandy.

"Well," he said with a big laugh, "We say plum brandy, not slivovitz. Slivovitz is usually a little rough, low quality."

Though Austria has become well-known as a wine producer, this region near Linz is too cold and rainy for wine grapes. The soil and conditions, however, are some of the best for orchard fruit. Hans grows 70 percent of the fruit he distills, including pears, apples, cherries, and apricots, and gets another 10 to 20 percent from neighboring farms. "You have to work with the fruit, not against the fruit. For eau-de-vie, you need perfect ripeness for each fruit. If it's not fully ripe, there's not enough sugar and too much acid. But the challenge is that all this is different for every fruit."

The fruit ratios that Hans distills from are insane: twenty-five pounds of pears or apples to make one liter of eau-de-vie; almost forty pounds of apricots for one liter. Hans once made a tomato eau-de-vie from dozens of varieties of heirloom tomatoes. "The first and last tomato eau-de-vie in the world," he said. "Never again." He and the local farmer washed and peeled all the tomatoes by hand. It took more than sixty-five pounds of tomatoes to make one bottle, and they made three hundred bottles. "One liter cost five hundred euros! It was really only for some extreme clients."

We ate lunch as Hans does every day: with his family (including his mother and father and his children) and his entire staff, the meal cooked by his wife. The farm has been in Hans's family since 1956. In 1990, Hans had been kicking around for several years as a young grad student in Vienna when his father called and said he had to come back home to the farm. "I said, 'I will only come home if I can plant fruit trees.' But, to be honest, I had never even seen a distillery before I started." In 1994, he distilled his first pear Williams eau-de-vie. He only had fifteen trees, and only made one hundred bottles, but with that batch he won a championship in Austria as the best pear Williams. Soon, prestigious restaurants from Vienna were calling with orders.

"But for me, the money is not the motive," he said. "I want to be the best distiller in the world. This is my life. I have no traditions. We have learned everything on our own. Each year we try something a little bit different. A little bit finer, a little more elegant, a little more pure.

"I have learned more from wine producers than spirits producers," he said. "In Austria, we have about forty thousand distillers. There are three or four that are perfect, maybe ten very good, and maybe twenty that are just good. And then there are 39,970 shitty distillers. My ten-year-old daughter knows more about distilling than these guys."

"Are there any distillers you respect?"

"I can't tell you . . . None!" he boomed.

And then it was time for the tasting. It felt like something I'd been waiting my whole life for. Hans's eaux-de-vie are like nothing I've ever sipped, and I spent more than three hours tasting about thirty different bottlings. Carrot eau-de-vie? Ginger eau-de-vie? Rowanberry eau-de-vie? Plum brandy that's been aged six years in mulberry wood casks? He served me one made from wild raspberries, handpicked in Serbia, sixty-five pounds to make one liter. He only made six bottles, and Helmut Lang bought three bought of them. "This is the most expensive eau-de-vie in the world right now, eighty euros for 350 milliliters." The most fantastic of all for me, though, was the quince. Let me read you my scribbled tasting notes from the quince: "Fucking amazing. End of story."

It wasn't just the aromatics that were so compelling, which is often the case in mediocre eaux-de-vie. The flavor was spot-on. "For me, a spirit is not a perfume," said Hans. "It is something to drink. It must have the flavor of the fruit." I really did not want to leave, but eventually Hans had to take me back to Linz, and I had to leave my little eau-de-vie fairy-tale land.

"Why is eau-de-vie such a hard sell in the United States?" I wanted to shout as we drove back along the Danube. Well, to be fair, price is a major issue. If you find Hans' eaux-de-vie in the States, they usually carry price tags of fifty to one hundred dollars, and that's for a half-sized 350-milliliter bottle.

Hans knows firsthand how challenging the U.S. eau-de-vie market is. The first time Hans came to America to sell his eau-de-vie, in 2001, he and his partner dressed in traditional Austrian costume. "No one wanted to buy our eaux-de-vie," he said. "They wanted to buy our costumes."

Desert Brandy

I thought I knew pisco pretty well. We're friends. I started drinking pisco sours about a decade ago, right around when the ceviche trend was up and coming. In fact, as a critic for a city magazine in the early 2000s, I was moved to call the pisco sour "infinitely more elegant" than either the caipirinhas or mojitos that most bartenders were still just learning how to make. Pisco: a grape-based brandy—clear, not aged in oak—with a bracing and rough 80-plus-proof kick if you drank it straight, which you never did. You used it in a pisco sour or a pisco punch. The Peruvians and Chileans were always arguing over who invented it and who should control the name. Beyond all that, what else did you need to know?

Then I went to Peru, and realized that I hadn't really known very much at all about my friend pisco. I was traveling with a few bartenders from San Francisco: drinks writer Jordan Mackay, and three fellows—Walter Moore, Carlos Romero, and Duggan McDonnell—who planned to launch a premium pisco called Campo de Encanto in 2010. On this trip, Romero, the master distiller, and Moore and McDonnell, his American partners, were developing their *acholado*, or blended pisco.

Lima is a great culinary hot spot, with a cool, overcast Mendocino-like climate. But we rolled out of Lima on a bus ride south. No bathrooms on this five-hour ride, but all the B and C American action movies you could hope for. After Vin Diesel in *xXx*, we took bets on what movie would come next. My money was on *Iron Eagle*, with Lou Gossett, Jr. I lost when a dubbed *Superman III* began. The landscape soon turned to desert. We passed the historic port of Pisco and arrived in the viticultural center of Ica, which is surrounded by giant mountains of sand. There is almost no rainfall there. Who knew you could grow grapes in such a place?

We stayed at the oasis of Huacachina, an old resort filled with dune buggies and backpackers. It was weird, sort of like a cross between a hippie ski town and Mos Eisley, with sandboarders instead of skiers and dune buggy drivers who drove like Han Solo. As we sat in a café, we watched one dune buggy driver skid down the dirt street. "You don't want that guy to take you up into the mountains," said the guy at the café. "He's a drunk."

Huacachina is said to be haunted by a witch in the middle of the lagoon who eats men at night. At least one man goes missing every year, according to legend. At night, one of my traveling companions wandered alone down to the water and claimed—totally freaking out—to have seen the witch. The jury is out on whether that sighting was pisco related. Perhaps it stemmed from excessive consumption of a coca leaf–infused pisco? Anyway, the freak-out was ill-timed, since we were expected at a house party in Ica. So I asked the Peruvian distiller, Romero, to reassure our friend that the witch was simply a myth. "But it's true," Romero insisted.

"Are you serious?" I said.

"Yes, it's true."

"Okaaay," I said. I tried a different approach. "Well, one man goes missing every year, right?"

"Yes."

"Well, has anyone gone missing yet this year?"

"What do you mean?"

"Well," I reasoned, "if one man has already gone missing, if the witch already has her quota, then you can reassure our friend that he won't go missing."

We finally did get to the house party in Ica, actually a birthday party for the seventy-year-old mother of the team's Peruvian business partner. A band played and several bottles of pisco were passed around. However, only one glass was passed around for thirty people. No matter where we went—house parties, bars, distilleries—and no matter how many people we were with—four, twelve, thirty, fifty—we were only ever provided one shot glass. The tradition, in Peru, is that you pour yourself a little pisco from the bottle, pass it to the next person, take your shot, then pass the glass. I don't care how popular pisco becomes in the States, that is one Peruvian custom that will definitely not make the leap north. Regardless, on that night, I filled up my shot glass, and then passed it to my right or to my left, either to a septuagenarian gentleman or his teenage grand-daughter. The night ended at a karaoke bar in downtown Ica, where I sang an amazing rendition of Lady Gaga's "Poker Face." A video of this actually existed, but, fortunately or unfortunately, the guy who shot the video had his laptop stolen on the bus ride back to Lima. So the world will never know whether or not I have a future as a Lady Gaga impersonator.

Peruvian pisco, it turns out, is just as strange and surprising as ski towns in deserts, drunk dune buggy drivers, thirty people drinking from the same glass, and the calculus of witch sightings. Which means, I guess, that pisco gives us a unique sense of place, a taste that springs from a land and its traditions. (Ding ding ding: paging Señor Terroir!) The spirit is also pretty ancient, with records of the earliest Spanish settlers drinking it in the sixteenth century.

The country has more than three hundred pisco producers, and the diversity of tastes pressed from the odd varietals of desert grapes is staggering. Quebranta—tannic, nonaromatic, and very dry—is the predominant grape, grown along with aromatic varieties such as Italia, Torontel, and even Moscatel. All these grapes make pretty terrible wine. But once distilled and left to rest for a few months, they create a white spirit that's as complex as a white spirit can be. It's important that pisco be produced only from the first press of grapes, and not from the skins, stems, and seeds, as is grappa—and as, unfortunately, are many low-quality piscos. Quebranta pisco is labeled *pisco puro*; acholado is a blend of Quebranta and other aromatic grapes and is often more expensive. The dry, nonaromatic Quebranta is the preferred grape of Peruvians; it's used most in blending, and it's probably what most Americans have experienced in their pisco sours. But some younger-generation distillers are experimenting with a higher ratio of the aromatic grapes in their acholados.

After dinner one night, our group tasted a single-varietal pisco made from only the Italia grape. The result was a floral digestif with subtle, fruity notes. The Peruvians among us didn't like it. Many of the Americans, including me, liked it very much. This was a pisco you could enjoy straight, and frankly, it was a better digestif than all but the very best grappas. We suggested that Americans would prefer an acholado with a higher percentage of these aromatics. But that spirit set off a debate that would continue for days. When blending for the American market, should the producer hold true to what a Peruvian connoisseur recognizes as a fine pisco? Or should the acholado reflect what an American palate would recognize as an elegant and approachable distilled spirit? I initially encouraged Romero, Moore, and McDonnell to veer toward the latter with Campo de Encanto. But an event on the last evening of our trip complicated my position in the debate.

That night, the local agricultural university in Ica asked if the group would meet their students and talk about acholado pisco, and perhaps the American palate. All of us were asked to blend our own acholado samples from among single-varietal piscos made from four different grapes. We would then pass our samples around to the students and professors, who would rate them. I relied heavily on the softer, aromatic grapes like Italia and Torontel, and much less on the Quebranta. Each of us was asked to name our pisco—I called mine Iron Eagle.

The students loved my acholado, emptying the first sample quickly. I blended another batch for the professors. The lone female professor came over to me, smiling, to say she liked Iron Eagle. The male professor, however, as well as a guy who was an official judge for the Peruvian pisco authority, did not like my pisco. Nor did Romero, nor did another distiller who was present. The female professor came to Iron Eagle's defense: "Oh, this is the pisco for me!"

"Face it, dude," said Jordan Mackay. "Iron Eagle is a chick pisco."

A Round of Drinks:
Terroir and Cocktails

Once spirits are bottled and shipped from their place of origin, many will eventually fall into the hands of crafty American bartenders. At that point, there's no telling where, and into which cocktails, they may end up. The following drinks—some traditional, some New Wave—all have traveled quite a ways from their humble *terroir*.

PALOMA

Serves 1

> In Mexico, Paloma cocktails are more popular than margaritas, and for good reason: grapefruit flavor mixes perfectly with tequila, better than lime juice alone. A traditional Paloma is made with a grapefruit soda such as Squirt. But this refreshing version calls instead for freshly squeezed white grapefruit juice and club soda, to add fizz.

3 ounces freshly squeezed white grapefruit juice

2 ounces blanco or silver tequila

¹/₂ ounce freshly squeezed lime juice

¹/₂ ounce agave nectar

Sea salt, to rim the glass

Club soda

1 lime wheel, for garnish

Fill a cocktail shaker two-thirds full with ice. Add the grapefruit juice, tequila, lime juice, and agave nectar. Shake well and strain into an ice-filled Collins glass rimmed with sea salt. Top with a splash of club soda, and garnish with the lime wheel.

Recipe by Tad Carducci of Tippling Bros., a New York-based consultancy

NOUVEAU CARRÉ

Serves 1

This is an inventive tequila riff on the New Orleans classic Vieux Carré. Añejo tequila is not normally used for mixing; pairing it with herbal-honey Bénédictine and the bright white-wine-and-citrus notes of Lillet Blanc is certainly strange. But somehow those ingredients fit together in this bold and complex cocktail.

1¹/₂ ounces añejo tequila

³/₄ ounce Bénédictine

¹/₄ ounce Lillet Blanc

2 dashes Peychaud's bitters

Lemon peel twist, for garnish

Fill a metal cocktail shaker halfway with ice. Add the tequila, Bénédictine, Lillet Blanc, and bitters. Stir until frost forms on the outside of the shaker, then strain into a chilled cocktail glass. Garnish with the lemon peel twist.

Recipe by Jonny Raglin of Absinthe Brasserie & Bar, San Francisco

RESTRAINING ORDER

Serves 1

Aperol—a bright orange, low-proof Italian aperitivo—has the uncanny ability to enhance and balance many disparate flavors and make everything taste better, including tequila. In this cocktail, it's part of an unlikely combination that includes celery bitters. Be sure to use a reposado tequila in this recipe, and do not neglect the garnish; a fat orange peel twist is critical for the right aromatics.

1¹/₂ ounces reposado tequila
³/₄ ounce Aperol
3 or 4 dashes celery bitters
Orange peel twist, for garnish

Fill a mixing glass halfway with ice. Place 2 or 3 large ice cubes in an old-fashioned or rocks glass. Add the tequila, Aperol, and bitters to the mixing glass. Stir vigorously for 20 to 30 seconds, then strain into the glass with the ice cubes. Twist the orange peel over the drink to release its oils, then rub it around the rim of the glass and drop it in.

Recipe by Colin Shearn of Franklin Mortgage & Investment Co., Philadelphia

BRASSERIE LEBBE

Serves 1

Eau-de-vie, generally poured as an after-dinner digestif, is challenging in cocktails. But as used here, it makes a cocktail that would be wonderful served earlier, perhaps even as a replacement for the mimosa at brunch. Neyah White of Nopa in San Francisco named the drink after a Belgian producer of *saison* farmhouse ales that have pear and yeasty notes, as this cocktail does. It works best with champagne, rather than other sparkling wines.

³/₄ ounce pear eau-de-vie
³/₄ ounce Licor 43 or Tuaca
¹/₂ ounce freshly squeezed lemon juice
3 ounces dry champagne

Fill a cocktail shaker halfway full with ice. Add the eau-de-vie, Licor 43, and lemon juice. Shake vigorously for 30 seconds, then strain into a champagne flute. Top with the champagne.

Recipe by Neyah White of Nopa, San Francisco

HANS PUNCH UP

Serves 8

This punch, by Adam Bernbach at Proof, is named for a guy Adam got into a fight with one New Year's Eve. Be sure to use pear eau-de-vie or poire Williams brandy, not pear liqueur; the liqueur would be too sweet for this recipe.

16 ounces pear eau-de-vie or poire Williams brandy
16 ounces honey syrup (page 219)
8 ounces freshly squeezed lemon juice
8 dashes Angostura bitters
8 ounces sparkling wine
8 mint sprigs, for garnish

Combine the pear eau-de-vie, honey syrup, lemon juice, and bitters in a large glass pitcher. Add about 1 cup of ice and stir vigorously. To serve, fill 8 highball glasses with ice; divide the punch among them, and top each with 1 ounce of sparkling wine. Stir gently, and garnish with mint sprigs.

Recipe by Adam Bernbach of Proof, Washington, D.C.

PISCO SOUR

Serves 1

This variation on the classic pisco sour is made in a blender and was adapted from a recipe by Eduardo Huaman Tito at Hotel Mossone in Huacachina, Peru. It was recently voted the best pisco sour in Peru. The blender helps achieve a nice froth; no shaking required. In Peru, the drink is made with 3 ounces of pisco, but I recommend 2½ ounces for the American palate. Be sure to use Key limes.

2½ ounces pisco
1 ounce freshly squeezed Key lime juice
1 tablespoon confectioners' sugar
1 medium egg white
1 dash Angostura bitters, for garnish

Combine the pisco, lime juice, sugar, and egg white in a blender. Process for 30 seconds, until frothy. Add a handful of ice and process for 1 minute, then pour into a highball glass. Garnish with the dash of bitters atop the foam.

Adapted from a recipe by Eduardo Huaman Tito of the Hotel Mossone, Huacachina, Peru

VICEROY

Serves 1

This cocktail was originally created for Campo de Encanto acholado (or blended) pisco—the pisco whose development I witnessed on my trip to Peru. The white-wine-and-citrus aperitif Lillet Blanc is a perfect complement to the grape-based pisco.

1½ ounces pisco
1 ounce Lillet Blanc
½ ounce freshly squeezed lime juice

$1/2$ ounce simple syrup (page 218)
$1^{1}/2$ ounces tonic water
Mint sprig, for garnish

Fill a highball glass with ice. Add the pisco, Lillet Blanc, lime juice, and simple syrup. Top with the tonic water and stir gently. Garnish with the mint sprig.

Recipe by Duggan McDonnell of Cantina, San Francisco

CHAPTER 8

OF POLITICS AND RUM

WHO CAN SAY ANYTHING THAT GIVES YOU THE MOMENTARY WELL-BEING THAT RUM DOES?

—*Ernest Hemingway*

D RINKING TRENDS COME AND GO, but tiki will always be with us. It keeps returning every few years or so, like the mustache, or animal-print fabric, or knee-high leather boots. Tiki drinks occupy a space somewhere in the Venn diagram of the American psyche where escapism, irony, and kitsch overlap, cutting across so many cultural divides. Hipster wannabes with badly drawn tattoos love tiki. Shoppers at Urban Outfitters love tiki. Suburban cougars on the prowl love tiki. Guys in Tommy Bahama shirts who listen to "Cheeseburger in Paradise" love tiki. Marlene Dietrich loved tiki. Richard Nixon loved tiki.

Who doesn't love tiki? Only one person immediately pops to mind: Donald Trump, who shuttered Trader Vic's in the late 1980s after he bought the Plaza Hotel. He called the famed tiki bar "tacky." Yes, Donald

Trump called something "tacky." You see, this is the strange sort of mind space we get into when we start talking tiki.

The late 1980s might have been one of the few times in late-twentieth-century America when tiki was decidedly out. So it's odd that my first experience with tiki drinks happened during that period. But if you were a college freshman in Boston, as I was, and you didn't have a fake ID, there is a good chance you and a group of friends might have ended up some night in a Chinese restaurant, perhaps in a part of town that was once called the Combat Zone. And you and your friends might have ordered a drink called a Scorpion Bowl, served in a large volcano bowl with a flaming shot of 151-proof rum in the center, from which you all drank with long straws. Perhaps you ordered more Scorpions, and there were races. Perhaps that turned into another one of your "bad night in college" stories. Anyway, because of my own Scorpion Bowl experience, I sat out the last tiki resurgence, back in the late 1990s and early 2000s.

But wait long enough and tiki—much like my old, grunge-era flannel shirts—comes around again, as it did in the late 2000s. Some of the classic-cocktail crowd feel tiki is a classic enough genre that's been overlooked. Luckily, this new generation of fine bartenders will be making sure that drinks such as the Mai Tai, the Zombie, the Navy Grog, and, yes, the Scorpion Bowl are made the right way, or improved as necessary.

The fact is, though tiki is often inseparable from tacky, tiki bars were conceived in the 1930s and 1940s as upscale nightspots. During their heyday, famous tiki joints such as Don the Beachcomber's in Hollywood and Trader Vic's in Oakland were the kinds of places where you put on your finest and hobnobbed. Don the Beachcomber, in particular, was the Spago of its day. Celebrities such as Bing Crosby, Greta Garbo, Howard Hughes, and Orson Welles dined on Cantonese cuisine, which Don termed "Polynesian." (This was why, by the late twentieth century, lowbrow Chinese restaurants were the only ones serving such tiki drinks as Scorpion Bowls. At a certain point, Chinese restaurants realized they were already serving "Polynesian" food, and so they decided to start serving the drinks, too.)

"Tiki was a very unironic big night out," said Jeff "Beachbum" Berry, who has spent the last decade researching tiki culture and writing a series of tiki books, including my favorite, *Sippin' Safari.* "There wasn't anything kitschy about it at the time. It was an escape. In the 1940s, people didn't travel. A tiki bar was where the midcentury Organization Man went to escape his white-collar job, his big mortgage, and the threat of nuclear annihilation." It's no wonder Tricky Dick would drag the likes of Henry Kissinger out to the Trader Vic's in Washington for Mai Tais.

Rum, of course, is the foundation on which tiki drinks are built. It makes sense, since rum also fuels so many aspects of the warm island fantasies that flow deep in America's cultural veins. Rum is the drink of umbrella cocktails and Love Boat cruises, of steel drums and Club Med, of dreadlocks and sex on the beach. "Where I go, I hope there's rum!" sings Jimmy Buffett and his Parrothead followers. Rum exudes romantic danger: think pirates and smugglers and guerillas and Hemingway and *la revolución.*

When I was visiting Hans Reisetbauer in Austria, after we'd finished the hours-long tasting of some the finest eaux-de-vie on the planet, Hans asked me, "Would you now like to taste something really special?"

"Special?" I said, dazed. "More special than the eau-de-vie that's made from thirty kilos of wild raspberries picked by hand in Serbia?"

He smiled. "Would you like to taste a rum from the cellar of Fidel Castro?"

"Of course," I said.

He left me in his tasting room and returned a few moments later, lumbering in with a heavy clay jug covered in straw. "It's from 1928."

As the story went, Hans had a friend who imported cigars from Cuba and had become friends with Fidel's cellar master. Hans had accompanied this friend on a trip to Havana and was invited to tour Fidel's cellars. The cellar master offered to sell Hans any spirit that caught his fancy, so Hans chose this jug of rum. It cost him five thousand dollars to finally bring it back to Austria.

Now, he poured two glasses. The rum, clocking in at 120 proof, was wild and smoky, yet totally smooth on the finish. "This isn't a clear distillate," Hans said. "It's actually a dirty spirit. But sometimes it doesn't matter. This is a classic. End of story."

As we sipped, I thought about this rum from 1928. Presumably, Fidel had come by this rum somehow after La Revolución. Perhaps he appropriated it from one of the mobster-run casinos of old Havana? Maybe from the cellar of a wealthy elite who fled to Miami? Perhaps from the Bacardi family before they fled to Puerto Rico? Or maybe even from the cellar of the corrupt President Batista, whom he overthrew? Did he and Che have a swig of the stuff while they strategized?

Rum is always a short half step, or closer, to politics. Case in point: The Cuban government and Bacardi have been fighting for years over control of the Havana Club brand name, which Cuba sells internationally through Pernod Ricard. Of course, because of the embargo, Tio Samuel won't let us have Havana Club, so I usually drink it in Europe.

Hans poured another glass of the rum. "Maybe Hemingway drank rum like this?" I asked, hopefully. I mean, if we're talking Cuba and politics and rum, Mr. Hemingway can't be far behind in the discussion. By now, we all know of Hemingway's affection for the daiquiri, the "authentic" framed handwritten notes in Havana bars that read, "My mojito in La Bodeguita, My daiquiri in El Floridita," the pissing away of his later years on a bárstool. We know it was post-revolution Cuba that finally broke Papa's heart. Yet Hemingway's Cuban period remains beloved of drinkers.

The poet Derek Walcott once wrote about this facet of Hemingway's legacy: "The seaside bars from the Bahamas to Tobago are full of boiled executives downing drinks and looking out with unshaven machismo to the lather-line of the reefs, their scuba gear conspicuously heaped like infantry weapons. They grunt about groupers and fire coral, as if Hemingway weren't dead and all the sharks and stingrays that never attack the locals hadn't gone with him."

I am not immune to this type of rum-soaked romanticism. I'll admit it: When I was in my twenties, I fancied myself a vaguely Hemingwayesque character—so much so that some writer friends had teasingly referred to me as "young Hemingway." It was not a compliment in grad school. Afterward, I spent a good deal of time in Latin American nations that were tottering shakily toward stability—Nicaragua, in particular.

It was during this period that I took up serious rum drinking. Bottles of Flor de Caña rum were three dollars for the white and only six dollars for the seven-year-old Grand Reserve. I remember stocking up during a visit in 1996, during the heated election between former Sandinista president Daniel Ortega and right-wing candidate Arnoldo Alemán. All the bars in the country were shuttered for three days while they tallied the votes. Rum was our only dinner one night when my friend Brian and I got caught up in a demonstration in Matagalpa, a Sandinista town in the highlands (we were escorted back to our hotel by police in riot gear, who told me, "Matagalpa is closed tonight, *jefe*"). In Granada, the day the bars opened our driver, Julio, met us at our hotel, so drunk on rum at 8:00 a.m. that we had to pile him into the backseat and drive him back to Managua. There, we drank rum and tonics with wealthy young men who were celebrating the Alemán win at a private casino in what seemed like someone's house. Years later, Alemán would be convicted of pilfering over $100 million from the nation's coffers.

We must thank Ortega and the Sandinistas, however indirectly, for the outstanding quality of Flor de Caña. When the Sandinistas seized power in 1979 after overthrowing the Somoza dictatorship, the junta set extremely strict price controls—particularly on rum. Rather than sell its best rum under this system, Flor de Caña decided to store it away, letting it age in casks. When the Sandinista government fell in 1990, they owned a huge stock of some of the finest aged rums in the region. Some of those Sandinista-era rums are now on the market as twenty-plus-year-old bottlings.

During the 1990s, Nicaragua struggled to become a tourist destination, "the next Costa Rica," as travel writers like me called it. Often it seemed so close but so far away. One night I was at Charly's Bar in Granada, packed with tourists, surveying the vibrant scene. (Charly's, oddly, had a wall dedicated to the 1980s heavy metal band the Scorpions; the German owner was a dead ringer for one of the band.) Anyway, I suddenly felt a hand smoothing a flyaway hair over my left ear. I swung around, and to my surprise, it was the friendly young Nicaraguan woman tending bar. "Sorry," she said. "Your hair was out of place and I was just brushing it back for you." She laughed really awkwardly, letting me know she meant nothing wanton by the gesture.

I assured her it was no problem and ordered another round. "There are a lot more foreigners in town these days, aren't there?" I said. "A lot more gringos."

"Oh yes," she said, pouring a drink. "And why not? We're all friends now, after all."

Then, another night, I found myself in the bar of Managua's Hotel InterContinental, drinking a twelve-year-old Flor de Caña. All around me, businessmen—some in bad suits, some in flower-print shirts trying to look tropical-casual—talked in hushed tones. They had been warned by their waiters not to walk the streets, to take only specific taxis, to visit only the fashionable bars guarded by men with shotguns and AK-47s.

I was approached by a man who was either an Ernest Hemingway wannabe or a Jimmy Buffett wannabe (it's often difficult to spot the difference). This guy wore a bushy mustache, shorts, sandals, a beaded necklace, and a Tampa Bay Devil Rays baseball hat.

He bought a shot of Flor de Caña, drank it, and, without so much as a hello, asked me, "Do you know any good strip clubs?"

"No," I said.

"Whorehouses?"

"No."

"Well, what the hell are you doing here in this country, then?" he asked.

"Just visiting," I said. "What are you doing here?"

"Whatever the hell I want to."

In late 2006, Nicaragua had a contest to name its *trago nacional*, or "national swig." The impetus seems to have been a sense of cultural envy: Cuba had its mojito. Mexico had the margarita. Why didn't Nicaragua have its own cocktail? One of the contest judges, the French ambassador to Nicaragua, was quoted in the *New York Times* as saying, "Nicaragua needs a new identity that doesn't have anything to do with revolution. This is a chance." The winning cocktail, the Macua, is pretty tasty: equal parts white rum and guava juice, with lemon juice and simple syrup.

The last time I was in Nicaragua, in 2007, happened to be only a few months after the unveiling of the Macua. Though I saw a number of promotional cards with the recipe, I did not see one person order the drink. There had been some light criticism in the Managua newspapers that the drink had to be made with Flor de Caña rum, the contest sponsor. But there were other, more important things going on in Nicaragua at that time, such as another ugly presidential campaign that, this time around, saw Daniel Ortega return to power. At most of the bars I went to in Managua, people were just drinking beer or Flor de Caña rum by the bottle, like always.

I'm always intrigued when a city or nation is moved to create some representative cocktail of place. The last time I saw it was in the spring of 2009. The Tourism Authority of Thailand made what it called "a move to give the Thai tourism and hospitality industries a much-needed boost." So what game-changing action did they take in the midst of a global economic collapse? Offer deep discounts on flights and hotels? Rebrand the nation with lavish full-page ads in travel magazines? Privatize the national airline? No, nothing like that. Here's what happened: they invented a new cocktail. It's called the Siam Sunray, and it involves vodka, coconut liqueur, lemongrass, ginger, and Thai chile peppers. "Successful signature drinks are one way to fast-track holiday destinations onto the world tourism map," said the authority in a joint statement issued with the Thai Hotels Association.

I've seen it happen around the world, from developing nations to our nation's capital. We've seen some older, classic drinks recently resurrected as signature cocktails with some success. Every summer, for instance, the D.C. Craft Bartenders Guild raises awareness about the Lime Rickey's rightful place as Washington's native cocktail. In 2008, the state legislature of Louisiana, in a grandiose move, voted to designate the Sazerac the official cocktail of New Orleans.

I wonder about this nearly universal desire for a signature drink to call one's own. We'd all love to have a drink named after ourselves, like Hemingway's daiquiri, the Papa Doble. But I don't know if you can just invent one out of thin air. I wish I could be a fly on the wall in one of these tourism authority boardrooms when the signature cocktail discussions happen: "Okay, people, we're not leaving here until someone comes up with our new official drink. Look, Brazil has its caipirinha, and Peru has its pisco sour. In Spain, they dump fruit and brandy into red wine and call it a national drink. For god's sake, even Martinez, California, has a cocktail they claim is the precursor to the martini. Think outside the box!"

Nothing sells escapism like a good umbrella drink, but rum is so much more than that. I'm thinking specifically about the sipping rums that I taste every year when I attend TasteDC's big annual Rum Festival, held at the Woman's National Democratic Club during the hot Washington, D.C., summer.

Annual sales of premium rum are up about 40 percent since 2002, and I've come to think of rum as one of the most complicated and fascinating spirits in the liquor store. Still, a rum tasting is quite different from a wine tasting. What is a rum tasting like? Let me quickly dispense with a few of your more pressing questions:

- No, neither Captain Morgan Spiced Rum nor Malibu coconut rum is served.

- Yes, there may be a $279 aged rum on offer.

- No, there is never a frozen daiquiri nor a blueberry mojito nor a Bahama Mama to be found.

- No, no one described anything as "grassy" or "fruit forward" or "mature yet owns the promise of youthfulness."

- Yes, I've seen several young women drawing smiley faces on their tasting sheets to mark the rums they liked and frowny faces to mark the ones they didn't.

- Yes, I overheard someone ask, "So, Guatemala . . . that's where, Central America, right?"

- Yes, there are numerous middle-aged men wearing Jimmy Buffet–esque island-print shirts, including one shirt I saw with pictures of bongos.

- No, there is not a lot of spitting going on.

All of which makes for a much more fun event than most other tastings I attend. Rum is, of course, a sugarcane-based spirit, but it has many variations. Some (say, from the English-speaking islands) are darker and fuller and use more molasses, while some (say, from the Spanish-speaking nations) are lighter and use less molasses. Some, made purely with sugarcane juice (say, from the French-speaking islands) use no molasses. Then there are varying amounts of barrel aging. The quality and complexity of rums overall has improved dramatically since the days of Hemingway: some of them have a fiery, smoky finish; others display more rounded hints of vanilla or caramel. The range is diverse.

With so many nations represented in the room—from Venezuela to Haiti to Martinique to Barbados—there are bound to be some regional rivalries. Once, I chatted near the hors d'oeuvres table with an international couple, the wife from Trinidad and the husband from Guyana. "Have you tried some of our rums from Trinidad yet?" asked the woman, insisting I get myself a taste of 10 Cane rum.

I asked her husband what he'd tasted. "Well, since I'm from Guyana," he said, "I've been tasting mostly the rums from Guyana." At my enthusiastic prodding, he sampled one of the Guatemalan rums and told me, with a shrug, that he was unimpressed. I then moved over to one of the stars of the evening, from Guyana: a seventeen-year-old rum, aged in Syrah casks, produced by Murray McDavid ($89). I noticed that the people with whom

I tasted the Murray McDavid drifted back to that table several times during the evening. I could see why the guy from Guyana had been so smug.

I'm always amazed at how expensive rum has gotten over the past decade: Zacapa 23 from Guatemala ($41), Mount Gay Extra Old from Barbados ($42), and the Santa Teresa Antiguo de Solera from Venezuela ($37) are just a few examples. Of course, the Cask 1623 rum produced by Pyrat, with its outlandish $279 price tag, was . . . nice? (And by "nice" I mean "not worth the money.") I began looking around for bottles that might convince a rum newbie or skeptic that the spirit is sophisticated and versatile. I found several outstanding aged rums for less than $30. You cannot go wrong with any of these: Pampero Aniversario Añejo from Venezuela at $29; Mount Gay Eclipse from Barbados at $27; and my old friend, seven-year-old Flor de Caña Grand Reserve at $24.

"Is aged rum the new single-malt Scotch?" my editor once asked. Hmm . . . perhaps? I find myself turning much more often to rums, served neat or on the rocks, than I do to other high-end sprits. A similar tasting challenge is there. Sometimes it takes a little time to wrap one's mind around a spirit. Take, for instance, rhum agricole from Martinique.

"Since when do you spell rum with an 'h'?" a friend asked when I served him a tasting flight of rhum agricole.

"It's French," I explained.

"Figures." He took his first sip. "Okay, I'm out of my comfort zone," he said. "Since when does rum taste like fresh-cut grass?"

"So," I said. "Is that your tasting note? This rum with an 'h' is grassy?" My friend extended me his middle finger.

I could empathize, and I felt for a moment like the dreaded Scotch snob pushing a big, smoky peat monster on a newbie (which I guess would go hand in hand with rum being the new single-malt Scotch). Anyway, rhum agricole may be the most complex rum of all. Only a handful of distilleries on Martinique and Guadeloupe are governed by an AOC, bestowed by the French government in 1996. Most other rums are made from molasses, but rhum agricole must be produced from 100 percent fresh, pure sugarcane juice. Some of the distilleries insist that their sugarcane be pressed within an hour of being cut in the fields.

Rhum agricole is distilled at a lower proof than other rums to capture more of the natural qualities of the sugarcane. The result is that rhum agricole becomes another spirit that can actually claim terroir.

It's an acquired taste, and honestly I didn't get it at the outset. The white took some experimenting to learn to mix with, and I thought the aged versions seemed a little too grassy. Or vegetal. But soon enough I started to truly appreciate rhum agricole. Learning to love rhum agricole is really no different from learning to appreciate complex wines such as Barolo or Châteauneuf-du-Pape—and it's infinitely easier than learning to love, say, Italian amari. So distinct is rhum agricole from other rums that the San Francisco World Spirits Competition recently instituted a separate category for the spirit.

"It's like the difference between Scotch and bourbon," said Ben Jones, a fourth-generation member of the Clément family who imports both Rhum Clément and Rhum J.M. from Martinique and has become rhum agricole's biggest booster in the United States. "It's just a different flavor profile." Lower distilling temperatures make for a huge contrast with molasses-based rums. "Once you cook the sugar, you've cooked off all the terroir and the finer qualities of what the sugarcane has to offer," Jones said.

After finally wrapping his mind around rhum agricole—extra "h" and all—even my friend had to agree.

There is at least one "h" rhum, however, that is not AOC controlled: Rhum Barbancourt from Haïti. And every time I see the fifteen-year-old bottle sitting on a liquor store shelf in the States for $44, it makes me sad and conflicted. I usually buy it, out of a sense of pity and remorse. Probably no one can taste Haitian rum and not think of the devastation and human tragedy of the earthquake in January 2010.

For me, it runs deeper. I can't ever taste it without thinking of my own visit to Haiti, back in 1999. I was visiting along with two friends, Kevin and Míchel. We'd all been greeted by the creaky brass band on the tarmac at the airport, and then by the construction sign at customs that read, "We Are Sorry To Welcome You In This Condition." We loved that bottles of Barbancourt cost only eight dollars. And we found it intriguing that everyone sitting beside us at the blood-red blackjack table in the El Rancho Casino in Pétionville was a "businessman" from Colombia with bodyguards. But our first evening eventually turned squirrelly when Míchel won eight hundred dollars in a slot machine and then was told by the cashier he'd be paid not in dollars or gourdes, but in something called "Haitian dollars"—a nebulous denomination that amounted to less than one hundred dollars. When he started to protest a little too loudly and drunkenly, several guys with machine guns came over and escorted him out. As I followed, a faded pink five-dollar chip fell out of my pocket, and a teenage prostitute dove to the carpet in front of me to grab it.

The next day, as we puttered along in the bumper-to-bumper Port-au-Prince traffic, rolling over occasional streams of raw sewage, Saintil, our driver, explained to us that his favorite actor was Shaquille O'Neal. He particularly liked Shaq in the movie *Steel*. Saintil made a quick short-cut through a dodgy alley, and we passed a mangy dog fighting with an enormous pig—literally paw and snout—over the right to eat a pile of garbage. After the shortcut, we were back to a standstill, surrounded by the vibrant reds and blues and yellows of the crazy *tap-taps* carrying sardined passengers in the overcrowded streets, windshields emblazoned with "Christ Is The Big Captain," "Lamentations 3:26," and "Sylvester Stallone."

As we pondered Shaquille O'Neal's thespian work, Saintil surprised us again by saying he often longed for a day when Papa Doc Duvalier—with his voodoo mysticism and his murderous secret police, the Tontons Macoutes—would be returned to power and end the utter chaos and lawlessness. Saintil said this even though, at forty-nine, he was certainly old enough to remember firsthand the violence of the Duvalier regime. "Many people believe that Papa Doc is still alive," he said. "No one actually saw him buried in his coffin. People say they've seen him, late at night, walking the streets of Port-au-Prince."

We were on our way south to Jacmel and needed to exchange dollars for gourdes, so Saintil cut out of traffic and sped through several backstreets. He eventually pulled the truck through a metal gate at a gray, nondescript warehouse, passed several armed guards, and parked. The four of us entered a dimly lit backroom where a woman and two men were counting piles upon piles of money—gourdes, dollars, and any number of other currencies. Without a word, the woman quickly took our twenties and fifties, counted out gourdes, and handed them to us. The two men never looked up as they continued to wrap piles of bills in rubber bands. Three minutes later, we were escorted back outside and straight to the truck by one of the armed guards. "Let's just not ask questions," someone said. Back in the truck, we all took big swigs of Barbancourt.

The trip to Jacmel, which was only about forty-eight miles away, took over five hours, on pockmarked roads through parched, treeless, eroded mountains. After an early detour through the slums of Cité Soleil—which the U.N. has called "the most dangerous place on Earth"— we were all a little rattled and in need of another drink. When Kevin and Míchel requested a stop, Saintil pulled over at the Snack Bar de l'Immaculée Conception.

By the time we arrived in Jacmel, it was early evening. Guides, guys guarding over our truck, and people selling fruit and wooden sculptures swarmed outside our hotel. We hired a boy no older than twelve to take us around town, and almost immediately, he tried to also interest us in the services of his slightly older "sister." Guides would continue to press many services on us over the next several days. At one point, when we needed to find a telephone, we had to hire three guides, one for each of us; then when we entered the neighborhood where the telephone office was, we had to hire another local guide for our guides. When we finally did arrive at the telephone office, we hired another guide to open the door and lead us into the building. So in the span of about six blocks, we'd placed five guides on our payroll.

Walking past the colonial buildings in the main square that night, one could almost imagine the port in the days when orange peels were exported to France to make top-shelf Cointreau. The town was Haiti's major port in the nineteenth century—more important than Port-au-Prince. But that was all long ago. Gone from Jacmel was the sweet fragrance of orange peels drying in the sun on flat rooftops. Those citrus smells, according to Saintil, created a powerful, exotic aphrodisiac. Years ago, as a boy, he lived in one of the rural villages near here, before he moved away to Port-au-Prince. He told us this as we lounged at a beachside bar and drank fifteen-year-old Barbancourt rum and watched garbage wash up in the surf. In Jacmel's soft breeze, you smelled something less than promising, something you couldn't quite place: Burning garbage? Sweat? Diesel exhaust? Simply the smell of things falling apart?

Carnival began at breakfast the following day. We watched a parade of children in costumes pass by our hotel's patio. Boys in purple tunics and fake swords danced in circles. Children with face paint and men with huge papier-mâché masks of dragons and lizards and spirits zigzagged down the road. A girl of about five danced on a stick that was levitated by a half dozen teenage boys while an older man pounded on a drum. Three men who'd doused themselves with motor oil as makeup and donned bull's masks cracked long black whips in the middle of the street. After each performance, we placed gourdes in the dancers' outstretched hands.

Later, we walked to the beachside bar, and my friend Kevin purchased, for a simple glass of rum, a straw hat painted fluorescent green and orange. Our bartender, the same one who'd run out of rum the night before and charged us for using our own, told us that cruise ships would soon be returning to Jacmel, calling there as they did thirty years ago. When we scoffed and pointed out all the garbage and metal debris littering the harbor, the bartender said, "Cruise ships already call at Cap Haitien in the north. The cruise companies just don't tell the Americans that they're coming to Haiti. They say it's a 'secret Caribbean island.'" It's true about Cap Haitien. If your cruise ship has stopped for a boozy afternoon on a "private island" called Labadee . . . well, you've actually been in Haiti.

Saintil suggested we go see a Carnival cockfight that was happening on the outskirts of town, and we reluctantly agreed. As our truck approached the cockfight pit, a fight had already begun. Under the thatched roof, men cradled roosters, and each of the birds' heads was covered with a sock or a rag so they wouldn't be provoked to bare their talons before the fight. We bought tickets and squeezed past barefoot spectators who spilled off the wooden benches and leaned on one another to see two roosters tearing each other into a bloody mess. The fight took an agonizing twenty minutes, with the crowd cheering each time one of the cocks staggered backward after a blow. Finally, one of them fell, and we watched money change hands.

We waited in the sun for the second fight, watching a friendly, toothless old man and his son sharpen their rooster's claws with a rusty knife. We stood trying to decide if we wanted to continue to sunburn ourselves or squeeze back under the roof. We watched a woman ladling a red homemade liquor out of a huge washtub. Nearly one hundred men drank out of the same rusty metal cup. We broke open our bottles of Barbancourt and passed them around.

Finally, as the hot stench of sweaty bodies stuffed in tight quarters under a sunbaked thatched roof reached its peak, the two cocks began fighting. But just as one rooster lunged for the other, the friendly toothless old man leaped into the ring and stood screaming with outstretched hands. The whole pit erupted in Creole curses and yelling. Saintil translated the argument to us as if this sort of thing happened every day: The old man who jumped in the ring shouted that the opposing rooster was under a voodoo spell and that a zombie walked among the spectators at the cockfight. The old man declared that he was a powerful man and insisted upon standing in the ring to ward off the effects of the zombie. Of course, the other men around the pit didn't like the idea of the old man standing in the middle of the cockfight and took issue. Another half hour of arguing ensued, with a lot of shoving and pointing. Finally, the fight was canceled. A young boy walked through the crowd, carefully counting bills out of a paper bag, paying back those who'd gambled. Judging from the tenor of the now-angry cockfight crowd—and in tune with my sudden desire to join PETA upon return home—we decided to return to Jacmel before the next match started.

Later that evening, Kevin, Míchel, Saintil, and I sat at our hotel's patio bar with more Barbancourt and listened to a ragtag band consisting of ten men and only three instruments: a bongo, a homemade banjo, and a pair of maracas. The old man with the maracas, the band's leader, danced and sang haunting Creole ballads. His white belt, cinched tight around his frail waist, looked as though it could never keep his baggy pants from falling down. Later, when he was drunker, the bandleader would fall down, backward, over his own wooden chair. "*Donnez quelque chose pour la musique*" (Give something for the music) read a handwritten sign.

As we ordered more rum, Kevin innocently requested a once-popular song he only half remembered from when he'd honeymooned in Haiti in the late 1970s. But when the band suddenly broke into the chorus of "Duvalier, Duvalier," nearly half the bar cleared out. The only one still dancing was a prostitute in a dirty brown dress. A dozen boys who loitered in the street kept tapping us on the shoulder, over the patio railing, with their palms out.

Our twelve-year-old guide returned. Míchel told him to get lost, but Kevin had another idea. This boy was barefoot, and for a couple days we'd all noticed how raw and injured his feet looked. Kevin took out four twenty-dollar bills, gave the boy one of them, and told him to go buy a pair of shoes with the money. "If you come back tomorrow at breakfast wearing a new pair of shoes," he said, "I'll give you the rest of the money."

The next morning, over mangoes and coffee on the hotel patio, we saw the boy clomping across the square. He was wearing a brand-new pair of what must have been size-thirteen basketball shoes. He could barely walk in them without tripping, and at one point he walked right out of them. But he was beaming, and he stomped up onto the patio and toward our table. He tapped Kevin on the shoulder and put his hand out. Kevin counted the bills into his hand.

When we returned to Pétionville, we attempted to visit the Barbancourt distillery. Saintil drove us, in the morning sunshine, high above Port-au-Prince to the stone ramparts of the Jane Barbancourt Castle. The thick, wooden door was locked, and so we banged with the huge metal knocker.

After three knocks, the castle door slowly opened, and we were met by . . . a woman in pink curlers and a nightgown. "You want to taste *rum?*" she said. There was a flurry of activity, and the woman's clearly hungover (or strung-out) boyfriend served us a huge plate of mangoes and coffee while the woman searched the castle for the key to the tasting room. She handed us a brochure that had to have dated from the Duvalier-era 1960s—with oversaturated photos of lush green mountains that now were totally defor-ested. The tasting room looked like a cheesy midcentury version of Medi-eval Times, with chairs and a bar cut out of barrels. The couple dusted off a few ancient bottles of *Jane* Barbancourt rum—not at all what we'd been drinking. Of course, this visit had been a big mistake. We later learned that there are two branches of the Barbancourt family that split many years ago. Some got the distillery, while others got the castle.

After I returned home from Haiti, I tacked a quote above my desk that has hung there for over a decade. It's from the seventeenth-century English churchman Thomas Fuller: "If an ass goes traveling, he'll not come home a horse."

Lately, I've been drinking Rhum Barbancourt again, because I think it's important to remember that some spirits, particularly rum, often come from troubled places. If we think about the terroir of spirits, we should also think about the people who struggle in that terroir. The Bar-bancourt distillery suffered major damage, losing around four million dol-lars in the January 2010 earthquake. But within six months, I was glad to hear that the distillery, with its 250 workers, is back up and running—optimistically hoping to recoup its loses within a few years. As for the Jane Barbancourt castle, I have heard nothing.

Years after I visited Haiti, I was tasting with a young Calvados pro-ducer from Normandy named Guillaume Drouin, who told me he'd worked for two years at the *real* Barbancourt distillery before he took over his father's Calvados distillery. Drouin was then an oenologist and he followed his girlfriend to Haiti. "The guy at Barbancourt said to me, 'Well, I don't have a job for you. I don't know what you'd do. But we only get an oenologist on the island about once a century, so I'd be foolish not to find something for you to do.' So I started working there."

I told Guillaume my story about Haiti as we were tasting his family's very rare and expensive apple brandy. I told him I'd always felt very conflicted about that trip: about how I'd wanted to help, at the very least by bearing witness, but how in the end I'd just been a ham-handed visitor. "I felt the same way," Guillaume said, who said it was extremely awkward to be the boss, as a *blanc* from the former colonizer. "After I came back to France, I was depressed. I left there and returned to my comfortable life. But how was I supposed to forget about what I'd seen in Haiti?"

I'd never met many people who'd been to Haiti, and it helped Guillaume and me strike up a rapport right away. That and the fact that his family's Calvados was one of the most sublime spirits I'd ever tasted. "You should come visit us in France sometime," Guillaume said. A few years later, I did.

A Round of Drinks:
Yo Ho Ho

A rum and tonic or a Dark and Stormy (rum, ginger beer, and a squeeze of lime) are the usual ways I enjoy rum in a drink. Another easy rum cocktail idea is Martinique's traditional Ti' Punch (short for *petit punch*, or "little punch"): drizzle a bar spoon full of cane syrup into an old-fashioned glass, cut a small disk from the side of a lime and squeeze it into the glass, add one and a half ounces of rhum agricole and a chunk of ice, and serve. (And watch out for the little punch it packs.)

I've taken to using unaged rhum agricole from Neisson or Rhum Clément as my go-to white rum because of the wild, vegetal layers of flavor it adds to cocktails. As the rhum ages in oak casks, the grassy, funky qualities are tamed a little, creating a spirit that approaches the depth and complexity of a fine cognac. For everyday drinking, smooth and mellow Rhum Clément VSOP is the gold standard, at about thirty-five dollars a bottle. La Favorite Ambré, Neisson, and J.M.'s VSOP are excellent choices in the same price range. For those who are looking for a real splurge, I highly recommend the Rhum J.M. Vieux 1997 vintage. Even at around one hundred dollars, it is still an unbelievable value. With its explosion of aromas and tastes—nutty, herbal, chocolaty, slightly fruity—it is one of the finest spirits I've tasted on the spirits beat.

PAPA DOBLE

Serves 1

> **2 ounces rhum agricole**
> **¹/₂ ounce freshly squeezed lime juice**
> **¹/₂ ounce freshly squeezed grapefruit juice**
> **¹/₄ ounce maraschino liqueur**

Fill a cocktail shaker halfway with ice. Add the rum, juices, and maraschino liqueur. Shake well for at least 60 seconds, then strain into a chilled cocktail glass or an ice-filled old-fashioned glass.

MACUA

Serves 1

Named after a tropical bird native to Central America, the Macua was declared the national drink of Nicaragua in late 2006, after a countrywide competition that took place during the heat of that year's ugly presidential campaign. This long drink is light, tart, and only a bit sweet: the perfect drink for a warm afternoon. Goya's guava juice is good to use, though guava nectar from Jumex is acceptable (the drink will be yellow instead of pink). Though white rum works best, an aged rum is also nice.

> **2 ounces rum**
> **2 ounces guava juice**
> **1 ounce freshly squeezed lemon juice**
> **¹/₄ ounce simple syrup (page 218)**
> **Orange slice, for garnish**

Fill a cocktail shaker halfway with ice. Add the rum, guava juice, lemon juice, and simple syrup. Shake well for at least 30 seconds, then strain into an ice-filled highball or Collins glass. Garnish with the orange slice.

EL PRESIDENTE

Serves 1

Popular in Havana during the 1920s and 1930s, the Presidente cocktail reportedly was offered to President Calvin Coolidge by then Cuban President Gerardo Machado. Coolidge, mindful of Prohibition back home, declined the drink. You should not. It has more in common with a martini or Manhattan than with standard tropical rum drinks. Be sure to use a good aged rum, like Venezuela's Pampero Aniversario, Nicaragua's Flor de Caña seven-year-old Grand Reserve, or—if you can find it—Havana Club Añejo from Cuba.

1 1/2 ounces aged rum
3/4 ounce dry vermouth
3/4 ounce Cointreau
1/2 teaspoon homemade grenadine (page 216)
Orange peel twist, for garnish

Fill a mixing glass two-thirds full with ice. Add the rum, vermouth, Cointreau, and grenadine. Stir vigorously for 30 seconds, then strain into a cocktail glass. Garnish with the orange peel twist.

RUM MANHATTAN

Serves 1

There are many versions of a Rum Manhattan floating around, but I like this one because it calls for aged rhum agricole, which is rum distilled from pure sugarcane juice in Martinique or Guadeloupe, such as Rhum Clément VSOP, Neisson Réserve Spéciale, or Rhum J.M. VSOP.

2 ounces aged rhum agricole
1 ounce sweet vermouth
¹/₂ teaspoon maraschino liqueur
1 dash orange bitters
Orange peel twist, for garnish

Fill a mixing glass halfway with ice. Add the rum, vermouth, maraschino liqueur, and bitters. Stir vigorously for at least 30 seconds, then strain into a chilled cocktail glass. Garnish with the orange peel twist.

Recipe by Derek Brown of the Passenger and the Columbia Room, Washington, D.C.

Now for a couple of offerings to the tiki gods.

Done right, tiki drinks seem to make the summer last just a little bit longer. So, what makes a tiki drink a tiki drink? They all have several common elements. The most obvious is that they have very complicated, multifaceted recipes, some with as many as twelve ingredients. "With these drinks, you're getting a complex culinary creation. It's really easy to mess up and make these drinks badly," says tiki expert Jeff "Beachbum" Berry.

Most tiki drinks are rum-based and have a citrus component, and a hallmark is the blending of numerous rum styles. You'll often find three or more types of rum—a light, a dark, an aged, a smoky Guyanese Demerara—all in the same recipe. Berry says, "When I first looked into these recipes, I thought, 'Why do I have to buy thirty different types of rum?' One recipe called specifically for a 94.1 proof rum. I mean, why did it have to be exactly 94.1? It's crazy. But it works. There's almost a scientific formula behind all these recipes." Tiki, for instance, is just about the only cocktail genre that calls for 151-proof rum. Berry says he's tried to maneuver around the overproof rum, but the drinks just don't have the same zing. "If you try to make a Zombie without the 151, it doesn't fly," he says. I concur.

Beyond the rum, good tiki drinks always balance flavor with some kind of sly flavoring agent, often a unique spice or secret-recipe syrup. "There's a strange, teasing layer of flavor that you can't quite put your finger on," according to Berry. "You're getting pushed and pulled in different directions." Berry has spent many years trying to decipher the mysterious recipes of Don the Beachcomber, which Don kept in code so his bartenders couldn't steal them. One example: An ingredient in the Zombie is "Don's Mix," a blend of fresh grapefruit juice and cinnamon-infused simple syrup. A more common tiki flavoring agent is orgeat, an almond-flavored syrup with hints of orange flower and rose water, another long-forgotten but essential ingredient in a Mai Tai.

Finally, the presentation and novelty factors are high. And we're talking about more than little umbrellas. Classic tiki drinks come out elaborately flaming, sometimes adorned with flowers, sometimes in a ceremonial bowl. "They wanted you to talk about these drinks over the watercooler on Monday," Berry says. "The Zombie was the Cosmopolitan of its day." I find that amazing, almost unbelievable, considering how high-octane the Zombie is.

ZOMBIE

Serves 1

> Be warned: Even Don the Beachcomber limited his customers to two Zombies a night, and that was during an era when very strong drinks were commonplace. The original 1934 Zombie recipe is a beast. Don's more refined 1956 version is included here.

> 1 1/2 ounces pineapple juice
> 1 1/2 ounces gold rum
> 1 ounce dark rum
> 3/4 ounce freshly squeezed lime juice
> 3/4 ounce maraschino liqueur

¹/₂ ounce Don's Mix (2 teaspoons freshly squeezed grapefruit juice,
1 teaspoon cinnamon-infused simple syrup; page 219)

¹/₂ ounce 151-proof rum

¹/₄ ounce falernum, preferably John D. Taylor's Velvet Falernum

¹/₄ ounce homemade grenadine (page 216)

¹/₈ teaspoon Pernod

2 dashes Angostura bitters

³/₄ cup ice cubes

Mint sprig or pineapple slice, for garnish

In a blender, combine the pineapple juice, gold and dark rums, lime juice, maraschino liqueur, Don's Mix, 151-proof rum, falernum, grenadine, Pernod, and bitters. Blend on low speed just to mix, then add the ice and blend on high speed for 5 seconds. Pour into a Collins glass or tiki mug; garnish with the mint sprig or pineapple slice.

Adapted from Don the Beachcomber's original recipe by Jeff "Beachbum" Berry

MAI TAI

Serves 1

If a bartender uses orange juice and/or grenadine in your Mai Tai, he or she is making it wrong. Almond-flavored orgeat syrup is the key. In fact, the reason the Mai Tai evolved into such a laughably bad cocktail is mostly due to the disappearance of orgeat syrup by the late twentieth century. There are now a few small producers of orgeat, but the good news is that making your own is relatively easy.

1 ounce aged Jamaican rum, preferably Appleton VX

1 ounce amber rhum agricole, preferably Rhum Clément VSOP

³/₄ ounce freshly squeezed lime juice, reserving a spent half lime for garnish

¹/₂ ounce Cointreau

¹/₂ ounce orgeat syrup (page 220)

¹/₄ ounce simple syrup (page 218)

Mint sprig, for garnish

Fill a cocktail shaker halfway with ice. Add the Jamaican run, rhum agricole, lime juice, Cointreau, orgeat syrup, and simple syrup. Shake well, then pour (unstrained) into a double old-fashioned glass or wineglass. Garnish with a mint sprig and the spent shell of half a lime.

Adapted from Trader Vic's original recipe by Jeff "Beachbum" Berry

Piña colada simply means "strained pineapple" in Spanish. That being the case, it's always seemed odd to me that coconut elbowed its way in to become the dominant flavor of this poolside favorite. It's an astonishing act of hubris, really, for Señor Coco López and his canned Cream of Coconut to have hijacked the blender away from pineapple. Now, I bear no ill will toward Señor López. If you happen to enjoy Coco López, by all means, have at it. Certainly, the version that Isaac was blending up for Charo on the lido deck of the Love Boat was loaded with coconut cream, and we all still love Isaac. But perhaps I can persuade you to try a lighter, fresher, and more pineapple-y version of the drink.

But first, I think we should delve into the somewhat murky history of the piña colada. It has been deemed the official drink of Puerto Rico, and during the 1950s a number of the island's hotel bartenders claimed they created it. The most oft-repeated story is that the drink was invented at the Caribe Hilton Hotel. As legend has it, one night in 1954—during a strike of coconut cutters, no less—a bartender cut the top off a pineapple, hollowed out the fruit, dumped in Coco López mix and rum, and served it with a straw. It may or may not be a coincidence that Coco López came on the market around 1954.

Truth be told, all of those Puerto Rican claims are dubious. There are references to the piña colada in periodicals and books in the 1920s and 1930s, and most point to Cuba as its origin and pineapple as the primary ingredient. Even Trader Vic's classic bartending guide included a piña colada recipe containing only rum and pineapple juice. Meanwhile, a Trader Vic drink called a Bahia, with coconut cream, more closely mirrors the modern-day piña colada. Regardless, the cream-of-coconut version became the one that captured the fancy of Americans. In the 1970s and 1980s, heavy cream and dark rum were added to the mix, and we had the supersweet, milkshakelike libation that became the clichéd standard. This, of course, was the Tom Cruise in *Cocktail* era, when cocktails in general became so cloyingly sweet.

When it comes to making a piña colada, I want to preach two things: fresh pineapple juice, and coconut water instead of coconut cream. No Coco López. For the purest piña colada, I favor a recipe of three parts pineapple juice, one part coconut water, and one part rum. With that basic 3:1:1 ratio, you'll discover a drink that's a world away from what typically comes out of the blender. I usually don't strain my pineapple juice after pureeing it (making mine a *piña sin colar*, I guess) since I think this helps the drink holds together a little better. For the coconut element, coconut water gives the drink a lighter, more complex, nuttier flavor. You can make piña coladas with all types of rums, but my favorite version uses rhum agricole, the Martinique rum made from pure sugarcane juice, from brands such as Rhum Clément and Neisson. The fresh cane notes mingle well with the pineapple and coconut and add a level of—dare I say it—sophistication.

PIÑA COLADA

Serves 4

> **¹/₂ pineapple, peeled, cored, and cut into chunks, plus 4 small slices for garnish**
> **4 ounces white rhum agricole**
> **4 ounces coconut water, such as Zico or Vita Coco**
> **3 cups ice cubes**

Place the pineapple chunks in a blender and puree. Measure out 1¹/₂ cups (12 ounces), then freeze any leftover puree for another use. Combine the pineapple puree, rum, and coconut water in a blender, then add the ice. Blend on high speed for about 1 minute. Pour into 4 Collins glasses. Garnish each with a pineapple slice, and serve with straws.

CHAPTER 9

THE ANGELS' SHARE

EXUBERANCE IS BETTER THAN TASTE.

—Gustave Flaubert

I DON'T KNOW WHY I WENT TO the Hemingway Bar during my last trip to Paris, but I did. Maybe I wanted to see if there were still Americans who bought into that old 1920s fantasy vision of Paris. Or maybe I was just looking for trouble. Anyway, let me be clear, the only reason to go to the Hemingway Bar, which is in the Ritz Hotel, is to watch utter ridiculousness in action. Cocktails at the Hemingway Bar start at €30. Glasses of 1834 cognac sell for €1,250. The Guinness-certified "world's most expensive cocktail," the Ritz Sidecar (with caviar), sells for €1,250. On the walls hang tons of Hemingway memorabilia, including a creepy photo of Papa, ailing, without a beard, from the late 1950s, and, disturbingly, his twelve-gauge Browning rifle mounted above the bar—which may or may not be in poor taste seeing as a gun like this is how the man killed himself. I ordered a Leperliac, purportedly "a hunting cocktail created in the Armagnac country," which called for Armagnac, mint, "white French clarified grape juice," and champagne. Okay, I thought, for €30 they must have at least pressed the grape juice themselves, right? No. Pierre, the bartender, grabbed a plastic bottle of store-bought grape juice, the French version of Welch's, and poured it into the shaker, along with a weak, free pour of the brandy and the sparkling wine. He offered me a newspaper and chips, as if that would make up for things.

As I was drinking my banal Leperliac, I felt someone rub my back and ask me to scoot over one bar stool. It was an American woman from Manhattan named Joy, seventyish but you could tell she'd been a beauty in her day. Joy was accompanied by a slightly younger couple from South Carolina. The husband told me he was "in the timber and real estate business." Joy took my hand as if I were her oldest confidant and whispered in my ear, "I've known these people for years and I can never understand a word they say." My newspaper was open on the bar, to an article about the president, and Joy whispered, "We don't really like Obama. But my father always said, 'Don't talk politics or religion.'" They'd all flown in to Paris for the weekend, for a friend's birthday, and had been staying at the Ritz.

These people could have been minor characters out of *The Sun Also Rises*, or one of Fitzgerald's novels, except for one major omission: they knew very little about their liquor. They'd been served by the white-jacketed charlatan Pierre the night before, and Joy clearly was charmed. "How does he just know all the measurements?" she squealed. "Isn't he just the best bartender?"

The guy from South Carolina didn't know what he wanted. "Grey Goose and a squeeze of lemon is usually my fly-fishing drink," he said. Then he halfheartedly told me he liked whiskey. Since I was about to visit Normandy the next day, I suggested maybe he should try a Calvados. "What is that?" he said. Pierre served him a small glass, and the guy winced: "Wow, that's got some real vapors."

"Don't get those French 75s like Pierre made us last night," said Joy "Those will put you under the bar."

At which point, I knocked over the remainder of my €30 drink onto the bar. "Look," Joy said, "I've made him nervous." She whispered, "Are you staying at the hotel?"

"No," I said. "Seven hundred euros a night is a little rich for me."

"Seven hundred! You couldn't get a very good room for that!"

Did people like this still exist in 2009? They clearly did. And some of them still tossed good money at spirits. In December of 2009, the landmark 427-year-old Parisian restaurant La Tour d'Argent cleaned out its cellar and auctioned off eighteen thousand bottles, including some extremely rare bottles of cognac. Three bottles, dating to 1788, sold respectively for $37,000, $31,000, and $27,300. The same week, at Christie's in New York, a bottle of fifty-year-old Glennfiddich Scotch sold at auction for $38,000. Just over a week later, Bonhams in New York auctioned off the coveted Willard S. Folsom Collection of Old and Rare Whiskies. Among the 895 bottles on sale, more than fifty Scotches sold for at least $1,000 apiece—including a fifty-year-old Dalmore and a fifty-year-old Balvenie, each of which sold for over $7,000. This flurry of high bidding had raised a few questions for me. Such as: Isn't there a financial crisis going on? Or: Why does the value of booze go up while the value of my portfolio remains in the toilet? Or: Have spirits become better investments than real estate, classic automobiles, and fine art?

I'd visited France a few months prior to those big sales, in September, and I was there to witness a different auction, the annual La Part des Anges auction in Cognac. At La Part des Anges, the bigwigs of the local spirits industry bid on very rare cognacs—the name means "The Angels' Share," the nickname for the amount of the cognac that evaporates in a barrel as it ages over decades. But before I headed to Cognac, I had a stopover in Paris and then planned to visit Guillaume Drouin's Calvados distillery just before the September apple harvest was about to begin.

While in Paris, I stopped in at Au Verger de la Madeleine, a well-respected dealer in rare wines and spirits. I wanted to play some real Liquor Store Archaeology: I'd come looking for the coveted Chartreuse Tarragona, the version that had been made in Spain from 1903, when the Chartreuse monks were expelled from France, until 1989, when the monks closed the distillery. Olivier Madinier, one of Au Verger de la Madeleine's managing partners, told me he had three bottles in his cellar. It was the middle of a Saturday afternoon, but he rolled down the gate and locked up the shop, then he and I descended into the dank, dusty cellar in a tiny elevator. We strolled past rows of thousand-euro bottles of Bordeaux, and then there were the bottles of Tarragona I'd heard so much about. Three of them. Each selling for eight hundred euros. Calling them "mythic," Madinier said, "For connoisseurs, it's more complex. It's rare, but it's good to drink. This is very important for us. Our clients are not only collectors. They like to drink the spirits." I told him I wholeheartedly endorsed this philosophy. Madinier held one of the Tarragonas in his hands, and I prayed silently that maybe he might pop it open and give me a taste. I'm not sure whether or not he thought I might buy a bottle—I wish I could have, but eight hundred euros is too rich for my blood. So Madinier and I stood silently for an awkward moment. Then he put the bottle back, we crowded into the little elevator and went back upstairs, and he reopened the shop.

I showed Madinier my auction catalog for La Part des Anges. Some of the estimated cognac prices seemed outrageous: a Frapin for €2,800, a Pierre Ferrand for €3,000, a Martell for €3,500. He paged through the catalog quickly and shrugged, seeming to say, "nothing special here." A dozen or cognacs with several-thousand-dollar price tags sat on his shelves, including a Delamain (Le Voyage) in a Baccarat crystal decanter for €6,500. Madinier told me that collectors certainly like to buy these pricey bottles. But if someone comes in and just wants a cognac to enjoy, he often steers them toward something like Jean Fillioux Rèserve Famil-iale. At around $200, it's definitely pricey as hell, but it feels like a down-right bargain compared to those at auction. "If you like to drink cognac, this is what we recommend," he said of Fillioux's family reserve.

Madinier pointed to a bottle of Delamain from 1840 on his shelves. "We once opened a bottle of this." He sighed. "Only a few hours later, it was bad." He let that fact silently sink in for a moment.

"Why?" I said.

"I don't know," he said, with a shrug. "Maybe it was the keeping. But at the end of the day, it was bad." With a chuckle he said, "I guess you have to drink it rapidly. I got to taste some before it went bad."

"How was it different?" I asked.

"There are so many different flavors. Leather . . ." Then he just clammed up, as if even trying to put words to the taste would be a kind of heresy. "There are flavors you just can't find in a younger cognac," he said.

I stared dumbly at him. I hoped he'd go on. "Really?" I said, not knowing what to say,

"Yes," he said. "It was . . . amazing."

"Well," I said, "it sounds like maybe it's impossible to describe?" No response.

"So . . . would you say that it's impossible to describe?"

He now looked at me as if I were profoundly stupid. "Yes." And that was all he said.

This, of course, was nothing new. One way or another, I always feel stupid when I'm in Paris. I have a long history of it.

The first time I had a "legal" drink was in Paris, on the French Club's trip to France during my senior year of high school. I finagled my way onto the trip: I hadn't taken French and knew not one word of French, but there were open slots and a girl I really liked named V. was going. Her boyfriend, however, was not. This was my very first trip outside of the United States, and it surprises me how little I recall of the travel itself. Of course, it was mostly a forgettable tour-bus hell. I do remember being given seventeen minutes at the Louvre and then over two hours at a department store called Printemps. But the most significant thing about this trip was that, though we all were eighteen, or younger, our parents had signed permission slips stating that, given France's more liberal liquor laws, we were allowed to drink alcoholic beverages—hard to believe in this age of extreme sensitivity to legal liability, but things were a little different in the 1980s. Anyway, the idea was that we students would enjoy a *moderate* amount of wine with dinner, and this would enhance our immersion into French culture. That was the theory.

In practice, here's what happened: On the morning of our arrival, almost as soon as we checked into our hotel, more than two dozen hormone-crazed teenagers marched to the nearest supermarket, loaded up on beer and vodka, and stashed it in our hotel rooms for later. At dinner that first night, in a bland, overpriced restaurant full of other tour-bus groups, we sipped the obligatory table wine. Then, when our teacher-chaperones suggested some kind of moonlight boat ride on the Seine or whatever, the majority of us did a big pretend yawn—*Oh, the jet lag . . . I think I need to go back to the hotel.* Luckily, some of the teetotalers agreed to go with the chaperones. The rest of us made a beeline back to the hotel, where a raging party quickly got underway, and within thirty minutes we had the angry hotel manager shouting threats at us.

Our hotel must have been in the Ninth Arrondissement, because it was only a short walk to the notorious nightclub district of Pigalle. After the hotel manager's threatening outburst, a group of kids started saying, "Dude, let's go to those bars we saw in Pig Alley!" V. and her friends were going, and so I followed along. I remember wandering through a seedy square with lots of flashing neon and signs for XXX live nude shows and guys playing accordion on the street and shady touts trying to get us to come inside this club or that. It was like nowhere I'd ever been before, but it also wasn't entirely foreign. Here's the thing: I was a good, dutiful, honors student. I'd read all the books the teachers had assigned and looked at all the paintings they'd told us to, including the ones which depicted a decadent and depraved Paris. I was not quite eighteen, and still blissfully unaware of so many things—including how awful and touristy Pigalle is—but it all felt immediately like something familiar, somewhere I wanted to be.

This was long before the days when everyone had a digital camera or a Facebook page, so I have no photos of this evening, but I can vividly imagine what our small band of a half dozen high school students from the Jersey suburbs must have looked like: big hair and banana clips and tight acid-washed jeans for the girls; mullets and kelly green varsity jackets and tuck-and-roll jeans for the boys. Inside a random bar—where, I swear to god, they were playing what I now know was Edith Piaf—we ordered beers, and a crew of dodgy middle-aged Frenchmen got very interested in the girls. These guys were classic: thin mustaches and scarves, smoking by inhaling through their noses. "You make kiss with me and I buy you drink," one said to V.'s friend. She did, and the men started buying us all drinks. Weird drinks: pastis, Suze, Chartreuse. Drinks we'd never heard of. Drinks that forced us to make a face, which of course delighted these middle-aged Frenchmen. After our third pastis, I remember telling V., like a jaded man of the world, "This isn't so bad; it's like sambuca." Soon enough, the Frenchmen got a little grabby, and one of my classmates in his varsity jacket got a little chippy and threatened to kick "some French ass," and so we decided it was time to leave the bar and return to the hotel.

We walked back through the chaos swirling around Pigalle, in the glow of the pastis. As we walked by a transvestite club, one of the guys in the varsity jackets yelled, "Dude, those girls are guys!"

"Oh, relax, dude," I said. I had V. on my arm—she'd made it clear the boyfriend at home was no longer an issue, and that what happened in Paris would stay in Paris. All it took was three pastis and we'd thrown off the shackles of our bourgeois suburban existence. We were freakin' Continental now. If someone had given me a Gauloise, I would have smoked by inhaling through my nose.

Back at the hotel, I crawled into bed with V. as her friend slept in the bed next to us. We kissed and began to strip. Wow, this was going straight from naughty Moulin Rouge to full-on Henry Miller! But within four minutes reality intervened, and the teacher-chaperones were banging on the door. And then I was out in the hallway, half-dressed, being yelled at by the French teacher, who was threatening to send me home. Apparently, our permission slips only covered so much decadence.

After Paris, I headed off to drink Calvados in Normandy, which I'd been looking forward to for a long time. Some years before I'd taken on the spirits beat, near the end of a tedious and unsuccessful autumn work trip, I found myself dining alone in the Italian restaurant of an airport hotel in Lyon, France. It wasn't a bad restaurant, but neither was it uplifting. I ate a passable lasagna and drank an average Rhone red as I and the other solitary diners silently watched the bar's television, where a soccer game was mired in a scoreless tie. For days, it had been cold and rainy, and I was pretty depressed.

Then came the dessert menu. I don't often order dessert, but at that moment I also did not want to go back to my room. So I ordered tarte Tatin. And then, scanning the after-dinner drinks list, I lighted upon Calvados, which at that time I'd never tasted. All I knew was that Calvados was an apple brandy from Normandy, and because I had already been thinking about apples for dessert, I ordered one. The tarte Tatin arrived, and it was okay. Then came the Calvados, a Christian Drouin Hors d'Age. From the initial swirl, sniff, and swallow, the liquid was a revelation to me: love at first sip. Suddenly, I felt warm and happy, and I laughed at myself for being down. I mean, please, I was on a business trip to France, not Des Moines. I must have spent the entire second half of the soccer game with that glass, and I went back to my room a little less lonely.

I tell that anecdote chiefly because I'd like to suggest that more restaurants take better care in developing their after-dinner drinks menus. Where else are people supposed to learn to taste fine, top-end spirits? Yet there frequently is a lack of creativity or even thought put into these offerings. A fine restaurant that would never think of putting a middling bottle on its wine list or a banal drink on its cocktail menu will too often stock the after-dinner menu with boring, overpriced staples. How many have interesting eaux-de-vie, or aged rums, or extra-añejo tequilas, or cask-aged Norwegian aquavits, or amari, or fortified wines that aren't port or sherry? Perhaps the after-dinner drinks menu is too often left to the sommeliers, many of whom—even some of the best, it must be said—suffer from a lack of spirits knowledge. Maybe the bartender should usurp this job from the sommelier. Anyway, that night in the airport hotel started me on a journey that resulted in Calvados becoming one of my favorite spirits—and perhaps my absolute favorite during the colder months.

I will admit I was predisposed to liking Calvados. I'd already had an apple brandy in my life: New Jersey's finest homegrown spirit, Laird's straight apple brandy. I came of age on Laird's applejack (aka Jersey Lightning), a blend of apple brandy and neutral spirits that is the less expensive cousin of apple brandy. I have a friend, Larry, who grew up near the Laird's farm and actually visited it on a fourth-grade field trip. And so, when I sip Laird's apple brandy—even the excellent aged versions—I'm still taken back to concealed flasks at bonfire pep rallies and homecoming games.

I find it unfortunate that applejack and apple brandy are not more widely embraced by contemporary drinkers. Applejack is essential in two classic cocktails, the Jack Rose and the Pink Lady. And back in the eighteenth century, it played a key role in our young nation's drinking life. A mug of applejack was a fairly common morning tipple for the colonists, and Laird's, in business since 1780, is the country's oldest distillery. George Washington wrote the Laird family asking for its applejack recipe, and Abraham Lincoln served applejack for twelve cents a glass in his Springfield, Illinois, tavern.

Although I love Laird's, once in a while, like our Founding Fathers, I am nagged by the idea that I'm somehow not as cultured as I should be. And so, like Jefferson and Franklin, I began looking toward France— although in this case it was merely to take the next step toward the world's finest apple brandy. Calvados was declared by Liebling, in *Between Meals*, to be "the best alcohol in the world." In Liebling's opinion, Calvados "has a more agreeable bouquet, a warmer touch to the heart, and more outgoing personality than cognac." Though he did admit that "not everybody has had the advantage of a good early soaking in the blessed liquid."

I arrived at the Drouin distillery—which produces both the Coeur de Lion and Comte Louis de Lauriston brands—near the town of Pont-l'Évêque on a beautiful September afternoon. Calvados can be produced in only three AOCs in Lower Normandy, where it is distilled from fermented cider that's pressed from about fifty local apple varieties. Pays d'Auge, where Drouin is located, is considered to be the finest Calvados AOC in Normandy.

Guillaume Drouin, thirty-one years old, is one of several Calvados distillers in Normandy, all of them part of a new generation in their twenties and thirties who have taken the reins of their family distilleries. I also visited thirty-nine-year-old Jérôme Dupont, who will take over for his father at Etienne Dupont, and Jean-Roger Groult, the twenty-seven-year-old heir at Roger Groult. This youth movement in Normandy feels timely and important, especially because Calvados's reputation has suffered over the years, even in France.

Fifty years ago, there were two thousand Calvados producers. Now there are only about one hundred. In the eighteenth century, Calvados was widely exported, even more so than cognac. But, according to Drouin, King Louis XIV, who was a friend of the cognac industry, made a decree that Calvados could not be exported, and could only be sold in Normandy. By the early twentieth century, 90 percent of Calvados was made by farmers for personal consumption and was drunk unaged. If a farmer did put Calvados in a barrel to age, it was as an investment for his old age, when it would be sold to a big producer. Jérôme Dupont, for instance, talked me about his grandmother inheriting barrels of his grandfather's Calvados, which were seen as "savings."

"Calvados has a bad image in France because there was a lot of shitty Calvados on the market for years," Drouin said. "My father's generation thinks Calvados is a drink for eighty-year-olds, because that's what our grandfathers drank. But the generation that takes Calvados in their morning coffee is disappearing. People my age, they have absolutely no opinion on Calvados. So maybe there's an opportunity there." I saw the challenge firsthand one night in the nearby seaside town of Trouville, where Drouin and Jean-Roger Groult were pouring Calvados-and-tonics during a party at a trendy bar. Just the week before, the local newspaper had featured the "New Generation of Calvados," and the producers had cringed because the journalist used the old slang term *calva*, with its connotations of moonshine. But when I asked some young partygoers if calva meant anything to them, they told me, "Nah. Calvados, calva, it doesn't mean anything except something to drink." And this, I remind you, was in Normandy.

Drouin took me out into his family's orchard, where he showed me some of the tiny, odd varieties of apples used to make Calvados. These are not shiny supermarket apples for eating out of hand or baking a pie with. They're blemished and often bitter tasting—in fact, of the dozens of varieties that grow in Normandy, about 70 percent are bitter or bitter-sweet. The apples are fermented into cider, which is then distilled twice and put into a barrel to age.

"The way people make cider is very empirical," Drouin said. "There is no scientific knowledge. I am trained as an oenologist. I've been working with wine, but I've never faced a challenge like making cider." Besides working for Barbancourt in Haiti, Drouin had worked as a winemaker in the Languedoc region as well as in Australia and South Africa. So when he returned home, he thought he had Calvados all figured out. "I was so overconfident, I lost half of the cider because I thought I knew what I was doing." One major mistake is that Drouin used too many sweet varieties in his blend, and his cider lacked the tannins and structure that would protect it against oxidation. After that first year—and after facing the wrath of his father—he began respecting the traditions. At least a little more. He is still applying his training with innovations such as finishing the spirit in port and sherry casks, and even in casks previously used for the fortified wine Banyuls.

"Usually people who like Calvados like spirits with personality," Drouin said. "Calvados has a strong personality." We hear so much about Scotch and cognac, and rightly so. But Calvados provides a similarly sophisticated and complex experience. Calvados can be expensive: Drouin's Hors d'Age sells for around $80; good vintages can sell from $200 to $500; and I once saw an 1865 Calvados from Huet on the shelf at Au Verger de la Madeleine for €2,800. Still, the basic reserve is much more affordable than cognac or Scotch. For the most part, Calvados is more modest. It's usually described as "rustic" and having a "big heart," and though these are clichés, they're also pretty true. It evolves in the glass as few spirits do. With a good Calvados, you sip and then smell and sip again two minutes later or ten minutes later or twenty minutes later. Each time, it's as if you're drinking a different brandy. "If I really want to understand a spirit," Drouin said, "give me a bottle, two hours, and a good friend."

Drouin and I spent a good two hours tasting through a wide range of his Calvados. The most memorable were the vintages, particularly the 1973 and the 1963. Of the 1973, Drouin said, "This is a classic. If someone says they want an old-style Calvados, this is it." As for the 1963, it was honestly one of the strangest, most complex spirits I'd ever tasted— forest, mushroom, spice, but also crisp, tart apple notes, and then a long, mellow finish that lasted in the mouth for hours. It was one of the greatest things I've ever sipped, and it shows how significantly aging transforms a spirit. "This is a whole meal in a glass," Drouin said. "When this was younger, it was probably volatile and unbalanced. But taste it now!" I can only hope to age this well myself. Even Pacult called the 1963 "a bona fide masterpiece . . . will live long in my memory as one of the greatest spirits/brandy experiences I've ever had."

But Drouin's finale may have outdone the 1963: we tasted his 1939 vintage. "This is one of the rarest in the world," Drouin said. "It's the only Calvados on the market that's certified from before the Second World War." That, of course, is because when the region was occupied, whatever the Germans didn't destroy, they drank.

Later, when I met Drouin's father, Christian, he told me that Calvados has always been a hard sell in the United States. "When I first started selling Calvados in the States, I would meet veterans who knew it as a harsh spirit," the elder Drouin said. "They would write letters home about this fierce apple spirit." I did not doubt this story. When I published a column on Calvados, I received a number of emails from WWII veterans like this one:

> I was in a small town in France, near the Belgium border on Christmas
> Day 1944. (I was with the 17th Airborne Division trudging through
> the snow to keep the German Army from reaching the Meuse River.)

Since the GIs in my squad knew I could speak a few words of French, they asked me to find someone who could get us some wine or other alcoholic spirits to celebrate the occasion. Unfortunately, there were no adult males in the town (due to German murder of civilians) who could fill our request. I asked an eight-year-old boy with whom I became very friendly. I don't know where he went but he returned with two bottles of Calvados! We had to pay $10 a bottle . . . but it was worth every penny! One bottle we had to give to our Platoon Leader-Lieutenant. Perhaps, it wasn't the best Calvados . . . It was quite strong . . . but very good.

Still, the younger Drouin seemed excited about the prospects for a new wave of Calvados in the States. "In America," he said, "people may not know anything about spirits. But at least they're excited to learn. In France, people think they know everything, but they don't."

"I used to think Calvados was something second to wine," Guillaume said. "To be honest, when I was younger, I was a snob. Then I had some wine friends taste my father's Calvados, and they were, like, 'Oh, my gosh, I can't believe your family makes this. It's so complex and amazing.'" He grabbed a bottle of the 1973 vintage. "Look," he said. "This is simply more complex than wine, more complex than a Lafite Rothschild."

Despite the spirit's sophistication, what struck me most about visiting these distillers in Normandy was their total lack of pretentiousness. At Groult, for instance, Jean-Roger still uses wood fire to fuel the stills. "I learned from my father and he from his father. We like to keep this . . . *savoir-faire*." Groult also uses decades-old barrels that are never quite empty, meaning the rootstock, too, may be decades old.

While I was visiting Groult, Jean-Roger's sister, Estelle, stopped by the tasting room with an apple pie she had just baked. I ate the pie, and I sipped Groult's lovely thirty-plus-year-old Doyen d'Age. From the tasting room, we could see apples ripening, ready to fall from the trees. The wood fire burned in the distillery room. The Calvados was aging quietly in the dark rooms as it had for decades. That moment represented everything I love and admire about fine spirits.

So many of the things people value are hard to define. In the fall of 2008, I attended the famed white truffle festival in Alba, Italy. For several days, a friend and I ate truffle shaved on more things than seemed reasonable or necessary (one €35 dish was simply truffle shaved on a baked egg), wandered among the truffle hunters in a very pungent convention center, and debated endlessly how to describe the white-truffle experience. We tossed around the usual descriptors: earthy, woody, rooty, garlicky, foresty. We chuckled about the unfortunate comparison once used by food writer Corby Kummer in *Gourmet* magazine to describe his first taste of truffle as a youth: "It tasted of parts of the body I urgently wanted to know better." But in the end, we agreed that part of the fungus's allure was that it defied description.

That's why, the first time I visited Cognac, I was happy to discover the concept of *rancio*. Rancio is the term for a peculiar flavor that the finest cognac takes on as it ages. It is, of course, impossible to describe. Nutty? Mushroomy? Cheesy? Gary Regan, author of the classic *The Joy of Mixology*, calls rancio "lactic" and likens it to the flavor of soy sauce; I do not disagree, though there also might be hints of toffee or almond. Beyond flavor, rancio also connotes a certain mouthfeel—the way the cognac presents on the tongue and finishes with an almost walnutlike oiliness.

Even for cognac producers, rancio is hard to describe. "It's a special taste," said Pascal Dagnaud, the master distiller at the small but highly regarded Ragnaud-Sabourin. "It's close to caramel, but a little bitter. It tastes a little like a bitter nut. It's a special taste."

At Ragnaud-Sabourin and Jean Fillioux, rancio was present in several offerings I tasted, as were dried fruit, spices, and dark chocolate. Rancio was most pronounced in Jean Fillioux's Cigar Club—and indeed in its Rèserve Familiale—and in Ragnaud-Sabourin's forty-five-year-old Florilège and Le Paradis, the last a blend of mostly century-old cognac with a small percentage of eau-de-vie that predated the mid-nineteenth-century phylloxera blight that destroyed so many European vineyards. These cognacs were as close to perfection as a distilled spirit could be.

One doesn't have to go to France to experience rancio, but sadly, in the States there are impediments. Cognac remains a mystery here for a few reasons. First, the really good stuff can be prohibitively priced. Case in point: Le Paradis will set you back about, oh, seven hundred dollars or so. Most of the cognac sold in the United States is either VS or VSOP. In very few cases do cognacs in those categories exhibit the elusive rancio, which generally appears after a decade or more of aging (and which, to me, is what separates a cognac you'd sip from one you'd mix in a cocktail). That is perhaps why boutique producers often do not make a VSOP. If you want to taste a bit of rancio on the cheap, something like Martell Medaillon VSOP or Hine Rare VSOP (both about forty dollars) are good. Otherwise, it might pay to invest eighty dollars or more in a bottle of XO. It's expensive, but it should last you a long time.

My first visit to Cognac came during strange, jittery times: just as recession was setting in. The "big four" cognac producers—Courvoisier, Hennessy, Martell, and Rémy Martin—had been riding high in recent years, with sales growing about 37 percent between 2001 and 2007. Cognac's popularity within youthful hip-hop culture generally is credited with the spirit's resurgence in the United States. In 2008, however, cognac sales stalled, and the larger producers organized what was called the International Cognac Summit to address the changing nature of cognac drinking, specifically the shift from after-dinner sipping among an older generation to its use in cocktails among a younger one. A team of international bartenders created a new cocktail, the Summit, as a symbol of that recognition.

I asked the distillers at Ragnaud-Sabourin and Jean Fillioux how they felt about the new focus on cocktails. Is it a good thing? "We're not interested in knowing whether it's a good thing or not," Dagnaud said.

When I posed the same question to master distiller Pascal Fillioux, he said simply, "I am not a mixologist. I like to drink cognac."

Other people I met in Cognac expressed unease. "I'm concerned about the future of cognac," said Véronique Reboul, who with her husband, Alain, grows wine grapes for several large cognac producers. We sat in their courtyard one afternoon, sipped Pineau de Charentes, the local aperitif. The Rebouls were big fans of Texas, having visited fledgling winemakers there in Cognac's sister city, Denison. There was a Citroën parked in the courtyard with a "Don't Mess With Texas" bumper sticker. "The younger generation is more interested in vodka. They perceive cognac to be Granddad's alcohol," said Véronique. "They perceive it to be expensive." Throughout France, throughout the world, I'd of course heard the same theme.

Back in the mid-2000s, before governments had more important things to worry about, a vodka war raged within the European Union. The so-called Vodka Belt countries of central and eastern Europe and Scandinavia declared that the spirit could be made only from grain or potatoes. A Finnish-backed proposal in the European Parliament sought to block distillers in the Netherlands, the United Kingdom, and France from calling their spirits "vodka" if they used nontraditional ingredients, such as fruit. The stakes were not small. Vodka, after all, is a twelve-billion-dollar worldwide industry.

In the end, the upstart nations prevailed, and they continue to sell their spirits as vodka. "Vodka War Lost," read the headline in the *Warsaw Voice*. "Would the French like champagne to be distilled from plums, and would the British accept whisky from apricots?" scoffed one Polish parliamentarian, who vowed to fight on.

Normally, stuff like disrespecting terroir gets blamed on Americans. So it was a small relief—a pleasure, really—to see the French get dragged into the fray. As they should have been. Some of the biggest names in the vodka business—Grey Goose, Cîroc, Citadelle—are produced around the legendary French distilling town of Cognac. To be fair, Grey Goose (created in 1997 specifically by Sidney Frank for the American market) and Citadelle are made with a traditional ingredient, wheat. But Cîroc and others use grapes in the distilling process. One can only imagine what sort of war France might wage if someone started bottling and selling a "cognac" from, say, West Virginia (perhaps made from ramps).

Of course, with the wild success of Grey Goose, many others have tried to capture the Cognac vodka magic. In early 2010, Sam's Club introduced a new vodka called Rue 33. According to Sam's Club, this vodka is "ultra premium" and "six times distilled and three times filtered." It is made in Cognac, France, just like Grey Goose, but true to Sam Club's form, this six-time distilled, ultra-premium vodka will be sold, economy-sized, in 1.75-liter bottles. Now, no matter how much eye-rolling goes on about romantic stories of elderflowers or monks or deer's blood, they're all a hell of lot better than, say, a boardroom-driven tale that goes, "Let's create some booze we can sell two aisles over from the diapers and the kitty litter, in 1.75-liter containers, at the seemingly affordable yet actually ridiculous price point of twenty-eight dollars."

But vodka is only the tip of the iceberg in Cognac. On one of my trips, I visited EuroWineGate, which most notably produces G'Vine gins as well as vodka. Company director Jean-Sébastien Robicquet is representative of a new generation of distillers who are trying to stay a step ahead of critics and trends. Robicquet worked for Hennessey and Hine before moving into white spirits and developing Cîroc—partnering with P. Diddy as the pitchman. Five years ago, as the vodka market became saturated, he saw an opportunity with gin, which also can be made from varying ingredients.

G'Vine uses green grape flowers, which were being snipped from the vine while I was there, as part of its botanical infusion. That goes against both the gin-making and wine-grape traditions in Cognac. The Rebouls were among the first vineyard owners to allow G'Vine to use their flowers. "I was under a confidentiality agreement, so I didn't say anything," Alain Reboul said. "But this is a very small town, and my neighbors were curious and were spying on me. The rumor was that I'd been working for a cosmetic company!"

The first G'Vine gin, Floraison, relied heavily on floral notes. Paul Pacult published a positive four-out-of-five-stars review, but wrote that he wished the distiller would "elevate the alcohol level" and "tone down the floral aspects one notch." So Robicquet adjusted the recipe for his second gin, the wonderful Nouaison, which has a stronger juniper kick.

"Pacult said we needed more juniper and a higher alcohol content. So we gave it to him. We've left him no choice but to give us five stars," Robicquet said, with a wink. Pacult winked back, giving them four stars again in *Spirit Journal*, only this time adding, "if I bestowed half stars, which I don't, I'd rate Nouaison Four and a Half." D'oh!

But the gin market was swiftly becoming saturated, and Robicquet was already brainstorming in different spirit categories. "All the know-how is grouped here in Cognac," he said. "People here know how to distill, how to bottle, how to express the greatest qualities of a product. If they can do it with cognac, there's no reason why they can't do it with any other spirit."

During my visit, Robicquet was checking out an experiment involving merlot grape flowers. After several attempts, he'd finally been able to extract the flavor he wanted. The success moved him nearly to tears, and he broke out champagne for his staff. "What will you do with this?" I asked. "Make another vodka?"

"No," he said.

"A gin?"

"No."

"An aperitif?"

"Who knows?" he said. "Something new."

A year later, I would meet him at Tales of the Cocktail. He would be presenting a tequila, in partnership with Carlos Camarena of El Tesoro, in which the tequila has been aged in Sauternes and cognac casks. A French tequila?

While in Cognac for La Part des Anges, I visited one day with Patrick Peyrelongue, the president of Delamain Cognac. Delamain is located in the small town of Jarnac, along the Charente River. A telltale black fungus that lives on cognac vapors coats most of the building facades as you walk the narrow streets.

Peyrelongue took me on a tour of his cellars. The key to making cognac, like many spirits, is in aging and blending. Delamain, like most houses, buys barrels of wine or eau-de-vie from growers, like the Rebouls. As with Calvados and its Pays d'Auge, Cognac has a sweet spot region within its AOC called Grand Champagne, and Delamain only uses wine from grapes grown in Grand Champagne. At a certain stage, the casks are sealed with red wax and locked in a room with two keys, one for the distiller and another for the BNIC (*Bureau National Interprofessionnel du Cognac*), the authority that governs the cognac industry. "I cannot get into my own casks," Peyrelongue said.

Peyrelongue popped open a cask dating from 1952 that was not locked up and poured me a glass. I tasted in the cool cellar. It was unbelievably smooth, and the hard-to-place rancio flavor and character were unmistakable. And it hadn't even had a chance to open up yet. "That's the magic of cognac," he said. "Early on, you take an undrinkable wine, and then you age it in a barrel. And fifty years later, you have a cognac like this. With a glass like this, you can spend a whole evening with it, warming it, smelling it, seeing how it changes. Unfortunately, it is nearly impossible to find a cognac like this, unless you want to pay so much money."

In his office, we tasted through much of Delamain's portfolio. The youngest cognac they release is an XO, which averages twenty-five years or more in the barrel. Consider that for a moment: even a cognac that has aged for two decades would not be ready for that blend. "It's still too young for us. Too much wood still," Peyrelongue said. Then we moved on to the Très Vénérable. "Very delicate, like a flower. When women say, 'Oh, I don't like cognac, it burns.' I tell them to try a glass of this."

"How much is this cognac?" I asked.

"Oh, I don't know," Peyrelongue said, with a dismissive wave.

"No, really," I said. "What price do you sell this for?"

He shrugged his shoulders. Now, for the record, I can tell you that the Delamain XO goes for about $100 and the Très Vénérable for about $250. Why I can find that in three seconds on Google but the president of the company didn't know is a mystery. Peyrelongue's indifference to price continued to bother me for the rest of my visit to Cognac.

On the afternoon before the auction, Delamain's neighbor in Jarnac, giant Courvoisier, held a press conference to unveil its L'Essence de Courvoisier, which would go on sale in only one store in the world, Harrods of London, for £1,800 (about $2,850). I immediately texted my editor: "Hey, Courvoisier's showing off a cognac that costs £1,800. Can I expense one?"

"Yeah, sure," he very snidely texted back. "Why not pick up two?"

Meanwhile, the crowd was gushing over the Baccarat crystal decanter suspended on a metal hoop. "Look at the bottle! How gorgeous!"

"But what about the liquid inside?" I asked.

"It doesn't really seem to matter," grumbled one of the other journalists. This is my main beef with expensive cognac in particular. Much of the perceived value is in the limited edition crystal decanter, with designs by Baccarat or Erté or Sèvres or whatever.

There is a delusional aspect to the cognac category's marketing, with its air of unattainable affluence and sophistication on one hand, and on the other, its dogged attempts to connect cognac with the general consumer. Only an hour before the unveiling of L'Essence de Courvoisier, the master distiller told me that Courvoisier Exclusif, which retails at around $45 to $50, was the best for mixing and that "bartenders like to use it behind the bar." First of all, there are definitely better mixing cognacs than this at the same price, or cheaper. But beyond that, if I want an affordable alternative, I can use a good brandy from somewhere else—say, a $25 Asbach Uralt from Germany or the best Spanish brandies at around $30—to mix in a Sidecar or a Stinger. When I suggested noncognac brandy alternatives to the representative for BNIC, the cognac authority, he said, "Ouch."

This is not a knock on cognac, which I enjoy very much. But the cold, hard reality is that good cognac is expensive. An investment, really. But at what return?

I don't know if I got any answers that night at the big La Part des Anges auction. The affair was black-tie—though in my case and the case of the other journalists in attendance, black-tie meant "wear a jacket for god's sake, and just don't embarrass yourself!"

The affair was on the banks of the Charente River, and boats ferried people across to the party. The Summit cocktail was served outside, amid dancing water, a string quartet, fireworks, and a shirtless man who danced with fire. Then we all went inside a gigantic tent for dinner and an auction. Through dinner, I was sitting with some people from Rémy Martin, a local car dealership, and the owners of a local bed-and-breakfast. But then, oddly, some condensation formed on the tent above me, and it started "raining" inside—on my head.

So as the auction was beginning, I decamped to another table, where some fellow writers were sitting with Alexandre Gabriel, the president of Pierre Ferrand. Gabriel's American wife, Debbie, laughed at me over the rain at my table, and said, "You're like Charlie Brown!"

More than a dozen cognacs went for more than $1,000 that night. I witnessed a Dupuy Folle Blanche sell for €2,700, a forty-year-old Delamain for €3,000, a 1975 Hine for €3,200, the Frapin Très Vieille Grande for €5,000. Martell in a crystal decanter painted with twenty-carat gold got snapped up for €5,500.

During the bidding, Gabriel had opened up a very special bottle of Pierre Ferrand, the seventy-year-old Ancestrale, and poured a few of us a glass. This was a real pour, too, not like the usual quarter-ounce pours that we usually do professional tastings with. This was a true glassful, to drink. And after about half an hour, another glass. Ancestrale does not have the pedigree of, say, the cognacs that were being auctioned at La Part des Anges, but it's certainly no slouch. If you find it for sale, it's usually got a price tag north of seven hundred dollars. Of course, being a professional, I'm happy to answer your questions about it. Was it amazing? Yes. Impossible to describe? Yes. Worth it? Hmm . . . that's not so straightforward.

Finally, a silly statue of an angel sold for €4,000, and the auction was over. No dancing afterward. No more drinks. Just *adieu, bonsoir!* "Well, it's not Paris," someone said. Gabriel could see that the journalists' night, however, was probably not over. There was still about half the bottle of Ancestrale left, so he asked me if I wanted to take it with me. "Really?" I asked.

"Yes," he said. "And I must be drunk. Because I've never given a bottle of Ancestrale to anyone that I've just met. But you seem like a man of good taste."

At that, I nearly doubled over with laughter. If you only knew, sir, I thought. Yes, dear reader, it's been quite a long, boozy road from my suburban Jersey youth to being the sort of man to be trusted with a bottle of seven-hundred-dollar cognac. Even here, having had my job for three years, and being looked to as some sort of expert on the topic of booze, I still felt like an imposter. I still felt like that kid sneaking a bottle of sambuca out of my parents' cabinet.

I shook hands with Gabriel, tucked the bottle under my coat, and walked out of the tent. I crossed the bridge over the Charente and stepped onto the bus that would take all of the journalists back to the town of Cognac. I settled into my seat and opened up my coat. Yes, to my disbelief, I was still sitting there with a bottle of seventy-year-old cognac. In Cognac. Every once in a while, I have a moment like this, when I need to pinch myself in wonder if this is really my life.

So what did I do? Well, old habits die hard. Dear reader, I popped that Ancestrale open and took a big, big swig—straight from the bottle. And then I smiled and took another one. Then I saw one of my fellow journalists sitting next to me looking very, very jealous. So, of course, what else could I do? I passed the bottle across the aisle. "Cheers," I said. Before long, it was all gone.

A Round of Drinks:
Apple of My Eye

Says Christian Drouin, Calvados producer, "I am always amazed when I go into a bar in the United States and the man or woman behind the bar takes my product, thinks for a few minutes, and then makes a cocktail on the spot. And usually the result is very interesting."

APPLE BRANDY OLD-FASHIONED

Serves 1

This drink wonderfully showcases your choice of apple brandy. Whether you use a Calvados or a domestic product such as Laird's apple brandy or Clear Creek Eau-de-Vie de Pomme, the spirit's unique characteristics and flavor profile will come through.

> **1 teaspoon pure maple syrup**
> **2 dashes Angostura bitters**
> **2 ounces apple brandy**

Combine the maple syrup and bitters in an old-fashioned glass, then add the apple brandy and 2 or 3 ice cubes. Stir gently for 10 seconds.

Adapted from a recipe by Misty Kalkofen of Green Street, Cambridge, Massachusetts

DELLA MELA

Serves 1

This drink features the brown, bitter, orange–flavored Italian soda called chinotto, which turns out to be a perfect companion for apple brandy. It allows for a wonderful, uncloying apple flavor to come through and smoothes out the brandy's rougher edges.

> **4 ounces chinotto soda, preferably San Pellegrino brand**
> **1 1/2 ounces apple brandy or applejack**
> **1 thin orange slice, for garnish**

Fill a highball glass with ice. Add the chinotto and apple brandy. Stir gently. Garnish with the orange slice.

Recipe by Jackson Cannon of Eastern Standard, Boston

JACK MAUVE

Serves 1

This variation on the classic Jack Rose calls for homemade grenadine. Since homemade grenadine will be purple rather than red, the Jack Rose in this case takes on a sort of mauve color—but more important, this version is much tastier. The original recipe calls for applejack; I recommend Laird's apple brandy or a nice Calvados for a sublime cocktail. With Calvados, though, use slightly less grenadine—about half an ounce.

1½ ounces apple brandy, applejack, or Calvados
¾ ounce freshly squeezed lime juice
¾ ounce homemade grenadine (page 216)

Fill a cocktail shaker halfway with ice. Add the apple brandy, lime juice, and grenadine. Shake vigorously, then strain into a chilled cocktail glass.

CORPSE REVIVER #1

Serves 1

1½ ounces brandy, preferably cognac
¾ ounce apple brandy, preferably Calvados
¾ ounce sweet vermouth
Lemon peel twist, for garnish

Fill a mixing glass halfway with ice. Add the brandy, Calvados, and vermouth. Stir vigorously, then strain into a chilled cocktail glass. Garnish with the lemon peel twist.

WIDOW'S KISS

Serves 1

This cocktail, first created in the late nineteenth century, involves two French liqueurs with romantic, and mysterious, company stories. Bénédictine is believed to be the world's oldest liqueur, dating to 1510. Made from brandy or cognac and a secret infusion of herbs, the recipe is closely guarded at the Benedictine abbey in Fécamp, Normandy. Chartreuse is made in the alpine town of Voiron, at a monastery called La Grande Chartreuse. There is little chance its secret recipe will ever be revealed. The only two Carthusian monks who know it have taken a vow of silence.

1 ¹/₂ ounces Calvados or applejack
³/₄ ounce Bénédictine
³/₄ ounce yellow Chartreuse
1 dash Angostura bitters
1 strawberry, sliced, for garnish

Fill a cocktail shaker two-thirds full with ice and add the Calvados, Bénédictine, Chartreuse, and bitters. Shake vigorously, then strain into a chilled cocktail glass. Garnish with the strawberry slices.

ACKNOWLEDGMENTS

FIRST AND FOREMOST, thanks to Joe Yonan, my editor at the *Washington Post*. It was he who made the brilliant decision to let me to write about booze for his section. Thanks also to my other wonderful Food section colleagues: Bonnie Benwick and Jane Touzalin for editing me to success every week—their fingerprints are all over this book; Jane Black for setting the writing bar high, but also for being the president of my fan club; and Leigh Lambert for sharing chuckles over the many unintentionally hilarious press releases we receive.

Thanks to Lisa Westmoreland at Ten Speed Press for seeing *Boozehound* as a worthy project, and huge thanks to Sara Golski, who certainly had her hands full editing me, yet shepherded this book through the process with aplomb.

My colleagues at The Smart Set, Jesse Smith and Brittany Tress, deserve my undying gratitude for putting up with me during all the travel and the writing. This book, in fact, wouldn't have happened without the amazingly generous support of Drexel University, in particular Dave Jones and Mark Greenberg. I should also give a shout-out to my "protégé" Emily Callaghan, whose talent and friendship is unwavering (even when her "assistance" at Tales of the Cocktail is shaky).

There are so many bartenders, drinks writers, and spirits people whose knowledge, generosity, and camaraderie is always greatly appreciated: Duggan McDonnell, Audrey Fort, Maggie Savarino, Jordan Mackay, Todd Thrasher, Derek Brown, Adam Bernbach, Gina Chersevani, Chantal

Tseng, Dave Wondrich, Jim Meehan, Neyah White, Jackie Patterson, Janell Moore, Camper English, Wayne Curtis, Charlotte Voisey, Nick Jarrett, Jeff "Beachbum" Berry, and Danielle Eddy, among many others.

I'd also like to thank some of my great drinking companions over the years: Trine Skjøldberg in Copenhagen, James Wood in Boston and Edinburgh, Vanessa Polk in the East Village, Kevin Meeker in Haiti, Italy, and Philly, Addy and Sonja and Hjalti in Reykjavík, the old Jersey Shore crowd (including Chris, Snap, Fran, and Game Girl), whoever played "apartment golf" that fateful night in Burlington, Vermont, and the whole gang at La Quercia in Pieve San Giacomo. I'm sure there about 9,999 more people who've bought me a drink in my lifetime . . . Don't worry, I haven't forgotten. I'll get the next round.

Thank you to Haddonfield, New Jersey, for being a dry town. It makes things a little more challenging to live here, keeps me on my toes.

An extra-special thanks is reserved for my family, including my in-laws, Jack and Mariann, who have hopefully forgiven me for taking their daughter away from California, and especially my own mom and dad, who surely could not have imagined the strange trajectory of their son's career, and yet have steadfastly supported it all the same. One thing, however, Mom: You once said that drinking wouldn't get me anywhere. Well, I hate to you inform otherwise . . . but . . .

Thanks to my brother Tyler, who has imbibed with me all over the world—from Iceland to the Netherlands to Portugal to Central America—and who may have the finest home bar of anyone in North America. And I would also like to give a shout-out to my youngest brother, Brad—though he is a teetotaler, we love him anyway.

I save the most love for those who put up with me every day, or at least when I'm not off tasting this or that. Cheers to my boys, Sander and Wes, who will only be allowed to read this book, and this acknowledgment, many years from now when they are twenty-one years old.

Finally, last in the acknowledgments but first in my heart, thanks to my beautiful, talented, and patient wife, Jen, my trusted first editor. Surely someday soon she can write her own gimlet-eyed book, called *Living with Boozehound*.

APPENDIX ⌒

HOME BARTENDING is a source of much anxiety, which is likely one reason why people don't experiment with new and interesting spirits. But really, making great cocktails in your kitchen is easy. Just keep a few basic truths in mind:

- **Always use fresh citrus.** Whenever a recipe calls for lemon, lime, orange, or grapefruit juice, squeeze the fruit yourself.

- **Never use premade mixes.** Remove "sour mix" from your shopping list. If you've only ever had a margarita made from a Day-Glo mix, then you have been living a lie. Besides, how much time and effort are you really saving? A real margarita only has three ingredients to begin with!

- **Always measure.** A cocktail is about the balance of flavors and textures, and ratios matter. Yeah, it looks cool to free pour, but most of the best bartenders measure out their drinks.

- **Never shake when a recipe calls for stirring, and vice versa.** It makes a big difference. Also, when a recipe says "shake well," for god's sake, shake *well!*

- **Always take care of your vermouth.** Don't be one of those people who thumb their noses at vermouth—it's an essential part of a cocktail maker's repertoire. Remember, vermouth is an aromatized wine, so you must keep it in the refrigerator and replace it every

month, because otherwise it will go bad. For this reason, I like buying small bottles for home use.

- **Never forget the bitters.** There's a reason the recipe calls for bitters. Bitters balance flavors and add texture to a cocktail.

Stocking the Basic Bar

Though this book has been mostly about obscure booze, you'll notice
that many of the cocktail recipes listed throughout call for more familiar
spirits. In fact, liqueurs, amari, and eaux-de-vie are most often the sup-
porting players in cocktails; almost all cocktails call for a base spirit in
one of the following six categories:

- **Gin.** I always stock a Plymouth gin, a traditional London dry gin like
Tanqueray or Beefeater's, and Old Tom gin.

- **Whiskey.** Bourbon and rye are essential, and there are plenty of
reasonably priced options. Buffalo Trace bourbon costs less than
twenty-five dollars and Rittenhouse rye less than twenty, to name
two go-to brands. An Irish whiskey like Bushmills or Redbreast is
also good to have on hand. And, of course, a single-malt Scotch
whisky—because if there's a single-malt drinker in your life, that's
likely all he or she is going to want.

- **Tequila.** You should always have a good blanco or silver, a reposado,
and an añejo. Good, 100 percent agave tequila is more expensive
than you think, but don't skimp.

- **Rum.** A well-stocked bar will have, at least, a white rum, an aged
rum, a rhum agricole, and a cachaça, the Brazilian cane-based spirit.
This may sound like a lot, but rums are complex, and each is distinct.

- **Brandy.** You'll want a good-value VSOP cognac, such as Pierre Ferrand Ambre, and a Calvados, apple brandy, or applejack; I've also started stocking the Peruvian brandy pisco.

- **Vodka.** Yes, despite my antivodka ranting, you should always keep a bottle on hand. You want to be a good host, and inevitably someone's going to come over and want a vodka tonic.

Beyond the Basic Bottles

After you've got the base spirits, you'll need to make some decisions about which liqueurs and mixers you'll want to keep on hand. Obviously, I've covered a lot of the popular liqueurs, from absinthe to Chartreuse to St-Germain to Tuaca, in my narrative. But here are several others that all good bars stock:

- **Orange liqueur.** Known as triple sec or curaçao or by brand name, these liqueurs are essential for so many cocktails, from margaritas to Sidecars. My personal preference is Cointreau or Combier.

- **Maraschino liqueur.** Not to be confused with the juice of "maraschino" cherries, this clear spirit pops up in both classic and contemporary cocktails. Luxardo brand is the oldest and the best.

- **Vermouth.** Always keep fresh bottles of three different varieties: dry, sweet (rosso), and white (bianco or blanc).

- **Campari and Aperol.** Many enjoyable recipes call for these two Italian aperitivi, and they're also both lovely with sparkling wine or club soda. I always have bottles of both in my fridge.

- **Bitters.** Always stock Angostura, Peychaud's, and orange bitters.

Other Key Bar Ingredients
to Keep on Hand

- Lots of ice

- Oranges, limes, lemons, grapefruit, fresh pineapple

- Tonic water, preferably Fever-Tree or Q Tonic

- Sparkling mineral water, preferably Apollinaris brand

- Club soda

- Ginger beer, preferably Barritt's, Reed's, or (if you like spicy) Blenheim

- Tomato juice

- Sparkling wine, such as prosecco or cava

- Agave nectar

- *Real* maraschino cherries from Luxardo (available online) or home-made preserved cherries (see opposite)

- Simple syrup (see page 218)

- Grenadine, preferably homemade (see below)

HOMEMADE GRENADINE

Makes about 2 cups

After making this simple recipe by Todd Thrasher, you may never go back to the bright red, artificial, syrupy bottled stuff. Be sure to use 100 percent pomegranate juice. After trying several brands, I found that the widely available POM was by far the best to use. As Thrasher says, "It's not going to be bright red, but that's a good thing." Use this in recipes like the Jack Mauve (page 208).

> **3 cups pomegranate juice**
> **1½ cups sugar**
> **1½ ounces freshly squeezed lemon juice**
> **Strips of zest from 1 whole orange (no pith)**

In a medium saucepan, bring the pomegranate juice to a boil. Add the sugar and lemon juice, stirring to dissolve the sugar, then add the orange zest. Immediately decrease the heat to medium-low and cook uncovered for 45 minutes, or until reduced by half.

Strain through a fine-mesh strainer, discarding the orange peel, and let cool to room temperature before using or storing.

The grenadine can be refrigerated for up to 2 weeks. For longer refrigerated storage (up to 2 months), add ½ ounce of 151-proof rum. Then, of course, the grenadine will be off-limits for children's drinks such as a Shirley Temple.

Adapted from a recipe by Todd Thrasher of Restaurant Eve, the Majestic, and PX, Alexandria, Virginia

PRESERVED CHERRIES

Makes about 65 cherries

These cherries, by Todd Thrasher, have a much more complex, sweet-and-savory taste than the neon-red maraschino cherries you find in jars at the supermarket. The cherries will keep, covered and refrigerated, for about two weeks. They're perfect in a Black Manhattan (page 42) or a Red Hook (page 43).

> **2 pints Bing cherries, pitted**
> **1 tablespoon salt**
> **2¼ cups sugar**
> **Juice of 1 medium lemon**
> **1 tablespoon almond extract**

Place the cherries in a shallow heatproof glass or ceramic bowl.

In a medium saucepan over high heat, combine 1¹/₄ cups of water and the salt. Bring to a boil, stirring to dissolve the salt. Remove from the heat; allow to cool for 10 minutes, then pour the liquid over the cherries. Cover and refrigerate overnight.

Drain the cherries, discarding the liquid, and rinse them with cold water. Wash the bowl in which the cherries were refrigerated and return them to the clean bowl.

In a small saucepan over medium-high heat, combine the sugar, lemon juice, and ¹/₄ cup of water. Bring to a boil, stirring to dissolve the sugar, then remove from the heat and add the almond extract. Pour the mixture over the cherries; let cool, then cover and refrigerate overnight, stirring occasionally.

Adapted from a recipe by Todd Thrasher of Restaurant Eve, the Majestic, and PX, Alexandria, Virginia

SIMPLE SYRUP

Makes 1¹/₃ cups

Simple syrup is integral to so many cocktails and is very easy to make.

1 cup sugar
1 cup water

In a small saucepan, combine the sugar and water over medium heat, stirring until the sugar dissolves. Bring to a slow, rolling boil, then decrease the heat to medium-low and simmer for 5 minutes. Transfer to a heatproof container and let cool to room temperature. Cover tightly and refrigerate until chilled through before using; store indefinitely in the refrigerator.

CINNAMON SYRUP

Makes ²/₃ cup

You can also make infused simple syrups by adding ingredients like citrus zests, split vanilla beans, and herbs like rosemary to the pan. This variation uses cinnamon; it's used in Don's Mix (along with grapefruit juice), which is a key ingredient in the Zombie (page 180).

¹/₃ cup sugar
¹/₃ cup water
2 (3-inch) cinnamon sticks

In a small saucepan, combine the sugar, water, and cinnamon sticks over medium heat, stirring until the sugar dissolves. Bring to a slow, rolling boil, then decrease the heat to medium-low and simmer for 5 minutes. Transfer to a heatproof container and let cool to room temperature. Discard the cinnamon sticks. Cover tightly and refrigerate until chilled before using; store indefinitely in the refrigerator.

HONEY SYRUP

Makes 3 cups

This is another variation on simple syrup, called for in recipes like the Hans Punch Up (page 155).

1 cup water
2 cups honey

In a medium saucepan, combine the water and honey over medium-high heat. Bring to a boil, stirring until the honey has dissolved. Decrease the heat to medium-low and simmer for 5 minutes. Transfer to a heatproof container and let cool to room temperature. Cool completely before using or storing in the refrigerator in a glass jar, where it will keep for 2 to 4 weeks.

ORGEAT SYRUP

Makes 2¹/₂ cups

This almond-flavored syrup is a key ingredient in many tiki drinks, such as the Mai Tai (page 181) and Navy Grog. Premade brands such as Fee Brothers, Torani, and Trader Vic's are available, but this version is much better.

3 ounces blanched almonds, coarsely chopped

1 ounce almond meal or almond flour

2³/₄ cups plus 1 tablespoon sugar

4 cups water

3 drops rose water

4 drops orange flower water

¹/₄ teaspoon almond extract

In a large saucepan over high heat, combine the almonds, almond meal, ¹/₂ cup plus 1 tablespoon of the sugar, and the water. Bring to a boil, then remove from the heat. Cover, cool to room temperature, and let sit overnight in the refrigerator.

Strain the liquid through a cheesecloth-lined fine-mesh strainer into a separate large saucepan over medium heat. Add the remaining 2¹/₄ cups of sugar, stirring until the sugar has dissolved. Bring to a slow, rolling boil, then decrease the heat to medium-low and simmer for 5 minutes.

Remove from the heat; let cool to room temperature, then stir in the rose water, orange flower water, and almond extract. Use a funnel to transfer the syrup to a bottle with a tight-fitting lid. Refrigerate for up to 1 month.

Adapted from a recipe by Rick Stutz, who blogs at www.kaiserpenguin.com

Essential Barware

You don't need to spend a fortune on fancy bar supplies, but you'll definitely need the following six tools:

- **Boston shaker.** This consists of two parts: a 16-ounce mixing glass and a slightly larger metal shaker that fits over the glass. It's a versatile tool, since it can be used for shaking or stirring in the mixing glass.

- **Strainer.** This fits over the shaker to keep solids (ice, fruit pulp) out of the cocktail glass. The most widely used is the familiar Hawthorne strainer, with its wire coil. But many bartenders also use a julep strainer, which looks like a big perforated spoon.

- **Jigger.** A small, hourglass-shaped, double-sided cup used to measure ingredients, with different volumes on either side (for example, 1¹/₂ ounces and ³/₄ ounce, or 1 ounce and ¹/₂ ounce). You'll need this since now you'll be carefully measuring your cocktail ingredients.

- **Bar spoon.** A long-handled spoon used to stir cocktails.

- **Juicer.** For all your fresh citrus juice, since you won't be using premade mixes anymore.

- **Channel knife or zester.** Used to make citrus peel twists, a garnish that many recipes call for. A vegetable peeler works equally well.

A Word on Citrus Peel Garnishes

When using the zester or peeler, be sure to work over the glass so that the oils are expressed into the drink as you peel. Make sure to avoid the bitter white pith that lies just under the colored outside of the citrus peel. When you've got your twist, squeeze it over the drink, rub the rim with it, then drop it into the cocktail.

Finally, a Little Rant about Glassware

The beginning of wisdom is to call things by their right names—so says an ancient Chinese proverb. So let us begin: A martini is served in what is correctly called a cocktail glass. A cocktail glass traditionally holds about 3 to 5 ounces of liquid. Nearly every martini recipe in nearly every cocktail guide ever published calls for about 3 ounces of spirits, diluted by a bit of stirring over ice, and served freezing cold with a garnish.

Wisdom therefore dictates that no martini needs to be poured into a glass larger than 5 ounces. Of course, that is not what the wise people at stores like Crate and Barrel say. I once found myself there, wandering the "drinkware" section, looking at rows of what they call "martini" glasses: the 9-ounce Roz, the 10-ounce Temptation, the 12-ounce Inga, even a 13-ounce stemless model. The smallest I could find was a 7-ouncer. I stared at all those lovely glasses and imagined how long it would take the average person to drink 12 ounces of gin and vermouth. That caused me to wince, and it led to two conclusions: First, wisdom does not begin in the drinkware section of Crate and Barrel. Second, the only reason to use a 12-ounce glass for a martini would be to accommodate one very, very large olive.

We are facing an epidemic of cocktails served in inappropriately large glasses. Anyone who's recently spent time at the local bar knows that cocktails are growing, often simply to justify a double-digit price tag.

"It's the mentality that bigger is better," said Charlotte Voisey, who visits bars all over the United States promoting Hendrick's gin. "But three sips in, the drink gets too warm."

A spokeswoman for Crate and Barrel told me that "martini" glasses in the 11- to 13-ounce range are the store's best sellers. When I asked why cocktail glasses have gotten so big, she retorted, "You know how they've supersized the McDonald's hamburger?"

When I suggested that the traditional way to drink a martini is in a glass of 4¹/₂ ounces or smaller, the spokeswoman asked, "Why would anyone drink a 4¹/₂-ounce martini?" Crate and Barrel considers 7 ounces to be the standard size.

Voisey blames the large-cocktail trend on ignorance and a false sense of value. "A small martini is a better value because you get to enjoy all of it before it gets warm," she says. "Two normal-size martinis would even be better than one big one."

Beyond creating an overpriced, warm drink, the large-glass phenomenon is not particularly healthy. If you don't take the time to measure—and few people do—it's nearly impossible to correctly gauge how much liquor you're pouring. People end up boozing much more than they realize.

Consider a 2003 Duke University Medical Center study in which college students were asked to estimate and pour standard measurements of different spirits into glasses of several sizes. The students, on average, overpoured shots by 26 percent, mixed drinks by 80 percent, and beer by 25 percent, the study showed. The larger the glass, the more they overpoured. Yes, I realize that for many college students, drink potency outweighs craftsmanship. But the best cocktails are carefully balanced, and the effect of an oversize glass on that balance has been worrying observers for decades.

"A too-large glass gives the drink more time to lose its chill and initial zest, and a half-filled glass looks unexciting, so an average-size cocktail glass of 4$^1/_2$ ounces is the most satisfactory," wrote Collette Richardson in the 1973 edition of *House and Garden's Drink Guide.*

Nearly four decades later, just try finding a 4$^1/_2$-ounce cocktail glass. In fact, most glassware called for in cocktail books has become exceedingly difficult to find. Retailers also are stocked with ridiculously huge double old-fashioned glasses, clocking in at 10 to 15 ounces. Finding the normal 6- to 8-ounce old-fashioned glass that most drink recipes call for is difficult but not impossible. I ended up buying a heavy-bottomed 6-ounce "juice" glass at Crate and Barrel that works fine.

In addition to the cocktail and old-fashioned glasses, a tall, slender 10-ounce highball glass and a 2-ounce cordial/shot glass are the essentials for a home bar. The best bet for finding them is at a bar- and restaurant-supply store or a yard sale. The search will be worth it.

INDEX ♋